The Power of the Story

Catastrophes in Context

General Editors:
Robert E. Barrios, University of New Orleans
Crystal Felima, University of Kentucky
Mark Schuller, Northern Illinois University

Catastrophes in Context aims to bring critical attention to the social, political, economic, and cultural structures that create disasters out of natural hazards or political events and that shape the responses. Combining long-term ethnographic fieldwork typical of anthropology and increasingly adopted in similar social science disciplines such as geography and sociology with a comparative frame that enlightens global structures and policy frameworks, *Catastrophes in Context* includes monographs and edited volumes that bring critical scrutiny to the multiple dimensions of specific disasters and important policy/practice questions for the field of disaster research and management. Theoretically innovative, our goal is to publish readable, lucid texts to be accessible to a wide range of audiences across academic disciplines and specifically practitioners and policymakers.

Volume 6
The Power of the Story: Writing Disasters in Haiti and the Circum-Caribbean
Edited by Vincent Joos, Martin Munro, and John Ribó

Volume 5
Making Things Happen: Community Participation and Disaster Reconstruction in Pakistan
Jane Murphy Thomas

Volume 4
Constructing Risk: Disaster, Development, and the Built Environment
Stephen O. Bender

Volume 3
Going Forward by Looking Back: Archaeological Perspectives on Socio-ecological Crisis, Response, and Collapse
Edited by Felix Riede and Payson Sheets

Volume 2
Disaster Upon Disaster: Exploring the Gap Between Knowledge, Policy and Practice
Edited by Susanna M. Hoffman and Roberto E. Barrios

Volume 1
Contextualizing Disaster
Edited by Gregory V. Button and Mark Schuller

The Power of the Story
Writing Disasters in Haiti and the Circum-Caribbean

Edited by Vincent Joos, Martin Munro, and John Ribó

berghahn
NEW YORK · OXFORD
www.berghahnbooks.com

First published in 2023 by
Berghahn Books
www.berghahnbooks.com

© 2023, 2026 Vincent Joos, Martin Munro, and John Ribó
First paperback edition published in 2026

All rights reserved. Except for the quotation of short passages
for the purposes of criticism and review, no part of this book
may be reproduced in any form or by any means, electronic or
mechanical, including photocopying, recording, or any information
storage and retrieval system now known or to be invented,
without written permission of the publisher.

Library of Congress Cataloging-in-Publication Data
Names: Joos, Vincent, editor. | Munro, Martin, editor. | Ribó, John, editor.
Title: The power of the story : writing disasters in Haiti and the
circum-Caribbean / edited by Vincent Joos, Martin Munro, and John Ribó.
Description: New York : Berghahn Books, 2023. | Series: Catastrophes in context;
 Volume 6 | Includes bibliographical references and index.
Identifiers: LCCN 2022053306 (print) | LCCN 2022053307 (ebook) |
 ISBN 9781800739567 (hardback) | ISBN 9781800739574 (epub)
Subjects: LCSH: Disaster relief—Caribbean Area. | Disaster relief—Haiti. | Disasters in
 literature. | Postcolonialism—Caribbean Area. |
 Postcolonialism—Haiti. | Racism.
Classification: LCC HV551.5.C227 P69 2023 (print) |
 LCC HV551.5.C227 (ebook) | DDC 363.34091729—dc23/eng/20230103
LC record available at https://lccn.loc.gov/2022053306
LC ebook record available at https://lccn.loc.gov/2022053307

British Library Cataloguing in Publication Data
A catalogue record for this book is available from the British Library

EU GPSR Authorized Representative
LOGOS EUROPE, 9 rue Nicolas Poussin, 17000, LA ROCHELLE, France
Email: Contact@logoseurope.eu

ISBN 978-1-80073-956-7 hardback
ISBN 978-1-83695-117-9 paperback
ISBN 978-1-80073-957-4 epub
ISBN 978-1-80073-768-6 web pdf

https://doi.org/10.3167/9781800739567

An electronic version of this book is freely available thanks to the support of
libraries working with Knowledge Unlatched. KU is a collaborative initiative
designed to make high-quality books Open Access for the public good. More
information about the inititative and links to the Open Access version can be
found at knowledgeunlatched.org.

This work is published subject to a Creative Commons Attribution
Noncommercial No Derivatives 4.0 License. The terms of the
license can be found at http://creativecommons.org/licenses/by-
nc-nd/4.0/. For uses beyond those covered in the license contact
Berghahn Books.

Contents

List of Illustrations   vii

Introduction. The Power of the Story: Writing Disasters in Haiti and the Circum-Caribbean   1
    Vincent Joos, Martin Munro, and John Ribó

Chapter 1. *Mòd Leta*: Haitian Understandings of Crises Past in Present   27
    Mark Schuller

Chapter 2. After the Storm: Hurricane Matthew, Haiti, and Disaster's *Longue Durée*   50
    Laura Wagner

Chapter 3. *Malediksyon*: (Neo)colonial Development, Disasters, and Countercapitalism in Northeastern Haiti   62
    Vincent Joos

Chapter 4. Post-Katrina Intrusions on African American Cultural Traditions in New Orleans   78
    Shearon Roberts

Chapter 5. Cat Bonds and Necrocapitalism in Haiti and Puerto Rico   98
    Jana Evans Braziel

Chapter 6. Wake Work in Post-Maria Puerto Rico and Beyond   120
    John Ribó

Chapter 7. Art and Politics Facing Disaster in the Caribbean: Defining a New Cultural Diplomacy   135
    Vanessa Selk

Chapter 8. Marvin Victor's *Corps mêlés* and the Writing of Disaster in Haiti 160
    Martin Munro

Chapter 9. Beyond Malediction and Prophecy: *Melovivi or the Trap* 175
    Alex Lenoble

Epilogue. Disrupting Permanent Catastrophe through Commemoration, Grief, and Action 188
    Vincent Joos, Martin Munro, and John Ribó

Index 195

Illustrations

Figures

4.1.	Flyer by Greater New Orleans Housing Alliance's march of 2 November 2019. Posted on Facebook on 23 October 2019.	88
4.2.	Screengrab of viral social media video of brass musician Eugene Grant's arrest on Frenchman Street, posted on Facebook by the Music & Culture Coalition of New Orleans and included in an editorial published on 18 July 2019.	90
5.1.	2017 and 2018 issuance for cat bonds. Source: artemis.bm.	102
5.2.	2019, 2020, and 2021 issuance for cat bonds. Source: artemis.bm.	103
5.3.	Fourth quarter cat bond issuances by year (2010–19). Source: artemis.bm.	104
5.4.	Cat bonds by geographical regional for Q4 2019. Source: artemis.bm.	105
5.5.	Cat bonds by sponsor (including unknown) for Q4 2019. Source: artemis.bm.	106
7.1.	*Lwa Goudou*, 2020, mixed media on paper in artist frame, 52x52 inches. © Edouard Duval-Carrié.	136
7.2.	Guy Régis Junior, *And the Whole World Quakes: The Great Collapse*. Reading at the Martin Segal Theater, directed by Kaneza Schaal, Caribbean Theater Project ACT, December 2019. © V. Selk.	143
7.3.	*Tout Saintes*, 2010, acrylic canvas, 36x24 inches. © Michael Elliott.	143
7.4.	*Imagined Spaces*, photography series, 2002. © Deborah Jack.	146

7.5.	*La Perla After Maria*, 23 minutes, Puerto Rico/Venezuela/Germany, 2018, film still. © Clari del Pilar Lewis.	147
7.6.	Guy Gabon, *#AllClimateRefugees*, installation, mixed media, part of *Echos imprévus* at the Memorial ACTe, Guadeloupe, 2017. © Bernard Boucard.	149
7.7.	Dominique Hunter, *And Then It Came*, 2017, installation, mixed media. © Mark Reamy.	151
7.8.	*White Noise*, 2019, Ceramic sculpture. © Morel Doucet.	153
7.9.	*Dismantling Sargasse Sea 3*, photography. © Louisa Marajo.	154

INTRODUCTION

The Power of the Story
Writing Disasters in Haiti and the Circum-Caribbean

VINCENT JOOS, MARTIN MUNRO, AND JOHN RIBÓ

> Big data is of no help when it comes to tracing the memories of the dead. It cannot record the voices of the deceased. But isn't that what humans have their imagination for?
>
> —Kiyoshi Shigematsu, writing about the Fukushima earthquake, 2013

Right after the 2010 earthquake that rocked the Port-au-Prince region and killed many people, a big data competition began between states and international organizations involved in the relief effort. The journalists Robert Muggah and Athena Kolbe, a year and half after the disaster, wrote that "in Haiti, fewer than 46,000 people were killed in the January 2010 earthquake. Or perhaps the death toll was more than 300,000" (2011). The Haitian state issued a high toll number of 230,000 deaths days after the quake. Aid agencies and states "allied" to Haiti criticized the flawed methodology of Haitian experts and waited a few months before announcing their own mortality count. The United States Agency of International Development, in May 2011, stated that between 46,000 and 85,000 people died in the disaster. This much smaller number had consequences: it minimized the need for assistance at a time when the $10 billion pledged by international donors had not been disbursed. Obliquely, it pushed nongovernmental organizations (NGOs) to reassess and sometimes shorten their missions in Haiti. In brief, the numbers battle was an academic exercise between different experts that directly and indirectly fueled ideological and logistical debates linked to the amount of aid needed. In a cynical fashion, we could now say, more than ten years after the earthquake, that these debates did not really matter. Despite the disbursement of billions of dollars, most of the reconstruction of infrastructures and buildings has not yet happened, and Haiti is today battered by overlapping political, economic, and environmental crises. However, the fact that gang violence resurfaced in 2018 or that some international NGOs' reconstruction projects failed spectacularly are not a matter of how much funding was disbursed. It has more to do with the fact that Haitians were silenced during the relief and reconstruction processes and that most aid actors did not take their desires and needs into account (McAlister 2012). It also has more to do with forms of structural violence that have increased disaster vulnerability since the beginning of the colonization of the Americas in 1492. Big data and quantitative analysis are poor frameworks to assess disasters. Numbers do not talk. It is only by listening to Haitian voices or to people who have lived in Haiti for many years that a fuller understanding emerges of the structural conditions that transformed an earthquake into a megadisaster.

In her recent work, Mimi Sheller writes similarly of how the earthquake made visible the "highly uneven interdependence and fragility of the complex mobility systems and infrastructural moorings that create the possibility for people to weave together everyday life" (2020: 1). Sheller is further critical of the "militarized and carceral response" to the "unnatural disaster," which deprived Haitian people any meaningful role in deciding how, or indeed where, their postdisaster future might be, as one of the primary aims of the US military was to make sure that there was no mass migration from Haiti to the United States (1–2). As such, the vast majority of Haitian citizens were unable to leave the country for medical care, or to visit family members, and many had no choice but to go to the camps hastily constructed for "internally displaced people," as if, in Sheller's words, "displacement were their identity" (2). As the response played out in a series of failures—the inability to move people from temporary shelters into transitional housing, the slow progress in shifting rubble and rebuilding housing—it became clear that such failures exposed what Sheller calls "the institutional scaffolding of mobility regimes that govern spatial mobility, including all the purposeful gaps and uneven distributions of mobility rights and 'network capital' that leave some groups most vulnerable to harm" (2). Focusing on another Caribbean site—Guyana following the disastrous flood of 2005—Sarah Vaughn is also concerned with the ways in which national and international agencies' reactions to disasters shape people's experiences, specifically in the case of a large-scale project to enhance irrigation and drainage infrastructures and the way such a project "alters understandings of settlement or the multilayered processes that contribute to dwelling and the habitation of a place" (2022: 1). Adapting to climate change, Vaughn insists, is for the people "a lived reality of settlement" rather than an "abstract risk" (1). This volume goes beyond quantitative debates to explore how race, gender, and class disparities fuel unequal and inefficient disaster responses that tend to lay the groundwork for crises rather than offer sustainable solutions. Following Vaughn, contributors use "counter-racial thinking"— an acknowledgment of race-based practices that takes distance from race-based politics and allows new engagements with the environment. As Vaughn writes, "counter-racial thinking not only offers a way to trace the racial political orders that lurk in the shadows of scientizing debates about climate change but also brings to the fore practices that insist on action across a variety of scales" (23).

This multidisciplinary edited volume focuses on narratives often hidden behind the "abstract risks" of academic and governmental discourse or obscured by statistical battles and planning strategies that are anchored in a crisis mindset. In the recent past, Haiti suffered many disasters—and hurricanes, political violence, earthquakes, and droughts continue to devastate this country. Not surprisingly, many scholars in this volume analyze the current situation in Haiti. They do so because studying Haiti—the region in the Americas that has suffered the most from (neo)colonial intrusions—reveals, to paraphrase the anthropologist Greg Beckett, the processes and structures that enable the repetition of disasters (2020: 252). The governmental debacles that follow hurricanes or earthquakes in Puerto Rico and the lack of sustainable postdisaster reconstruction in this island echo the structural issues that plague Haiti: the absence of centralized state institutions able to intervene during disasters; a lack of budgetary autonomy at all levels; and the systematic dismemberment of public education, health, and other institutions. As in Haiti, despite their many protests, the people of Puerto Rico are still treated as neocolonial subjects—second-class US citizens who remain placed under the tutelage of federal institutions that continue to impose forms of austerity that led to disaster vulnerability in the first place. As Mark Schuller recently wrote, what seem to be disparate regional disasters are structurally linked to one another and happen on a global scale. Indeed, we "risk reproducing a defensive, single-issue individualism, atomization, and compartmentalization—a 'whack-a-mole' approach to resistance"—if we cannot explain how racial capitalism and neoliberal abandonment of public services engender slow and fast, small and large disasters at once (2021: 4).

The list of disasters could unfortunately go on. Every disaster is unique, yet similar processes of gentrification and privatization of public services in postdisaster periods are to be seen in many areas of the Greater Caribbean region. Puerto Rico, Dominica, the Bahamas, or the US Gulf Coast, to take a few examples, did not recover from recent disasters. Instead, as in the Puerto Rico and Port-au-Prince examples, postdisaster periods in these regions have seen the intensification of neoliberal reforms. It is not only the physical landscape that bears the brunt of these catastrophes. Public services and the basic welfare dwindle with every postdisaster reconstruction phase while states act as police and actuary of corporations and large estate owners. Social scientists have well described these processes and have also explored how the slashing of state regulations and public investments render these areas of the world vulnerable to disasters. The Caribbean offers a case in point, as it was the first region in the world to be globally managed and as it has long served as an experimental platform for neoliberal reforms (Mintz 1974; Girvan 1975). As Yarimar Bonilla reminds us, the majority of Caribbean polities are nonsovereign societies, and "even those that have achieved 'flag independence' still struggle with how to forge a more robust project of self-determination, how to reconcile the unresolved legacies of colonialism and slavery, how to assert control over their entanglements with foreign powers, and how to stem their disappointment with the unfulfilled promises of political and economic modernity" (2015: xiii–xiv). The colonial legacies in this region, including what Bonilla calls the "common disenchantment with the modernist project of postcolonial sovereignty" (xiv), weigh heavily and call for historical insights on present crises.

Beyond restating the well-known ravages of neoliberalism in the Caribbean, this volume brings together cultural and literary critics, historians, and anthropologists to open a dialogue on the (neo)colonial legacies that constrain the sovereignty of Caribbean regions and that make disasters more forceful there than anywhere in the Americas. As this introduction demonstrates through the example of Hispaniola, these (neo)colonial legacies are rooted not only in historical dynamics of the Caribbean but also in discourses about disaster in the region. While Hispaniola is susceptible to seismic activity and hurricanes due to geology and geography, European and US colonial interventions created, exacerbated, and entrenched conditions that make the island particularly vulnerable to disaster still to this day. These catastrophic colonial interventions include but are not limited to the genocide, displacement, and enslavement of Indigenous and African peoples; the disruption, destruction, and reconfiguration of local ecologies, economies, and governments; and the establishment and maintenance of racial capitalism as the dominant socioeconomic system structuring the exploitation of labor and the extraction of natural resources on the island, in the region, and beyond. Moreover, the prevalence in Hispaniola's and Haiti's histories of disasters—natural, man-made, and both—have contributed to global discourses that characterize Haiti particularly and the Caribbean more generally as inherently disastrous. As this introduction and multiple chapters in this volume illustrate, such discourses have tangible material effects because they inform the strategies, policies, and actions of governments and NGOs, foreign and domestic. The purpose of this volume then is to acknowledge and grapple with the historical, discursive, and material aspects of how these (neo)colonial legacies shape disaster throughout the Caribbean and its diasporas. Given the broad historical, geographic, linguistic, and cultural scope of such an undertaking, this volume is necessarily a limited and not exhaustively representative selection of scholarship on disaster in the circum-Caribbean. The goal is that the work included in this collection will catalyze further collaborative research and interdisciplinary debate on the topic.

The Colonial Anchors of Disasters

As Bartolomé de las Casas made clear in his *Short Account of the Destruction of the Indies*, published in 1552, the colonization of the Americas is a history of genocide, plunder, and barbaric violence. The atrocities committed against Indigenous people of the Americas, along with the diseases brought by Spanish colonizers, decimated entire communities. The death toll was so great that cultivated land started to disappear, paving the way for a massive forest expansion that would cause the first worldwide human-induced climate change: a global cooling (Koch et al. 2019). They started the process that would link localized, yet massive, genocides to global economic and so-called natural disasters. Columbus and his men started to destroy Hispaniola from the moment they reached the shores of today's Haiti in 1492. Diseases rapidly devastated local populations and the barbaric Spanish enslavement and killing of Indigenous people led to their almost total disappearance in a matter of fifty years. Once Columbus returned to the island in 1493 to find his sailors at the settlement La Navidad, he discovered that Indigenous people had destroyed the colonial compound and, not surprisingly, killed his men. As archaeologist Clark Moore states, "[the Spaniards were] invaders. They made slaves of the Indians, stole their wives. That's why the Indians killed the Santa María crew and burned La Navidad" (Maclean 2008). However, because the Taíno cacique Guacanagaríx received Columbus and his men after the Santa María wreck and gave him gold presents in exchange for mirrors, brass objects, and clothing, the mirage of El Dorado floated over the Americas, making the region a prime destination for Spanish colonizers (Floyd 1973; Columbus 1960). During his three-week stay in 1492, Columbus forged a bond with Guacanagaríx, who authorized the sailors to settle in one of the villages he controlled. When Columbus came back in 1493 and found that rival tribes had killed his men, he and Guacanagarix made a military alliance. The minor cacique saw this alliance as a way to gain political power. In 1495, Guacanagarix and his three thousand soldiers helped the Spanish army of twelve hundred men wage a ten-month war against other Taínos in order to "pacify" them (Palmié and Scarano 2011: 119). At the end of this war, Columbus negotiated a settlement with Guarionex, the most important cacique of the region defeated by this new hybrid army. With this agreement, Taínos over the age of fourteen became "obliged to pay quarterly as much gold dust as filled a hawk's bell. This was the first regular taxation of the Indians and served as precedent for other exactions still more intolerable" (Almeida 2011: 29). People who did not comply could be killed, brutalized, or sold into slavery in Spain. Yet, as Joselyn Almeida mentions, the Taínos never completely submitted to the Spaniards and starved their oppressors, and sometimes themselves, by refusing to produce food. This short summary of Columbus's first major war in the Americas sheds light on the modus operandi for extracting resources and producing disasters in the Americas: coerced labor and taxation, enslavement, barbaric violence, and measured productivity would be the hallmarks of European colonialism, especially in the Caribbean.

This first colonization effort shaped economic, social, and religious interactions between Europeans and peoples of the Americas by instituting new human hierarchies that would become crucial to the extension of global capitalism. However, even though Spanish soldiers had major technological advantages, the Taíno population of Hispaniola never fully submitted to the Spanish crown and established practices of marronage and guerilla warfare. Maroon societies mastered subsistence agriculture and relentlessly fought against the nascent sugar plantation economy started in Hispaniola by Columbus. This is a key point for scholars writing in this volume: while it is important to describe the processes of colonial theft and destruction, it is equally important for us to point to the networks of resistance and solidarity that formed first in response to colonialism and later to imperialism and neoliberalism. Yet, as many scholars note here, life in the Caribbean could not be reduced to the binaries of oppression and resistance or of disaster and recovery. For instance, on islands like Dominica, Hispaniola, or Saint Lucia, societies of peasant farmers have managed to live outside of capitalism on their own terms.[1] Describing these alternative ways of life, these different epistemologies and cosmologies, is key to this volume—and again, these cannot be reduced to mere reactions against (neo)colonial forces. By combining anthropological texts that use ethnographic insights with analyses of literature, music, or art, we aim to go beyond disaster narratives by exploring the multiple ways people engage with death, violence, and also with political action and hope.

Some of the analyses that follow track how racial capitalism has wreacked havoc in Caribbean worlds in the postcolonial era. Following Cedric J. Robinson and other luminaries such as Eric Williams, C. L. R. James, Walter Rodney, Sylvia Winter, Norman Girvan, and Lloyd Best, it is clear that the form of colonial capitalism that continues to fracture Caribbean societies and to render them vulnerable to disasters by forcing them into cash crop agriculture or industrial "development" is anchored in what Robinson calls racial capitalism—defined here as the process of making profits off nonwhite bodies. Racial capitalism well predates the transatlantic migrations and the slave trade beginning in the sixteenth century and is rooted in the forms of blood-based social differentiation that stratify labor and hierarchies in medieval societies. As Robinson writes, it is "important to realize that with respect to the emerging European civilization whose beginnings coincide with the arrivals of these same barbarians, slave labor as a critical basis of production would continue without any significant interruption into the twentieth century" (1983: 11). Our ensemble of texts enables historical comparisons that anchor large movements of people, forceful transformations of the landscape, and simple labor exploitation in colonial ideologies and practices.

Conquests, reshuffling of borders, expulsions, kidnapping and enslavement, and forced labor driven by extractive economies marked the "millennium" of European civilization and continue to shape the (post)colonial Caribbean. Sidney Mintz (1974) argues that the basis of the plantation economy—slave labor, monocrop agriculture, organized work tasks, and an ideology of economic growth—took form in the Mediterranean world before Columbus exported this model to Hispaniola at the end of the fifteenth century. The rupture of modernity is rather a reactivation of centuries-old practices and a powerful growth of an exploitative mode of production already present in Europe. What Europeans brought to the Caribbean, beyond diseases and genocide, is a particular mode of production based on chattel slavery (and later on racialized hierarchies of labor) that makes these regions vulnerable to social upheavals and political struggles, and to environmental disasters.

Privileging export monocrops such as bananas or coffee is detrimental to subsistence agriculture and local food security. Haiti presents a clear-cut case in this regard. Politicians and experts alike have repeatedly accused Haitian peasants of being the agents of the mass deforestation of the island. Likewise, many scholars have reproduced the myth that only 1.5 percent to 2 percent of Haiti is covered by trees, which makes the deforestation crisis seemingly irreversible. There is a deforestation problem in Haiti: from the harvest of precious woods in the colonial period to the mass deforestation engendered by land grabs during the 1915–1934 US occupation, (neo)colonial powers have transformed parts of the country into semideserts (Anglade 1981). It is not the peasant's production of charcoal that is driving deforestation, but *longue durée* cash crop agriculture. As Alex Bellande has astutely shown, 30 percent of Haiti is covered by bushes and trees (2015). Bellande demonstrates that peasants are essential actors when it comes to the environmental well-being of Haiti. Peasant farmers have contributed to recent reforestation efforts and know how to work with sustainable methods; they cut invasive trees and bushes for charcoal production and protect trees that are beneficial to subsistence agriculture. Bellande argues that "reboisement"—a strategic and concerted planting of trees, such as avocado, mango, or breadfruit, that are prized by farmers—should be the key method for reforestation efforts. In brief, Bellande, by arguing for reboisement, proposes a method that includes the needs of peasant farmers and of local ecosystems. Agricultural polycultures in the Caribbean are crucial for food security—it is a risk-adverse form of agriculture that is far more beneficial to local populations who export monocrops that are subject to diseases and to global price fluctuations. Bananas, for instance, are an instable and dangerous monocrop that puts Caribbean populations at risk. Beyond global market instabilities brought by distant and varied crises, banana plantations are today threatened by fungal diseases that could halt the economy of many regions relying on this crop worldwide (Cohen 2011). Moreover, the production of bananas in the French colonies of Martinique and Guadeloupe brought new health crises to the fore. As Malcolm Ferdinand has shown, the widespread use of chlordecone as a pesticide in banana plantations from 1972 to 1993 contaminated 90 percent of the inhabitants in those islands. Many are now at risk of having cancer and other major diseases linked to the state-sponsored French use of chlordecone (Ferdinand 2022). The racialized modes of production favored in plantation economies continue to ruin the Caribbean today and set up this region for upcoming disasters. Our goal with this volume is to bring historical complexity and to reckon with racist and exploitative systems that continue to devastate our planet and to create false categories of "natives" that are pitted against one another.

Writing about Disasters: The Power of the Story

Nothing, writes Mark Anderson, "shakes one's worldview more than the experience of a natural disaster." Disaster is by definition "conceived of as a rupture or inversion of the normal order of things; natural disaster denotes that moment of disjuncture when nature topples what we see as the natural order of human dominance" (2011: 1). In the case of an earthquake, the metaphorical solidity of the land, fundamental to the construction of identity, is uprooted, "sweeping the ground from beneath our feet and reducing to rubble our literal and conceptual edifices" (1). The effects of natural disasters depend not only on the inherent forces of nature but also on the economic, social, and cultural conditions in which human communities exist.[2] Traditionally invested with divine or supernatural meanings—as messages from God or nature—natural disasters call for interpretation, and these interpretations are largely determined by the culture of the human community, as the events themselves have "no inherent meaning discernable by humans outside that which we assign them" (3). These meanings change according to the particular place, but also over time, and in places like Haiti that are prone to natural disasters, it may be that meanings not only change but dissipate, to the extent that they become relatively meaningless, or at least impossible to decode in any coherent way.

In the five centuries since its colonization by the Spanish, the island of Hispaniola has had a particularly long and periodically intense history of seismic activity. The Enriquillo fault in southern Hispaniola forms a continuous geomorphic lineament with the Plantain Garden fault in eastern Jamaica, and the history of human settlement on the island shows that towns have often been built close to the fault: in 1579 there were five towns located within 10–20 kilometers of the fault; in 1628, 1630, and 1633 there were five; and in 1725 there were fourteen (Bakun, Flores, and ten Brink 2012: 18). There were nine hurricanes reported in Hispaniola between 1494 and 1548, but the first reported severe earthquake, on the north of the island, was on 2 December 1562 (18). The first recorded earthquake in southwestern Hispaniola (modern-day Haiti) was in 1701, and this was followed by two major earthquakes in 1751, and a further event in 1770. The nineteenth and twentieth centuries were by contrast relatively quiet periods: in the time between 1770 and 2010 there was only one recorded earthquake, measuring 6.3, in 1860 (19).

One of the fascinating aspects of the prerevolution earthquakes is that they appear to be shadowed by significant changes in colonial society, and to track the gradual movement to the outright revolution of 1791. In 1670, Louis XIV authorized the French slave trade, and in 1685 he signed the *Code Noir* (Black Code), the notorious law that was an attempt to regulate all aspects of slavery, and which, for example, prescribed three levels of punishment for runaway slaves: "branding with a fleur-de-lis, cutting the hamstring, and finally, death" (Miller 28). In between these dates, there were two earthquakes that devastated some plantations, and which thereby reduced economic gains. Subsequently, even the most minor of constraints against brutality in the Code Noir were ignored in the interests of restoring profitability, and by 1697 slaves "imitated a revolt" (Benson 2010: 87). "Small and failed for the moment," Benson writes, "It was a sign of things to come: Makandal's revolt and the ultimately successful revolts of Toussaint and Dessalines" (87). Of course, these "revolts" were complex, drawn-out events that culminated in the major revolutionary war of 1791–1804 and constituted some of the most significant acts of anti-imperial, anti-racist resistance in human history.

The 18 October 1751 event was described by Moreau de Saint-Méry as a "furious earthquake . . . which began at 3 o'clock in the afternoon," and which, among other effects, led to the discovery of "mineral waters that spurt from several sources" (94). The earthquake dealt a "deadly blow" to the town of Azua, "by overturning houses and bringing the sea up to the point where the town was built" (Moreau 96). In fact, the town was destroyed and thereafter moved northward to its present location, while the city of Santo Domingo also suffered severe damage. Contemporary accounts described "such a strong earthquake . . . from its impulsive subterranean roar felt and violent motion on all the churches and buildings, such that all of those of masonry in this city reached their total ruin" (Bakun, Flores, and ten Brink 2012: 24). There were also reports of a tsunami associated with the earthquake, but these may have been confused with the effects of the five Caribbean hurricanes of 1751 (25). There was a second major earthquake the following month, on 21 November 1751. This event caused severe damage to Port-au-Prince and the plain of Cul-de-Sac (25). Around the same time, François Makandal's campaign of liberation began. Accused by colonizers of making poison from harvested plants, Makandal coordinated attacks against slaves considered to be enemies, and slave masters. By developing an extensive network among slaves in the northern province, Makandal in effect "helped set in motion a cycle of paranoia and violence that continued in Saint-Domingue for decades" (Dubois 2004: 52).

On 3 June 1770, an earthquake was felt across the entire island and destroyed Port-au-Prince. The major quake had in fact been preceded by ten smaller events between 1765 and 1770. The plains of Léogâne, Port-au-Prince, and Petit Goave suffered considerable damage (Bakun, Flores, and ten Brink 2012: 26). More than five hundred people were killed in Port-au-Prince, the sea rose dramatically, and on the affected plains all the sugar works were destroyed (Southey 1870: 407). The historian Georges Corvington wrote of the effects on the stratified population: "Blacks, soldiers, settlers rich and poor were all turned into mere people, leveled by common misfortune" (1970: 88). Moreau describes this as a "terrible earthquake," which caused serious damage to property and led to a small river's level rising by nine feet and overflowing onto surrounding fields (Moreau 714). He also reports further quakes on 20 September 1770, 29–30 September 1786, 2 December 1787, and 5 January 1788, only a few short years before the beginning of the slave revolt. Moreau also writes of extremely wet rainy seasons between 1782 and 1785, of a very dry year in 1786 (713), of hurricanes in 1775 and 1788, and of a comet that was visible in the sky for seven days in 1766 (714), so that one has the sense of a particularly turbulent time of natural disasters and other extrahuman events echoing, mirroring, and perhaps to some extent creating the rising spirit of revolt among the slave population. Nature, one imagines, revealed the fallibility of the colonial system and the limits of the whites' control over the land, and offered powerful images of destruction that were to be repeated and intensified across the cities and plantations of Saint Domingue during the long revolutionary war. In this sense, perhaps we can talk of Saint Domingue in the late eighteenth century as a "culture of disaster," one where natural disasters are not only physical events but also "agents of cultural formation." In effect, cultures of disaster come into being when "frequently occurring natural hazards are integrated into the schema of daily life" (Anderson 2011: 8).

Between the late eighteenth century and 2010, the only significant earthquake in Haiti occurred on 8 April 1860 and was accompanied by a tsunami (Bakun, Flores, and ten Brink 2012: 26). The 2010 event is considered to be a rerupture of the 1701 earthquake source zone and may herald a new period of seismic activity along the Enriquillo fault system (28). In the history of earthquakes in the region the 7.0 magnitude quake of 12 January 2010 was not particularly large, but it was certainly the most destructive and deadly, due in large part to inadequate building practices (28). The 2010 earthquake had in fact been predicted by a Haitian seismologist, Claude Prepetit, who wrote in 2009 of his "worst nightmare" that there would come earthquakes that would cause far greater damage and loss of life than in the past (2008: 8). He also makes a telling connection between different kinds of natural events in his argument that the catastrophic floods in the years preceding 2010 might well have triggered the seismological process that resulted in the 2010 earthquake (9). This is important as it suggests that natural catastrophes of different kinds can create the conditions for further disasters, and that the 2010 event is but part of a contemporary experience of ongoing, relentless disaster.

This experience is termed a condition of "permanent catastrophe" by the Haitian sociologist Laënnec Hurbon. Recognizing the apparent contradiction in the term, Hurbon writes that if every disaster supposes a rupture in time and experience, one should also be aware of the "before and after of the catastrophe" (2012: 8).[3] Disasters strike so often in Haiti—from the floods in Gonaïves in 2004 to the 2010 earthquake to the cholera epidemic to Hurricanes Sandy and Isaac in 2012—that the population "risks taking as natural every calamity" (9). One effect of living in permanent catastrophe is that the memory of the most deadly of these events, the 2010 earthquake, fades quickly and the event loses its distinctiveness. One has the impression, Hurbon wrote in 2012, that nothing happened on 12 January 2010, and that a "leap has been skillfully made beyond that date" (8). The constant denial and annulment of the disaster leads to the general "permanent installation in catastrophe" (9).

This condition of permanent disaster has important political dimensions, for as Hurbon argues at the heart of the situation "the leaders of the State seem to worry only about how to stay in power" (9). Disasters are moreover "godsends" for those in power in that they give the politicians a source of legitimacy, which otherwise they would not have (9).[4] There is even a "desire for disasters" in government, as these events allow the leaders to present themselves as victims to the international community, and to discharge their responsibilities in the economic, social, cultural, and political life of Haiti (9). To live in a state of permanent disaster means that individual events are not memorialized in a way that would consign them to the past and allow a sense of time other than that characterized by catastrophe: people live, Hurbon says, "without a perceptible future" and "in the condition of being superfluous (floating between life and death)" (10). Hurbon points out that the government has no interest in a memorial for the 2010 earthquake, and as such the disaster is not considered past but part of the catastrophic present (9). This in turn has serious consequences for notions of reconstruction, as to be in a permanent state of catastrophe is to forget any time in which disaster was not a daily reality, and to lose awareness of what was there before to be reconstructed.[5] As Hurbon puts it, the causes of permanent disaster are as much political as environmental (10). Indeed, the various signs of environmental degradation—deforestation, pollution, and so on—can be read as "the expression of the failure of the Haitian State" (10).[6]

Robert Fatton Jr. is similarly interested in the "politics of catastrophe," the roots of which he traces to colonial times, and in the authoritarian tradition generated by the French and subsequently mirrored in the "patterns of despotism" that have shaped Haitian political history since 1804 (2011: 158–59). In this regard, Fatton's concerns are similar to those expressed by Millery Polyné, who writes of the history of race and development and the particular ways in which that history determines the relative impact of similar natural events in the Americas, such as the earthquake in Chile in 2010 (2013: xviii). Analyzing print media following the events in Haiti and Chile, Polyné says that such writing "entrenches the reader into a discourse of Haitian life as antimodern, violent, and perpetually ill-equipped if one properly situates Haiti in the historical and regional context of anti-black, anti-Haitian prejudice" (xix). Nick Nesbitt largely echoes Polyné in his argument that the earthquake was "no mere natural event," and he denounces the "political catastrophe wrought from forcible underdevelopment and structural precariousness," which is for him the fundamental reason for the extent of human and material damage that followed the Haitian event (2013: 5).

Lamenting the historical and contemporary impotence of the state, Fatton further argues that the creation of a new and responsible state is crucial to any strategy of reconstruction (2011: 175–76).[7] Fatton's ideas are in turn echoed by the political scientist Jean-Germain Gros who states that "the destruction of January 12, 2010, was certainly caused by nature, but the scale of the destruction speaks to generations, if not centuries, of ineffectual government" (2010). In *State Failure, Underdevelopment, and Foreign Intervention in Haiti*, Gros shows how foreign economic interventions and the influx of international capital produce benefits for certain members of the elite but create obstacles to the building of a more equitable system of resource redistribution (2012). If Gros argues that internal constraints such as deforestation, demographic pressure, or the economic elite's disregard for the well-being of a majority of Haitians contribute to the failure of the Haitian state, he nonetheless argues that building a more just and democratic state is necessary and possible. "Working states save lives; failed states cannot. Thus, state making is a matter of life or death" (1).

Writing on the immediate postearthquake period, Patrick Sylvain considers the failure of a particular Haitian politician, President René Préval, to articulate the state vision of how Haiti should react to the disaster (2013: 87). Sylvain critiques the "executive silence" that followed the earthquake, most notably that of Préval himself, whose silence is judged to be unethical at a time of a catastrophic challenge (90). Such silence and inaction on behalf of the state's representatives is far from new. As Sylvain argues: "The landscape of indifference is so deeply rooted in the nation's history that silence by Haitian executives has created a political culture of ineptitude and passivity" (91).

In the absence of a functioning state and a coherent state discourse, Haitian intellectuals such as Hurbon have a particular prominence, and bear a particular responsibility. Indeed, intellectual discourse to a large extent compensates for the virtual lack of state leadership and the "executive silence" on issues of citizenship, politics, and human rights. Haitian literature in particular has traditionally functioned as a site in which are debated and explored many of the issues that the state ignores and appears unable to act on. As Dash writes, this is not a new phenomenon, as "literature served the function of critical consciousness in nineteenth-century Haiti" (1998: 49). Literature may also be one of the most privileged means for the outsider to gain direct access to Haitian ways of thinking and being. In her postearthquake memoir, Amy Wilentz writes of her relationships with various Haitian acquaintances, and how first appearances can be deceptive in that initial impressions of insiders being "available and transparent" are not always confirmed by subsequent exchanges. Wilentz writes of how she has "gotten beyond this barrier" with many of her Haitian friends. But with others she has not, and she has "stopped trying to get past the ramparts of the citadelle" (2013: 86). One might say that reading Haitian fiction and poetry offers one way of going beyond these kinds of interpersonal and intercultural barriers and establishing an intimate bond with a Haitian voice. However, at the same time, even literature remains at times opaque and impenetrable to the outsider (and perhaps also to the insider), and authors do not always, if ever, expose fully or directly their personal thoughts, nor should they be expected to. Nonetheless, as Anderson argues, natural disasters involve "human interaction with the environment and as such must be mediated through culture" (2011: 1). In Haiti literature has often been a privileged mediator in registering and memorializing natural and other disasters. Literature may also be related to forms of power in that "culture is never apolitical; rather politics represents the process by which cultural trends are formalized and institutionalized as political power" (2).

In effect, Anderson's ideas are similar to the arguments proposed by Michel-Rolph Trouillot in the first chapter of *Silencing the Past*, which is entitled, tellingly, "The Power of the Story." Trouillot challenges the "storage model of memory-history," the view of "knowledge as recollection" (1995: 14). Arguing that the past is never truly over, and that it cannot exist independently of the present, Trouillot contends that historical knowledge involves both the social process and the narratives of that process, and that theories of history "rarely examine in detail the concrete production of specific narratives" (22). Trouillot's argument that history and fiction are related in all societies effectively elevates the importance of literature, and it places a new emphasis on the concrete narrative processes through which history is told. Trouillot's interest lies less in determining what history is than in understanding how it works, for the definition of history changes with time and place, or as he puts it, "history reveals itself only through the production of specific narratives" (25). This in turn leads Trouillot to privilege the ordinary, the unexceptional, what he calls the "heroism of anonymous men, women and—too often forgotten—children going about the business of daily life" (2002: 205). The ordinary stories of such historical actors are important to Trouillot's effort to imagine a broader view of historical production than that acknowledged by most theorists, and to valorize what he calls the "field laborers" of historical production, the disparate groups and individuals "who augment, deflect, or reorganize" the work of professional historians and who include, crucially, artists of all kinds, including fiction writers (1995: 25). As such, fiction is a valid and dynamic means of creating historical knowledge; indeed, it is indispensable in acquiring the kind of deep, broad, and at times contradictory understanding of history that Trouillot writes of.[8]

Circum-Caribbean Disasters: Haiti and Beyond

Haiti is far from isolated in its experience of disaster; indeed, the idea of a dystopian present in the Caribbean at large is suggested in the visual art project undertaken in 2011 by the journal *Small Axe*, entitled "The Visual Life of Catastrophic History."[9] The project responds to the prominence of the theme of catastrophe in contemporary critical thought and artistic practice. The reasons for the prominence of catastrophe in contemporary thought and culture include the "wars without end" unleashed by "emperor-like sovereigns"; the personal and social effects of systemic financial collapse; the destructive force of natural events such as tsunamis, hurricanes, and earthquakes; and the "terrible spectacle" of the most vulnerable people fleeing in fear before "the total power of men and gods" ("Visual Life" 2011: 133). Together, these calamities create the "pervasive haunting sense" that we are living in "a perpetual state of emergency, not only in the very midst of seemingly uncontrollable disaster but also in a constant *expectation* of disaster" (133). Within this global catastrophic present, the Caribbean is "a measureless scene of catastrophe," a site particularly susceptible to calamities, to various natural disasters, and social and political atrocities (134). The statement further argues that the Caribbean was "*inaugurated* in catastrophe," in the "founding colonial catastrophe," which manifests itself still in societies structured with "tiny rapacious elites" at one end and "impoverished masses" at the other, and through "cynical, unresponsive governments given to authoritarian rule and corruption" (134). While Haiti is far from alone in living in a time of catastrophe, it may be considered, as the *Small Axe* statement argues, as perhaps the "*limit*-instance" of catastrophic history, of a "hard experience familiar to *all* our Caribbean" (134).

This edited volume brings new questions and new stories to the fore by exploring the aftermaths of disasters in a broad historical frame in order to shed light on the structural frameworks of pre- and postdisaster periods, with a special emphasis on the popular and sometimes intimate responses catastrophes generate. The activation or constitution of solidarity networks; the resurgence of political and social movements fighting against industrialization, gentrification, and institutions that foster displacement of local populations; the creation of new grassroots organizations meant to preserve local ways of life and cultures; and processes of grief, commemoration, and collective trauma are important features of postdisaster landscapes. Believing, like Trouillot, in the power of the story, our book offers a dialogue between social scientists and scholars who study contemporary literature and arts to help us reflect on the political, economic, social, and cultural shifts and structures that render regions vulnerable to disasters, shape recovery efforts, and transform collective memory.

Why should we connect the efforts to understand disasters made by humanities scholars and social scientists? What does this dialogue bring? In short, even when doing ethnographic work, it is difficult for anthropologists to account for the grief and trauma a disaster creates. Social science methods may convey the depth of an environmental and political crisis, but they rarely account for the aesthetic crises spurred by disasters in the domain of literary and artistic representation. Literary works, for instance, reveal less visible cultural shifts that change societies in the long term through processes that form collective memory. Many literary works published in the aftermath of the Haitian earthquake show, for example, how people tapped into religious and economic systems forged after the country's independence to commemorate their loved ones and to activate solidarity networks. Grasping these transformations in the human understanding of one's surroundings is crucial for social scientists and policy makers alike, as they convey a sense of who communities want to be and how they want to manage their environments and livelihoods in the future. As many recovery efforts show, experts on the ground often fail to understand local cultures and operate with abstract plans that are disconnected from the social and cultural norms of the places where they work. Analyzing aesthetic productions allows us to think about the lived dimensions of reconstruction periods. The Berghahn series Catastrophes in Context, anchored in the social sciences, is a fitting place for such a dialogue. The chapters that follow explore at once the structural and cultural dynamics of disasters. These texts offer accounts of the neocolonial violence that constitutes the framework in which disasters unfold and, in the meantime, provide reflections on the large and small changes that affect everyday people and their response to disasters. These responses framed in aesthetic works provide, in turn, fruitful accounts of postdisaster periods where alternative visions of the future can emerge.

The aim is to encourage debate and collaboration between scholars working on disasters from various disciplinary perspectives so that the volume will offer a rich and diverse set of arguments and analyses on the ever-relevant theme of catastrophe in the circum-Caribbean. The chapters are a selection of the most innovative papers presented at a conference held at Florida State University in February 2020 on the theme of disaster in the 21st-century circum-Caribbean. The conference was held to mark the ten-year anniversary of the Haitian earthquake, and the volume proposes a regional approach to disaster that draws connections between twenty-first-century experiences of catastrophe in the region. This comparative, regional perspective allows the volume to consider, for example, how different forms of disaster capitalism and colonial legacies encourage replacement of populations, displacing people who have longer histories in a place with others who will have temporary and surface relationships to that place, transforming them into sites of skimming visitation. Such population replacement has taken place in New Orleans after Hurricane Katrina, is being put in place bureaucratically in Puerto Rico after Hurricane Maria, and is a major concern for the small coastal communities in the Florida panhandle after Hurricane Michael. Likewise, megadisasters open new opportunities for political experimentation such as the complete wipeout of public education in New Orleans or the possibility of a permanent federal shutdown in Puerto Rico.[10]

This is a cross-disciplinary volume that combines and puts into dialogue perspectives on disaster from fields such as anthropology, history, cultural studies, sociology, and literary studies. The volume opens with three chapters written by cultural anthropologists committed to long-term ethnography in Haiti. Mark Schuller offers a broad overview of past and present disasters in Haiti in the first chapter of the volume. In "*Mòd Leta*: Haitian Understandings of Crises Past in Present," Schuller shows how the violence and dehumanization of the plantation world and of global capitalism engendered unequal exchanges that still hamper the region. The Caribbean is disproportionately beset by hazards and suffers for warming sea temperatures. Seen from the Caribbean, climate change is a violent continuation of slavery and displacement. Local "folk" theories long disaggregated "hazards" from "disasters," and community mutual aid and survival, which were adaptations to slavery, were precursors to "resilience"—in all its contradictions—long before it became popularized. From whose point of view do events become "disasters," and what is the "disaster" itself? Weaving ethnographic insights with a deep analysis of Caribbean theoretical and aesthetic practices, Schuller opens the volume by proposing to move toward a Caribbean epistemology of disasters based on the lived realities and experiences of Caribbean people and reflective of processes anchored in a long and violent past.

In the second chapter, Laura Wagner examines the relationship between two catastrophes: the earthquake of 12 January 2010, which struck Port-au-Prince and the surrounding area, and 2016's Hurricane Matthew, which struck Haiti's southern peninsula, particularly the Grand'Anse province. The former was an unprecedented urban disaster, which unleashed a massive, if failed, international aid response. The latter was a rural disaster, which received far less media coverage and humanitarian aid. The two events are connected, however, through patterns of centralization and rural-to-urban migration. This essay revisits Wagner's writing from shortly after the earthquake, which focused on Melise Rivien, a woman from the rural Grand'Anse who was a domestic worker in Port-au-Prince, and who died when the home in which she lived and worked collapsed during the quake. By following the lives of some of her family in the Grand'Anse, through Hurricane Matthew and beyond, this essay explores how things have, and haven't, changed in the ten years since the earthquake, and it asks what recovery means when the disaster never ends.

In the third chapter, Vincent Joos revisits the notion of *malediksyon* (curse), which journalists and experts often use to describe Haiti's cycles of disasters. Televangelists and economic experts often depict Vodou (and, obliquely, peasant cultures) as being an obstacle to modernity and progress. More secular versions of a cursed Haiti circulate as well. Indeed, by silencing the history of colonization and imperial domination that led to the massive deforestation of the country or the demographic centralization of its people in Port-au-Prince, it seems that an endless series of disasters strike Haiti randomly. Using ethnographic insights, Joos analyzes the blank-slate discourse that erases a violent history of nefarious foreign interventions that transformed Haiti into a region prone to disasters. In this chapter, Joos takes historical vignettes to show how the blank-slate mentality of explorers and experts of all kinds have transformed and, ultimately, ruined northeastern Haiti. Thinking of the island as a blank space is not only a tool to develop nefarious industries but also a powerful narrative strategy that is used to silence Haitians and to destroy the counterplantation systems upon which peasant farmers founded viable lives.

Chapter four shifts the attention to another key twenty-first-century disaster, as Shearon Roberts tracks how, fifteen years since Hurricane Katrina, New Orleans remains an important case study of how postdisaster recovery can be persistently unequal. This chapter examines how post-Katrina gentrification of African American neighborhoods impacted historical and cultural traditions that are both a source of currency (livelihood) and community building for Black residents. This chapter therefore examines 2019 social media and alternative media discourse by New Orleans residents around intrusions to cultural traditions by primarily new white residents, described as "transplants" residing in historically Black wards in the city. While mainstream media in the city have largely framed post–Hurricane Katrina gentrification of Black neighborhoods as a debate between "progress versus preservation," this study describes how native African American residents saw outsiders as increasing hostile law enforcement through profiling. The cultural tensions brought on by gentrification provide a window into how postdisaster recovery impacts marginalized groups. While native white populations in New Orleans have returned to the city close to their original levels, the same has not occurred for native African American residents fifteen years later. More importantly, cultural intrusions impact the livelihood of Black residents, whose informal and formal traditions are an economic means for these communities in a city that sells its culture, primarily Black culture, as its primary revenue draw for tourism.

In chapter five, Jana Evans Braziel furthers the analysis of the privatization and financialization of entire regions of the circum-Caribbean by focusing on the impact of catastrophe (cat) bond trading in Haiti and Puerto Rico. Braziel examines the collision of natural disasters and unnatural "structural adjustments" in the Greater Caribbean by interrogating neoliberal approaches to so-called "disposable" economies, for-profit debt refinancing, externally imposed austerity measures, and postdisaster rebuilding (or not) in the wake of Caribbean natural disasters. Taking the 2010 earthquake in Haiti, referred to in Kreyòl (Creole) by the onomatopoeiac term "Goudougoudou," and the 2017 fallout of Hurricane Maria in Puerto Rico as the two primary case studies, but also pointing to salient postdisaster parallels in New Orleans following Hurricane Katrina, Braziel dismantles the inhumane policies and dehumanizing impacts of contemporary necrocapitalism—the debased international trading in death and disaster stocks, or the for-profit investment in death capital. Braziel argues that the Caribbean, long the all-inclusive resort for the rich and famous, then the all-too-frequent site of offshore banking for corporate wealth, has now entered a perilous period of absolute necrocapital destruction before (and perhaps for) profit.

In chapter six, John Ribó tracks how people defend the dead in postdisaster landscapes. In her incisive meditation on black culture in the long afterlife of slavery, *In the Wake: On Blackness and Being*, Christina Sharpe asks, "What does it mean to defend the dead?" (10). Sharpe turns to the autobiographical to undiscipline her study, to validate the quotidian lived experiences of black and brown people, and to illustrate the numerous, labor-intensive manifestations of defending the dead from all manner of neglect and mistreatment—from the anodyne, slow violence of bureaucratic negligence, to the outright, state-sanctioned murder by police and military forces, to the symbolic oblivion of erasure. In response to these various modes of violence, tactics for defending the dead take different forms throughout the African diaspora. This chapter interrogates strategies for defending the dead in the neocolonial context of Puerto Rico through close readings of literary and cultural productions that stand as forms of "wake work." Here, Ribó argues that wake work cultivates an active, symbiotic, cyclical relationship in which the dead empower the living to defend the dead; this interdependent and dynamic relationship of the living and the dead alloys cultural production and political protest, suffusing popular culture with historical import and communal purpose.

In chapter seven, Vanessa Selk asserts that when a hurricane hits a country, a tsunami swallows an island, or an earthquake destroys a city, the priority of political authorities generally remains security, so as to ensure the safety of the population. The notion of emergency, resulting from a disaster, is hence commonly linked to that of safety: to avoid a crisis, an emergency alert mobilizes hundreds of government forces and services to protect a population. This applies not only to government forces within their own borders but also to diplomatic services in a foreign country, who have to collaborate with local authorities to ensure their citizens are safe. But what actions, Selk asks, are taken during a disaster by government or diplomatic services that usually do not deal with security or safety matters. Are culture and education relegated to nonpriority status during a catastrophe? Can cultural diplomacy play a key role in a humanitarian crisis? Can cultural diplomacy be led by nonofficial art organizations or artists themselves? Is art a matter of emergency? This chapter focuses on the limitations and opportunities for art and culture to thrive in spite, or as a result, of a disaster, thanks to political or diplomatic decisions abroad. Several pan-Caribbean examples and comparisons explain how political decisions related to culture can affect in different ways the perception of belonging to a region or a territory in a postcolonial context, and how disaster politics and communication can increase the value of artwork in the short term.

In chapter eight, Martin Munro asks: What are the effects of a catastrophic earthquake on a society, its culture, and its politics? Which of these effects are temporary and which endure? Are the various effects immediately discernible, or do they manifest themselves over time? What is the relationship between natural disasters and social change? What roles do artists, and writers in particular, have in witnessing, bearing testimony to, and gauging the effects of natural disasters? These are some of the fundamental questions raised by the Haitian earthquake of 12 January

2010, a uniquely destructive event in the recent history of cataclysmic disasters, in Haiti and the broader world.[11] The sheer scale of the destruction caused by the earthquake posed an unprecedented challenge to authors, as well as other artists. Although many authors expressed initially their feelings of helplessness and of the futility of their art, virtually all established and many new and original voices published works soon after the earthquake, some of whom write directly of the event, while others make no reference to it at all. There was and has been no single, unifying literary reaction to the earthquake; rather, there is a proliferation of works that share certain thematic preoccupations but which insist on the freedom to express those themes in original ways, thus making new and daring explorations of form a crucial part of the meaning of the event as it is processed through the workings of the individual text. If, as many authors initially said, art is useless in the face of catastrophe, that uselessness has a paradoxical value, in that it can be used to liberate an author from the potentially restrictive expectation to act as a faithful chronicler of a social event. In this chapter, Munro engages with a unique piece of writing: Marvin Victor's *Corps mêlés*, a quite brilliant first—and to date, only—novel that was hailed as one of the first "postearthquake novels," but which today is rarely discussed by scholars and risks being forgotten, itself a kind of tragically neglected ruin.

In chapter nine, Alex Lenoble furthers the literary analysis of disasters by analyzing *Melovivi*, a play written by Frankétienne, who was rehearsing his latest theater play on the day of the earthquake. In the play, against a background of disaster, two characters, A and B, talk and ramble in Frankétienne's unique language. In this postapocalyptic vision of a world in peril, the characters ponder the global ecological situation and the emptiness of grand discourses mouthed by pseudoexperts and international institutions. It is a world that goes around in circles, and where language reveals its vanity. In this chapter, Lenoble explores how Haiti, which is not named as such in the play, is in fact inscribed in a broader eco- and geopolitical space, where everything is interconnected. For the first time Frankétienne's work addresses issues pertaining to our current environmental crisis. Lenoble also argues that *Melovivi* is not a representation of events that happened or were about to happen; it does not deliver any intellectual knowledge or political analysis. The text of the play, the chapter argues, is only a support for a performance where living bodies express and transmit affects to other living bodies, in ways that suggest the transhistorical, transnational, transgenerational nature of Caribbean experiences of disaster.

Ultimately, without suggesting that disaster is the only way through which to approach the contemporary circum-Caribbean, the volume recognizes the importance of disaster in lived reality and seeks to deepen and broaden understanding of the theme by juxtaposing work from scholars across disciplines. Such collaboration and dialogue are rare, but we feel they are necessary as we address the multiple ramifications of living in and with contemporary disasters.

Vincent Joos is an assistant professor of anthropology and global French studies at Florida State University. His work has appeared in *Economic Anthropology, Transforming Anthropology, Vibrant,* and *World Politics Review*. His work focuses on postdisaster reconstruction in the Caribbean. He recently published his first book, *Urban Dwellings, Haitian Citizenships: Housing, Memory, and Daily Life in Haiti* (Rutgers University Press, 2021).

Martin Munro is Winthrop-King Professor of French and francophone studies at Florida State University. His publications include *Writing on the Fault Line: Haitian Literature and the Earthquake of 2010* (Liverpool University Press, 2014); *Tropical Apocalypse: Haiti and the Caribbean End Times* (University of Virginia Press, 2015); and *Listening to the Caribbean: Sounds of Slavery, Revolt, and Race* (Liverpool University Press, 2022).

John Ribó is assistant professor of English at Florida State University, where he specializes in contemporary Latinx literatures and cultures. His work has appeared in *Chiricú, The Journal of Haitian Studies, Cuban Studies,* and *ASAP*. He is currently completing his first manuscript, tentatively titled *Haitian Hauntings*.

Notes

1. See, for example, Michel-Rolph Trouillot, *Peasants and Capital: Dominica in the World Economy* (Baltimore, MD: The Johns Hopkins University Press, 1988), and Jean Casimir, *The Haitians: A Decolonial History* (Chapel Hill, NC: the University of North Carolina Press, 2020).
2. See, for example, Susan Bassnett's essay "Seismic Aftershocks: Responses to the Great Lisbon Earthquake of 1755" on the various interpretations of the Lisbon earthquake of 1755, which range from religious questions on the existence of God to Enlightenment-inspired rationalist understandings. Bassnett, Susan. 2006. "Seismic Aftershocks: Responses to the Great Lisbon Earthquake of 1755." Sites of Exchange: European Crossroads and Faultlines, edited by Maurizio Ascari and Adriana Corrado, Rodopi, pp. 177-88.
3. See also David Scott's interpretation of the collapse of the Grenada Revolution as "merely one significant *episode* in a larger story of generations of conflict in what is now imagined and represented as the cyclical pattern of a general history whose generative logic is catastrophic" (2014: 74–75).

4. Jonathan Katz suggests that disasters are also godsends for donors, who by late March 2012 had delivered less than half of the long-term funding pledged for 2010 and 2011. Donor countries, he argues, let President René Préval carry the blame for the lack of reconstruction (207). He also says that with the huge logistical costs of the relief operation, "much of the money was a stimulus program for the donor countries themselves" (206). He further critiques the overall achievements of the foreign relief programs: "Having sought above all to prevent riots, ensure stability, and prevent disease, the responders helped spark the first, undermine the second, and by all evidence caused the third" (278). Raoul Peck's 2013 film *Assistance mortelle* presents a cutting critique of humanitarian and development aid in Haiti. For a critique of "military humanitarianism" in postearthquake Haiti, see Jennifer Greenburg, "The 'Strong Arm' and the 'Friendly Hand.'"
5. See in this regard the excellent "Haiti Memory Project," an online archive of testimonies about the earthquake. The project, somewhat unlike Hurbon, "assumes that earthquake is a point-zero in the lives of individual Haitians and in Haitian history; it is a moment that divided time into 'before' and 'after.'" (The Haiti Memory Project website, Louie B. Nunn Center for Oral History, University of Kentucky Libraries, accessed 24 October 2013, https://web.archive.org/web/20131222134939/http://haitimemoryproject.org/the-haiti-memory-project/about/>)
6. See also Hurbon's (2012) critique of the "privatization of the state."
7. See also the other articles published in the March 2011 special issue of *Journal of Black Studies* on the theme of "The Haiti Earthquake of 2010: The Politics of a Natural Disaster."
8. J. Michael Dash explores these ideas further, and suggests that Trouillot in some regards did join the "family business" of writing fiction in his anthropological work. ("Neither Magical Nor Exceptional: The Idea of the Ordinary in Caribbean Studies," paper for Haitian Studies Association annual conference, Port-au-Prince, Haiti, 8 November 2013.)
9. In an early postearthquake article, Yanick Lahens insists that Haiti and its challenges are far from peripheral to global modernity: "In spite of those limits, despite its poverty, its political vicissitudes, its meager existence, Haiti is not a periphery. Its history makes of it a center. I have always lived it as such. As a metaphor for all the challenges that humanity must face today and for which this modernity has not delivered on its promises" ("Haïti ou la santé du malheur," *Libération* 19 January 2010, https://www.liberation.fr/planete/2010/01/19/haiti-ou-la-sante-du-malheur_605105/ accessed 23 November 2022).
10. See, for example, Katherine Browne, *Standing in the Need: Culture, Comfort, and Coming Home After Katrina* (Chicago: University of Chicago Press, 2015); Vincanne Adams, *Markets of Sorrow, Labors of Faith: New Orleans in the Wake of Katrina* (Durham, NC: Duke University Press, 2013); Steve Kroll-Smith, Vern Baxter, and Pam Jenkins, *Left to Chance: Hurricane Katrina and the Story of Two New Orleans Neighborhoods* (Austin, TX: University of Texas Press, 2015); Lynn Weber and Lori Peek, eds., *Displaced: Life in the Katrina Diaspora* (Austin, TX: University of Texas Press, 2015); Yarimar Bonilla and Marisol LeBrón, eds., *Aftershocks of Disaster: Puerto Rico Before and After the Storm* (Chicago: Haymarket Books, 2019); Hilda Lloréns, *Making Livable Worlds: Afro-Puerto Rican Women Building Environmental Justice* (Seattle: University of Washington Press, 2021); Ricia Anne Chansky and Marci Denesiuk, eds., *Mi María: Surviving the Storm* (Chicago: Haymarket Books, 2021); Marie T. Mora, Havidán Rodríguez, and Alberto Dávila, eds., *Hurricane Ma-*

ria in Puerto Rico: Disaster, Vulnerability & Resiliency* (Blue Ridge Summit, Pennsylvania: Lexington Books, 2021)
11. Among the effects of the Haitian earthquake listed by the Disasters Emergency Committee are 3.5 million people affected by the quake, 220,000 estimated deaths, 300,000 injured, and nearly 300,000 homes destroyed or badly damaged. ("2010 Haiti Earthquake Facts and Figures," Disasters Emergency Committee website, accessed 9 November 2021, http://www.dec.org.uk/haiti-earthquake-facts-and-figures.)

References

Almeida, Joselyn M. 2011. *Reimagining the Transatlantic, 1780–1890*. Farnham, England: Ashgate.
Anderson, Mark D. 2011. *Disaster Writing: The Cultural Politics of Catastrophe in Latin America*. Charlottesville: University of Virginia Press.
Anglade, Georges. 1981. *Atlas Critique d'Haïti*. Montréal: Groupe d'études et de recherches critiques d'espace, Département de géographie, Université du Québec à Montréal.
Bakun, William H., Claudia H. Flores, and Uri S. ten Brink. 2012. "Significant Earthquakes on the Enriquillo Fault System, Hispaniola, 1500–2010: Implications for Seismic Hazard." *Bulletin of the Seismological Society of America* 102 (1): 18–30.
Beckett, Greg. 2020. *There Is No More Haiti. Between Life and Death in Port-au-Prince*. Oakland, CA: University of California Press.
Bellande, Alex. 2015. *Haïti Déforestée, Paysages Remodelés*. Montreal: CIDIHCA.
Benson, LeGrace. 2010. "Art, Artists, and the Shaking of the Foundations." In *Haiti Rising: Haitian History, Culture, and the Earthquake of 2010*, ed. Martin Munro, 87–95. Liverpool, UK: Liverpool University Press.
Bonilla, Yarimar. 2015. *Non-Sovereign Futures: French Caribbean Politics in the Wake of Disenchantment*. Chicago: University of Chicago Press.
Casimir, Jean. 2020. *The Haitians: A Decolonial History*, trans. Laurent Dubois. Chapel Hill, NC: University of North Carolina Press.
Cohen, Alisha. 2011. *Bananas: Nutrition, Diseases and Trade Issues*. Hauppauge, NY: Nova Science Publishers.
Columbus, Christopher. 1960. *The Journal of Christopher Columbus*. New York: C. N. Potter.
Corvington, Georges. 1970. *Port-au-Prince au cours des ans*. Port-au-Prince: Henri Deschamps.
Dash, J. Michael. 1998. *The Other America: Caribbean Literature in a New World Context*. Charlottesville: University of Virginia Press.
Dubois, Laurent. 2004. *Avengers of the New World: The Story of the Haitian Revolution*. Boston, MA: Harvard University Press.
Fatton, Robert, Jr. 2011. "Haiti in the Aftermath of the Earthquake: The Politics of Catastrophe." *Journal of Black Studies* 42(2): 158–85.
Ferdinand, Malcolm. 2022. *Decolonial Ecology: Thinking from the Caribbean World*. Cambridge, UK: Polity Press.
Floyd, Troy S. 1973. *The Columbus Dynasty in the Caribbean, 1492–1526*. Albuquerque: Univ. of New Mexico Press.

Girvan, Norman. 1975. *Aspects of the Political Economy of Race in the Caribbean and the Americas*. Atlanta, GA: Institute of the Black World.
Greenburg, Jennifer. 2013. "The "Strong Arm" and the "Friendly Hand": Military Humanitarianism in Post-earthquake Haiti." *Journal of Haitian Studies*, 19(1), 95–122.
Gros, Jean-Germain. 2012. *State Failure, Underdevelopment, and Foreign Intervention in Haiti*. New York: Routledge.
———. 2010. "In Haiti, Recovery Hinges on Fixing Government." Public Broadcasting Service. Feb 8, 2010. https://www.pbs.org/newshour/show/in-haiti-recovery-hinges-on-fixing-government.
Hurbon, Laënnec. 2012. "Catastrophe permanente et reconstruction." *L'Observatoire de la reconstruction* 6: 8–10.
Katz, Jonathan. 2014. *The Big Truck that Went By: How the World Came to Save Haiti and Left Behind a Disaster*. New York: Macmillan
Koch, Alexander, Chris Brierley, Mark M. Maslin, and Simon L. Lewis. 2019. "Earth System Impacts of the European Arrival and Great Dying in the Americas after 1492." *Quaternary Science Reviews* 207:13–36, https://doi.org/10.1016/j.quascirev.2018.12.004.
Kolbe, Athena and Muggah, Robert. 2011. Haiti: Why an accurate count of civilian deaths matters. July 12, 2011. *Los Angeles Times*. Retrieved 11/23/2022. https://www.latimes.com/opinion/la-xpm-2011-jul-12-la-oe-muggah-haiti-count-20110712-story.html
Maclean, Frances. 2008. "The Lost Fort of Columbus." *Smithsonian Magazine* (January).
McAlister, Elizabeth. 2012. "Soundscapes of Disaster and Humanitarianism: Survival Singing, Relief Telethons, and the Haiti Earthquake." *Small Axe* 16(3): 22–38, https://doi.org/10.1215/07990537-1894078.
Miller, Christopher. 2008. *The French Atlantic Triangle: Literature and Culture of the Slave Trade*. Durham, NC: Duke University Press
Mintz, Sidney W. 1974. *Caribbean Transformations*. Chicago: Aldine.
Moreau de Saint-Méry, M. L. E. 1797. *Description Topographique, physique, civile, politique, et historique de la partie française de l'isle de Saint-Domingue*. Paris: Dupont.
Nesbitt, Nick. 2013. "Haiti, the Monstrous Anomaly." In *The Idea of Haiti: Rethinking Crisis and Development*, ed. Millery Polyné, 3–26. Minneapolis: University of Minnesota Press.
Palmié, Stephan, and Francisco A. Scarano. 2011. *The Caribbean: A History of the Region and Its Peoples*. Chicago: The University of Chicago Press.
Peck, Raoul. 2013. *Assistance mortelle*. Film. Producteurs : ARTE France, Velvet Film, Figuier Production, Velvet Film Inc., RTBF, Entre Chien et Loup.
Polyné, Millery. 2013. "Introduction: To Make Visible the Invisible Epistemological Order: Haiti, Singularity, and Newness." In *The Idea of Haiti: Rethinking Crisis and Development*, ed. Millery Polyné, xi-xxxvii. Minneapolis: University of Minnesota Press.
Prepetit, Claude. 2008. "Tremblements de terre en Haïti: mythe ou réalité?" Port-au-Prince, Haiti : Laboratoire National du Bâtiment et des Travaux Publics. https://lnbtp.gouv.ht/publications/Seismes%20en%20Haiti.pdf
Robinson, Cedric J. 1983. *Black Marxism*. Chapel Hill: University of North Carolina Press.
Scott, David. 2014. *Omens of Adversity: Tragedy, Time, Memory, Justice*. Durham, NC: Duke University Press
Sharpe, Christina. 2016. *In the Wake: On Blackness and Being*. Durham, NC: Duke University Press.

Sheller, Mimi. 2020. *Island Futures: Caribbean Survival in the Anthropocene*. Durham, NC: Duke University Press.

Shigematsu, Kiyoshi. 2013. *Mata tsugi no haru e*. Tokyo: Fushosha.

Schuller, Mark. 2021. *Humanity's Last Stand*. New Brunswick, NY: Rutgers University Press.

Southey, Thomas. 1827. *Chronological History of the West Indies, Vol. 2*. London: Longman, Rees, Orme, Brown & Green.

Sylvain, Patrick. 2013. "The Violence of Executive Silence." In *The Idea of Haiti: Rethinking Crisis and Development*, ed. Millery Polyné, 87–109. Minneapolis: University of Minnesota Press.

Trouillot, Michel-Rolph. 1988. *Peasants and Capital: Dominica in the World Economy*. Baltimore, MD: The Johns Hopkins University Press.

———. 1995. *Silencing the Past: Power and the Production of History*. Boston: Beacon Press.

———. 2002. "Culture on the Edges: Caribbean Creolization in Historical Context." In *From the Margins: Historical Anthropology and Its Futures*, ed. Millery Polyné, 189–210. Durham, NC: Duke University Press.

Vaughn, Sarah. 2022. *Engineering Vulnerability: In Pursuit of Climate Adaptation*. Durham, NC: Duke University Press.

Wilentz, Amy. 2013. *Farewell, Fred Voodoo: A Letter from Haiti*. New York: Simon and Schuster.

"The Visual Life of Catastrophic History: A Small Axe Project Statement." 2011. *Small Axe* 34: 133–36.

CHAPTER 1

Mòd Leta

Haitian Understandings of Crises Past in Present

MARK SCHULLER

Haiti typically garners attention from media, policymakers, philanthropic organizations, and activists in the US and other countries within the global north only during crises. Building on the excellent analyses from Haitian scholars like Michel-Rolph Trouillot (1990) and Gina Ulysse (2010) examining the ideological work that representations of Haiti do, this chapter focuses on how disasters are understood and commemorated as *events*. Disaster scholarship often disaggregates disasters from triggering events. This chapter interrogates events in another sense, as media construction. The earthquake of 12 January 2010 in Haiti inspired an unprecedented media signature, which as I argued earlier in this series (2016b) shaped the response. This signature continued in a ten-year commemoration as media event. As this chapter was edited in summer 2022, Haiti again returned to public conversation following the *New York Times*'s publication of "The Ransom," an interactive, in-depth look at Haiti's 1825 independence debt, which the *Times* modelled after the highly successful 1619 project. The *Times* has unparalleled resources for creating media events.

Between the time this chapter was drafted in 2020 and edited in 2022, a devastating series of disaster events beset the world's first free Black republic: in addition to COVID and its economic crisis, Haitian people have faced a constitutional crisis, state-sanctioned violence and human rights violations (both in Haiti and along the US-Mexico border), the assassination of the president, two earthquakes, and a deadly hurricane, with several more months in the hurricane season extended because of climate change. Outside Haiti, the public conversation either fused these crises in "exceptionalist" terms that denigrate Haiti or portrayed them as discrete, mutually unintelligible crises that are disconnected from foreign intervention.

By contrast, Haitian scholars, activists, aid professionals, and community leaders understand these events portrayed in isolation, the *kriz konjonktirèl* ("conjunctural" or intersecting crisis), as manifestations of the *kriz estriktirèl* (structural crisis), which has its roots in the brutality of plantation slavery and slaveholding powers' punishment for the Haitian Revolution that first ended it. As many in Haiti tell it, the past lives on in the present. These events all highlight the *mòd leta*, or "governance strategies," which is also a pun on the words *mò deta*, meaning deaths resulting from state violence, and an aspect of Achille Mbembe's (2003) necropolitics.[1] Haitian understandings thus challenge the focus on disasters as events, instead foregrounding the *longue durée* crisis of global racial capitalism.

This chapter centers Haitian understandings of disasters. I have been working alongside scholars, activists, and community leaders since 2001 as both a scholar and activist—as a visiting professor with a formal affiliation and as a member of activist collectives. My commitments to communities and movements have shaped and in many ways defined the formal research I have conducted. Since the 2010 earthquake I have led four large mixed-method studies focusing on various aspects of the international aid response and its hegemonic vehicle, nongovernmental organizations (NGOs). In addition to data from these formal research projects, this chapter is informed by relationships with Haitian professionals and activists developed over the decades, which have led to conversations and invitations to present and conduct further research. In particular, I was in Haiti on 12 January 2020, to offer solidarity. All quotes not otherwise attributed come from conversations with the author, and following disciplinary convention and to protect the confidentiality of individuals, people listed as only a first name in this article are pseudonyms.

Specifically, contrasting the foreign media event, this chapter shares how various groups within Haiti commemorated the 2010 earthquake. For people in Haiti the memory of the earthquake of 12 January 2010 is hard to forget. But decades of foreign intervention cast a large shadow, blurring the lines of what is a disaster. Under a thirteen-year UN occupation, activists referred to postearthquake aid as a humanitarian occupation,[2] what several foreigners called the "republic of NGOs" (Klarreich and Polman 2012; Kristoff and Panarelli 2010). The enormity of the catastrophe and the ways in which catastrophes are layered atop one another make it hard to talk about in any more than fragments, in Caribbean Nobel laureate Derek Walcott's sense.[3] This is how it was experienced, how it is understood: as fragments, still-uncleared rubble. And fragments in the other sense: Haitians are not homogenous. Honoring this humanity and complexity, this chapter presents analyses as fragments.

The Mainstream Disaster Narrative

This complexity was definitely flattened in what can be called the disaster narrative, structured by what's framed inside the story, what is not, who is positioned as victim, and who as hero (Schuller 2016b). The tenth anniversary of the earthquake provided an opportunity to reflect on failures of the international aid response. For for-profit capitalist media and many "alternative" media, the ten-year milestone centered on the question: where did the money go? The story got quite a bit more media play than I had initially thought, perhaps because of two of the main protagonists. Predictably Bill and Hillary Clintons' long shadow prevents other issues from being seen and discussed. Make no mistake: Haitian people are not huge fans of the world's pre-eminent power couple, whom Jonathan Katz dubbed the "King and Queen of Haiti,"[4] now dethroned.

But focusing on foreign failure once again relegates Haitian people and their analyses to the margins. Any discussion of the 2010 earthquake and the failed response needs to be grounded by the material realities, theorized by people's own mixed, complex, and at times contradictory understandings and analyses.

As Gina Athena Ulysse tweeted in 2020 as the tenth anniversary of the quake approached, "the world cracked open and once again Haiti was asked to lead change in the world." One clear example was resilience. After the earthquake, "resilience" was trotted out in a racialized, postcolonial context to either justify sending less aid because Haitian people need less, because of their extraordinary "resilience" (Ulysse 2011), or as cover for disaster capitalism, embodied by Bill Clinton's slogan of "building back better." Clinton used this cheerful phrase following the 2004 earthquake and tsunami in Aceh, Indonesia, whom humanitarian agencies widely regard as a success and the model for "humanitarianism 2.0." Perhaps signaling the importance of Haiti in a new era of increasingly frequent "natural" disasters—what some call the Anthropocene—the next Democrat to take over the White House, Joe Biden, used this same term to gain support for post-COVID investment in public infrastructure. The "better" in Haiti's case only became clear after tens of millions of dollars was spent on projects that favored Clinton donors in areas not affected by the 2010 earthquake, such as an industrial park and mining in the north and tourist development in the south.

Yes, let's talk about disaster capitalism (Klein 2007; Schuller 2008)[5]. Let's also talk about these obviously broken promises. But let's also look at what work this narrative is doing on the ground. The more we make it about the Clintons, the less it is about Haiti and Haitian people. Furthermore, the Clintons' failure in Haiti exemplifies the contradictions of doing well by doing good. The global capitalist system—and the racial order that its foundation in plantation slavery created—broke Haiti in the first place. Only the most naïve, most gullible—or those with the greatest personal interests at stake—could have believed that this very system could repair it.

People in Haiti knew better. A mainstream social democrat and future presidential candidate from the OPL (the Organization of People in the Struggle), Sauveur Pierre Etienne (1997), working out of an NGO, called the proliferation of NGOs an "invasion." Defining the radical position, UEH (State University of Haiti) professor Janil Lwijis—murdered minutes before the earthquake—argued that NGOs are a form of government, implanting foreign capital on Haitian territory (2009). The Haitian proverb expresses this so well: *rat mode, soufle.* The rat bites, and then blows on the wound, what Michel Agier (2003) called the "left hand of empire."

Not "Built Back Better"

Let's be crystal clear: Haiti was not "built back better."

It's the night of 11 January 2020, the day before the media circus. It's a little cooler than usual, with an occasional breeze. People are walking up and down the street. The bread merchant comes by, looking for a sale. Motorcycles zoom in the distance. As it's Saturday, there's not too much traffic on the main arteries.

Street merchants are *chèche lavi* (literally looking for life, making a living) today, the stands a little more stocked than they have been with seasonal produce. The *ti boutik* (mom and pop stores) selling soft drinks or beer as well as imported goods—literally everything else from cooking oil to soap, cornflakes, or bleach—are still empty. Proprietor after proprietor explained the same thing: they don't want to take chances going out to buy more merchandise. More importantly, *pa gen kòb*—there's no money circulating.

Occasionally a private water truck rumbles by, followed by the sound of the pump used for its delivery. Neighbors tell me that the public water utility hasn't provided water since the *gwo peyi lòk*—the countrywide lockdown or general strike—that began in September and lasted for over two months.

The goings-on in the neighborhood of Kriswa,[6] in the capital city of Pòtoprens, are instructive. The house next door lies empty, just its foundations showing where weeds aren't overgrown. All that remains of the structure is the reservoir. Neighbors from up the street come down to fill their five-gallon buckets. One by one, the large trees like the *flanbwayan*, over sixty feet tall, with bright reddish-orange blooms, have been cut down for charcoal. The *jeran*, the domestic workers of the house, have now set up shop in one faded plywood "temporary" shelter and two homemade tin dwellings. The family who lived there, Dr. Charles's, abandoned it to them long ago. Not only did the Charles family not have funds to reconstruct their house, as a family of ten children they couldn't agree on ownership.

Across the street is Lise's house. She comes by the neighborhood from time to time on her motorcycle, which another neighbor taught her to drive after the earthquake. She was here yesterday. Her house wasn't destroyed on 12 January 2010 but during an aftershock eight days after, killing her father. Unlike the Charles family she doesn't own another home, so she can't afford to let this house go. Of the original house, two rooms are still standing, which she can live in once she finishes fixing it up, reconnecting the plumbing and electrical systems. Like Sisyphus, Lise has been steadily working on the house since six months after the earthquake, ten years ago. She fought to get her house tagged "green"—habitable. But like most people here, she doesn't have a steady job; she lives from contract to contract with youth- or education-oriented NGOs. NGO contracts and therefore money to people like Lise have dwindled to almost nothing. But she, like everyone else around, is *degaje l*—getting by. Mostly she's worried that if she didn't come back from time to time someone else would take it from under her, like the house I lived in before the earthquake.

After the 2010 earthquake, my landlady, a Christian pastor, adamantly refused our assistance to repair her house, saying that only God could protect it. She only very reluctantly allowed another neighbor, a structural engineer who still shines a streetlamp for neighborhood students to study by, to evaluate her home and make recommendations. In the summer of 2019 a group of individuals, some of whom were affiliated with the state via the court and police, tagged the house and others in the neighborhood. Several years ago, my landlady disappeared, failing to pay the annual property tax. As of November, a few weeks ago, someone else has lived there. I'm not sure how long I can afford to stay here because my landlords—caring for a frail and aging father—attempted to double the rent last summer. Rents in the neighborhood have more than quadrupled over the past ten years. This is not only because of houses destroyed but a process of what Andrea Steinke (2012) called "humanitarian gentrification," wherein aid and aid workers inflate housing prices. After the earthquake several NGOs offered $2,500-per-month housing contracts for their foreign employees (at the time my monthly rent for a three-bedroom dwelling was $175), triggering a domino effect wherein foreign NGO workers displaced higher-paid Haitian professionals, who displaced lower-paid professionals, and so on down the system. Artificially inflated, rents did not go down again.

It's been ten years since *Goudougoudou*, the earthquake that ripped through Haiti's nerve center, leveling houses, schools, hospitals, and government buildings, trapping and killing many—the "official" count is

230,000, but that's been contested. The fact that there is still a question mark speaks volumes: not only about the enormity of the quake but also the incapacity of the Haitian state to conduct a census, not to mention the extremely low value granted to Haitian lives, particularly those in the majority of the population who have been impoverished. This very low value was evidenced in the mass grave site, with people thrown away like garbage into a big pit in an area called Titanyen, without a name, without an official identity card.

Titanyen is now the northern border of Kanaran, the so-called "promised land" where 250,000–300,000 people live, all since the earthquake, by some accounts the third largest city in Haiti. In many ways, Kanaran is a "bastard child" of the state and international NGO response to 12 January, in direct contrast to the planned relocation site aptly named Corail Cesselesse—endless coral. International NGOs like Oxfam negotiated a resettlement of 20,000 people from the Pétion-Ville Club, a symbol of opulence and exclusion. Managing the Pétion-Ville Club camp—which housed over 60,000 residents at its peak—was an organization cofounded by Academy Award winner Sean Penn. One of the most poignant images from Raoul Peck's film *Fatal Assistance* (2013) was people being loaded onto a bus and sent away. The look of disappointment on people's faces as they saw their destination, a desert, overcame the look of apprehension and fear as they boarded the bus.

As bastard child, Kanaran was shut out of resources. NGOs and international agencies promoted the idea that NGO camp management led to more aid. Indeed, in a quantitative study of indicators such as water, sanitation, and clinics in 108 camps, camp management proved the most statistically significant variable. However, NGOs only agreed to manage around 20 percent of the camps (Schuller and Levey 2014). One reason for this is NGOs' inability to control these spaces. Antonio, a career humanitarian who came to Haiti in 2010, said, "When you are looking at the camp in the middle of nowhere, it is a very closed environment you can control. When you are dealing with an urban environment you don't have as much control: it keeps changing and it keeps moving, and it's very different." While certainly not plentiful, the resources sent to Corail were in direct contrast to Kanaran's nothing. NGOs created a border between "have littles" and "have nots." This is the way aid is designed to be: a patchwork, fragments.

The "promised land" had been twice previously zoned by the government, in the 1940s and 1971, for an industrial park and even tourism (Louis 2013). Dusty, windswept, exposed to the hot Caribbean sun, the land was never developed and rarely even visited, with a few exceptions. On top of the mountain, a small group of Christian believers used it as a site for prayer rituals, naming it Canaan/Kanaran.

Following the earthquake, even such marginal space was at a premium. Whether because of the planned Corail pulling people and aid, or the prayer site, Kanaran became a refuge for people seeking shelter. A persistent rumor held that this land was available for people to squat on, and an estimated thirty thousand people pitched bedsheets right after the earthquake. Churches built out of scrap wood also sprung up almost immediately in the disaster's wake. Abandoned by both the state and international aid agencies, Kanaran became a space of refuge for people displaced by force, like Jean Fils. Before the earthquake, Jean Fils lived in a popular neighborhood close to Haiti's industrial park. He was a sewing maching "operator" when he found factory work and offered his service as a mechanic when the factory closed, which occurred not infrequently. Born in a rural section of the Central Plateau, Jean Fils joined two million people of his generation in moving to the capital because of neoliberal push and pull factors (DeWind and Kinley III 1988; Dupuy 2005). When his cinder block house crumbled in the earthquake, he joined many of his neighbors, taking his family and whatever belongings they could salvage to the nearest open space. He, like a million and a half others, became a statistic: an "internally displaced person." This legal definition came later, after an aid NGO came by to do a census. The camp bore a name, Mozole, in Cité Soleil, which grew up to accommodate Haiti's working poor. PAPDA (Haitian Platform to Advocate for Alternative Development) director Camille Chalmers said, "Cité Soleil is a child of the industrial park" (Bergan and Schuller 2009).

In other words, ten years later, many people in Haiti lived this humanitarian occupation as a continuous legacy. As Laura Wagner (in this volume) writes, "the Earthquake hasn't ended."

Humanitarian Aftershocks

In addition to the ways in which it focuses disproportionate attention on the intentions—"good" or "bad"—of foreign actors, another concern I have with seizing upon this ten-year marker is the common sense—in Gramsci's (1971) definition—that the stories spun by international media and agencies appeal to, taking for granted the position of "Haiti as fucked up." Setting aside partisan swiping at the Clintons, images of the still-unbuilt National Palace or the uncleared rubble seem to do the work all by itself: nothing functions here. Sixteen billion dollars and nothing to show for it. Ergo, Haiti must somehow truly be beyond saving, as right-wing commentators, some less openly white supremacist than others, have long argued, from Moreau de Saint-Mery and Faustin Wirkus to Pat Robertson and David Brooks. This is an opportunity to examine the disaster narrative: Whose story is being shared? What is the disaster?

Foreign failures after the earthquake demand more serious interrogation of the long-term impacts of this "Fatal Assistance" (Peck 2013) or "Humanitarian Aftershocks" (Schuller 2016a).

Haiti *is* a graveyard of failed NGO projects. This is especially visible in the capital of the "republic of NGOs," Leyogann (Baguidy 2020), where faded and torn placards proudly announcing a still-incomplete project stick out like gravestones. However, in addition to asking where did the money go, we should be asking what did it do? Looking at what is missing prevents us from seeing the ruptures triggered by the aid.

Solidarity

What struck me most about 12 January 2010 was the enormous outpouring of solidarity from within Haiti itself, limitless and unparalleled. Even if foreign media didn't see it, many Haitian authors like Edwidge Danticat (2010), Yanick Lahens (2010), Gary Victor (2010), and Michèle Montas (2011) witnessed the same story: the Haitian people were the real heroes of the time. Neighbors shared their daily bread, clothing, water, cooking utensils, and household tools. People whose houses weren't destroyed welcomed family members, neighbors, organization members, and students, while community brigades pulled people out from under the rubble. People created an inventory of who had what quantity of oil or rice, what capacity their buckets or pots had to collect water, and teams offered first aid and reconnected electricity wires. Families in the provinces made many sacrifices to welcome more than 630,000 people who fled the "Republic of Port-au-Prince" (Bengtsson et al. 2011; Jean-Baptiste 2012).

What happened to this outpouring of solidarity? NGOs offering humanitarian aid encouraged the creation of the internally displaced persons camp, creating the identity of "IDP." People who lived in the camps outlined the process, such as Rose-Anne at Hancho: "Well, the camp committee, how it got here, it was when someone came here, a lady, she told us if we want to benefit something here there must be a committee here."

Humanitarian Subjects

Whatever process of community organization existed before the earthquake, now as IDPs Haitians ceased to be citizens and became humanitarian subjects. They had to follow the rules set out by the NGOs in order to receive their aid. The existing civic infrastructure was systematically and deliberately replaced by camp committees, creations of NGOs to "check the box" for "participation," in foreign aid professional Andrea's words. NGOs gave these unelected camp committees, who owed their existence to the NGOs, power to determine who received aid and who was a "legitimate" IDP. This was done "in order to avoid chaos," according to Antonio, a foreign camp management specialist. The discourse from many NGO and international aid staff at the time was one of fear or blame; when it was becoming patently obvious that the aid wasn't working, the first reflex was to blame local residents for being unruly or "faking it." Hillary Clinton's chief of staff, Cheryl Mills, echoed racist comments from Barbara Bush after Hurricane Katrina, saying that Haitian people were "better off" in the camps. Timothy Schwartz added fuel to the fire by declaring that less than a fifth of IDPs were "legitimate."

Almost immediately following publication of the news story that quoted this declaration, Delmas mayor Wilson Jeudy authorized violence to force people out of the camps on the public squares in the town, in his words to "liberate" the spaces. In rapid succession, beginning 12 May 2011, two days before President Michel Martelly took office, armed individuals ripped and set fire to people's tents in a camp called Orphe Shadda in Delmas 1 and in the public squares in Delmas 3 and in Kafou Ayewopò (the "airport corner," also the name of a plaza, where the main thoroughfare intersects the road to the airport). Fifty-one-year-old Thelucia Ciffren was killed in such a brutal act of state violence (Dupain 2012). Again, at the ACRA 2 camp in Juvenat, just before midnight on 16 February 2013, in advance of the Caribbean Community (CARICOM) summit at the nearby Caribe Convention Center, Anel Exeus was assassinated as an armed group set fire to thousands of people's dwellings and belongings. The fire killed a five-year-old.

This violence highlights what many in Haiti and particularly in the camps have deplored, namely that Haitian lives don't matter: *Se paske nou pa moun pou yo. Se bèt nou ye pou yo. Yo trete nou pi mal pase chen.* "It's because we aren't people to them. We are animals to them. They treat us worse than dogs."

"Mini-me"

Camp committees were in effect a mini-me of NGOs, created by them, in their image, reproducing their bureaucratic structure, authority, and top-down governance structures. Camp residents had mixed understandings of the committees; at some camps, such as CAJIT (the Youth Action

Committee of St. Thomas Court) or Kolonbi, a majority identified that they knew the strategies and that they could participate in meetings, and that they knew when they were. But many others were in the dark; for example, no one at the Nan Bannann camp knew how the committee was selected. Committees were overwhelmingly led by men. In the Hancho camp, the NGO required there to be a woman at the head. In every interaction my team and I had with this camp president, she displayed a clear lack of knowledge about the workings of the camp. These interactions were few because she didn't even live there. Camp committees were deputized with the power to distribute ration cards to the IDPs and maintain lists of worthy recipients (see Minn 2016). As the local representatives, fluent in their native language, they accompanied NGOs in their regular census of the population. This was done out of fear of disorder but also fear that somehow someone would slip through and game the system. The most animated a foreign aid worker would get during interviews was to retell such a "gotcha" moment. To put that in context, a $500 annual rental allowance for a Haitian IDP camp resident is only two *days'* worth of a foreign aid worker's per diem. But let's be honest with ourselves, flipping James Ferguson's (2005) phrase: perhaps we scholars are the "evil twin."

Often, camp committee members were members of a church hierarchy, led by a pastor. The NGO managing the Plas Lapè camp, where thirty thousand people lived for a time, was a religious NGO. The Salvation Army had established a base of operations in Haiti in 1950, in the neighborhood. The director handpicked the committee, who were members of his church. Nearly all were men, and *none* lived in the camp; most didn't even live in the neighborhood. Eventually—when foreign money for food aid ran out—the Salvation Army abandoned the camp, leaving two NGOs to duke it out for control. Camp residents disparagingly called the committee *pòch prela*, pockets of tarps. They were so corrupt in pocketing the aid, and their pockets were so big—like tarps—that Josselyn said, "when you are filling it, it never fills up." The language that people used to describe other camp committees clearly demonstrates their distance from the community: *chèf* (chief), *gwo nèg* (big man), and even *gang*. Exceptions to this distance from the population were instructive: CAJIT was literally "off the grid" until April 2010, not officially recognized in the Displacement Tracking Matrix and therefore shut out of aid. Having relied on their own efforts and not having an NGO boss, the camp committee was held in high esteem by residents.

With the attention of foreign actors on state corruption since the PetroCaribe scandal, the humanitarian occupation offers important historical context. While it is true that these actions were completed by Haitian people, the sets of local actors were created as groups, given rules to follow, and sometimes absolute authority on distribution decisions by international agencies.

Demobilization

Another problem with the "mini-me" camp committees is that these foreign creations displaced existing civic infrastructure (Schuller 2012b). Camp committees were in effect "genetically modified" organizations (Schuller 2012a).[7] For example, also in the Plas Lapè camp, this committee staffed by nonresidents displaced a people's organization with several thousand members that had been in the neighborhood since 1990, twenty years at that point. This was not unique to Plas Lapè; all over Port-au-Prince, NGO-created committees were put in direct competition with existing organizations and community leaders. For example, in CAJIT, even the elected local-level government council (CASEC), was excluded from the process. In 2012, an NGO began a process of constructing T-shelters and so created another committee to facilitate this distribution, casting CAJIT aside. Immediately people began talking about corruption of this NGO-created, top-down committee in terms of who received the construction, including the new president who reportedly had three shelters built for himself.

NGO aid and these genetically modified organizations demobilized the population. People's organizations, OP in the French or Kreyòl, had a long and sometimes contradictory history in so-called "popular" neighborhoods (where low-income people resided). The history of OPs began with the popular uprising against Duvalier and the iron fist he represented, against social exclusion, and against extreme poverty triggered by the then-new experiment with neoliberalism. At the core of OPs' *raison d'être* is protest, making demands (Dubuisson 2021). Whether through sit-ins, *bat tenèb* (banging on pots and pans, making noise to demonstrate their anger), or street marches, OPs changed the political landscape in Haiti's swelling capital. In addition to this *militant* approach demanding state services (the Kreyòl word – in this case gendered feminine, to refer to women activists – is more direct than *activist*), OPs also engaged in collectivist self-help projects like street cleanup, managing public water taps, fixing infrastructure projects, and having *ti sourit*, block parties. Central to OPs' civic infrastructure, their ability to transform the social landscape, was the ethos and practice of *kotizasyon*, members' voluntary contribution.

Foreign NGO aid after the earthquake disrupted this in several ways. First, creating (comparatively) well-resourced organizations—the camp committees—created new leaders and challenged the legitimacy of and public confidence in the OPs. Second, a humanitarian logic, often managed by explicitly evangelical NGOs, displaced the discourse of rights. NGO aid became charity, turning active citizens into "mouths to feed" or grateful, "worthy" recipients (Minn 2016), as demonstrated by a young woman living in the Hancho camp: "A foreigner, an NGO, comes to our aid here when God touches its/her/his heart. When that happens, we feel happy." Third, the practice of "cash for work" was the final nail in the coffin for the practice of voluntary, self-help collectivism. Marcel Mauss's *The Gift* (1990) discusses the problems inherent to power relations when a gift cannot be reciprocated. Called the "yellow T-shirt" phenomenon because of the highly visible teams wearing matching NGO garb, the expectation of being paid—albeit at or even less than Haiti's minimum wage—got people out of the practice of *kotizasyon* and volunteer labor (Ayiti Kale Je 2010). Sometimes called in Kreyòl *rèt tann* (lying in wait), the French word for this phenomenon, discussed at least in scholarly circles, is *assistancialisme*, the state of being a spectator, watching instead of acting (Thomas 2013). A neologism used by former French president Nicolas Sarkozy, decidedly not a fan of public assistance, the term translates into a "culture of dependency."

In Haiti people spoke of these genetically modified organizations as *wete trip, mete pay*, literally taking out one's guts to replace with straw—that is, as hollowed out. These committees, created by NGOs to be their deputies, are not able to speak up, nor do they even think to question the aid. Within social movements after the earthquake, one of the biggest insults is to be accused of *fè ONG*—"NGOing" (Schuller 2018). Seen in light of the commodification of projects and their visibility, some activists call out the fragmentation and stalemate of Haiti's current mobilization.

Increasing Violence

David Oxygène, the leader of one such OP (and currently one of the most visible) called MOLEGHAF—the Mouvement de Liberté d'Egalité des Haïtiens pour la Fraternité (Movement of Liberty and Equality of Haitians for Brotherhood)—identified divergent tendencies within popular neighborhoods and the OP sector. In a context of extreme poverty and horrible material conditions—Oxygène kept returning to these, which he names as products of imperialism and the inequalities and social exclusion that it engenders—people identified as "leaders" can either have democratic or "banditist" tendencies. For good or ill, armed individuals—call them "gangs" if you aren't concerned about the racialized connotations—are able to offer material resources and "security" (Kivland 2020). The problem according to Oxygène is that NGOs have systematically propped up this type of leader to the exclusion of democratic, bottom-up people's organizations. And this is not just in the Fònasyonal neighborhood where MOLEGHAF is based. Djems Olivier has documented this in other "red zones," such as Sitesolèy, Belè, and Kafou Fèy. Olivier's painstakingly researched dissertation (Olivier 2020) demonstrates specific ways in which NGOs create *gwo chèf*, fragmenting communities and reifying "turf," a process he calls "archipelization" (Olivier 2021).

Foreign actors seize upon the trope of "gangs"—not only journalists but the US government, the Organization of American States(OAS), and the so-called "Core Group"—the US, Canada, France, Brazil, the European Union and the OAS. Drawing on these racist stereotypes, President Jovenel Moïse attempted to cover up the November 2018 massacre in Lasalin, where Haitian human rights organizations reported seventy-three casualties at the hands of state affiliates seeking to suppress dissent.[8] While reading accounts of violence, it's important to remember their roots in the humanitarian occupation.

Disrupting the Family

NGO aid also disrupted the family. The traditional Haitian rural household structure survived the massive rural exodus triggered by neoliberal push-and-pull policies, which saw Port-au-Prince's population quadruple in two decades (Dupuy 2005). The *lakou*—an extended family compound with clustered sleeping spaces surrounding common outdoor living spaces—obviously had to be modified to adapt to popular neighborhoods and shantytowns, where families often live in single-room dwellings as small as ten feet by ten feet. But before the earthquake, Port-au-Prince households had, on average, 5.37 members, including cousins, aunties, and grandparents. This multigenerational household was a backbone of survival (Bastien 1961; Laguerre 1973). This flexible family unit facilitated security, with one person able to be home to keep watch on the space and children. Larger households also meant that resources could be pooled, with multiple people *chèche lavi*—again, literally "looking for life" or livelihood. Given the precarity of poor families and the volatility of the small formal labor market in the industrial park, most families—59 percent—engaged in commerce. This *lakou*-style family was the nucleus of solidarity. As was often explained to me: "When one of us has food, we all eat." Neighbors sent plates of cooked food as common practice.

Once in the camps, household size decreased to an average of 3.36, a reduction of two people per household. This decrease is greater in camps with more NGO aid. In CAJIT, which as noted earlier missed the train because they were invisible, the average household size went from 5.6 to 4.8, a 15 percent decrease, which approximates the official earthquake death toll. By contrast, households from one of the most NGOized camps, Karade, decreased from an average of 6.1 people before the earthquake to 3.6 after, over 40 percent.

While there may well be important local differences, foreign humanitarian practice offers an explanation. Despite its pretentions to "universality" humanitarian aid is rooted in so-called "Western" culture. Provincializing NGOs reveals the attachment to the patriarchal "nuclear" family that is the norm—if increasingly not the practice—in postindustrial nations like the US, Canada, France, the UK, and other donor countries. The same ration bag of rice beans, and cooking oil went to a family of two or eight. Given the rules of the game, families split up to maximize their chances of receiving a distribution. This division was magnified in the official relocation process of the approximately one in six camp residents who received some sort of relocation assistance. In a follow-up study in four neighborhoods in Port-au-Prince, almost half (47 percent) of people lived with different family than before the earthquake. Almost a third (32 percent) of people lived in a different neighborhood (Schuller 2012).

In Western Europe, the nuclear family evolved hand in hand with the Industrial Revolution; when families worked the land, more children and intergenerational households meant more hands to work. When crowded in cities, the household divorced from the unit of production but remaining the unit of consumption meant more mouths to feed. This cultural shift occurred over two or three generations in the UK and the US. This occurred over two *years* in Haiti. This has profound consequences considering that Charlene Desir (2011: 282) argued that the *lakou* is "a theoretical and social framework and integral part of the social fabric of Haiti."

Increasing Violence against Women

Among the most perverse outcomes of foreign humanitarian policies was an increase of violence against women. One of the gains of second-wave feminism was the promotion of Women in Development, or WID. In WID, women became primary beneficiaries of NGO aid. Not everyone shared the goal of women's empowerment, as voiced by Alain, who worked at USAID: "You give money to a man and he's as likely to spend it on beer or a lover as on his family. But if you give to a woman, you're guaranteed that she will prioritize feeding herself and her children." Specifically, after the earthquake, agencies followed the World Food Program guidelines that food aid be sent to women. This in effect solidified the role of women as *poto mitan,* or pillars of the family (N'Zengou-Tayo 1998). Caribbeanist scholars since Edith Clarke (1957) have noted that households are "matrifocal," which Hortense Spillers (1987), Angela Davis (1983), Saidiyah Hartman (1996), and Christina Sharpe (2010) argued has its origin in the brutality of patriarchy on the plantation. Giving food aid to *only* women not only encouraged families to split to give a seventeen-year-old the status of head of household to double their food aid, it also created the opportunity for "transactional sex."

NGOs set up the rules and empowered the perpetrators. Had the camp committees been democratic, or had NGOs encouraged or supported spaces for deliberation or participation in the camps, a system of distribution to women might not have created problems. However, NGOs employed a system of ration cards, in effect deputizing their committees to distribute the cards. Committees were dominated by men, including those whose power was gained by the gun—or Bible. This was a recipe for abuse.

Kolonbi camp resident Evrance, in her fifties, never received food aid. When asked why, she theorized, "It's because the guys in the committee choose young women with large buttocks." The researcher conducting this interview asked for clarification, making sure of what she heard. Evrance replied, "You heard me! Beautiful, beautiful, beautiful, beautiful asses." This was not unique to Kolonbi, as Plas Lapè camp resident Fabiola details. She didn't get a cash-for-work job digging canals: "This is a job for men. I didn't work in the project. We must have sex with them. Such an old woman like me, what can I do for them?" In the St. Louis camp, the Red Cross gave the camp committee president Esaie, a male, the responsibility to give the official list of who was a "real" resident and therefore eligible for relocation assistance valued at $500 or more. According to Sandy Nelzy (2013, 22), Esaie used this as leverage over at least two mothers, one of whom, Josiane, was married, to demand sex: "Because she refused the offer, [Esaie] stopped informing [Josiane] about the Red Cross visits to the camp and refused to include her name in the list he gave the Red Cross as to who would receive official relocation assistance." A study by Poto Fanm+Fi revealed that 37 percent of pregnant women reported performing transactional sex as a survival strategy (d'Adesky et al. 2012). For these reasons and others, violence against women was endemic in the camps. According to Small Arms Survey, two percent of women reported gender-based violence in Haiti 2010. In the camps, this figure jumps over tenfold, to 22 percent (Muggah 2011).

Haitian Understandings

Various collectives of artists, scholars, NGOs, and activists had their own commemoration of the 2010 earthquake. It's difficult to capture ten years, in no small part because of the magnitude of the earthquake. As noted above, this media event often seems like fragments. A loose coalition formed as the anniversary approached. Calling itself *Amouni*, "harmony," the group called for dispersed, decentered, local commemorations of the disaster. Beginning with the conception that *moun* (people) are the heart of *amouni* (harmony), the fuller name included *semans limyè*, seeds of light. Their declaration began by acknowledging the solidarity after the earthquake as the "foundation of the nation." Underscoring the spiritual dimension of harmony, the call for resistance took a cue from the musical term, acknowledging that harmony always is accompanied by *dezòd* (disorder) or a cacophony. From here the statement denounces the disorder of the capitalist system, "which is devouring people as well as the planet," and which prevents people from living in harmony with another, creating a wake of false consciousness. On the night of 11 January, the evening before the anniversary of the quake, dozens of young people, mostly men, gathered at a platform in the Fort National neighborhood. On the twelfth, events were spread from Kanaran to Plas Jeremi in the Kafou Fèy neighborhood.

At all the events I attended, at least one speaker mentioned the importance of people's material conditions. Centering conditions of the impoverished majority in Haiti (all of the speakers and events were in Pòtoprens) reprimands foreign media's focus on the political stage. Haiti's 1987 constitution guarantees the right to housing in Article 22, but the state has neglected its duties. People commented on the *lavi chè*, the rapid inflation and devaluation of Haiti's currency. On 6 July 2018, when the country stood up in revolt against the planned hikes in gas prices that the IMF had arranged with the government, the exchange rate was sixty-five gourdes (Haiti's currency) to the dollar. Less than a year later, on 9 June 2019, during a massive nationwide protest following the publication of a partial report of the PetroCaribe investigation, it was ninety-one to the dollar. Many speakers foregrounded education, health care, water, and electricity.

Commentators questioned what constituted the disaster. Human rights attorney Mario Joseph pointed out that Haiti has been hit with earthquakes before, including Port-au-Prince in 1751 and Cap Haïtien in 1842. Joseph defined the lack of state preparation and response as the disaster. As David Oxygène of MOLEGHAF and others said, "It didn't begin with January 12, and it didn't end with January 12." A leader with KOD-15, in

Kanaran, called this neglect a form of state violence (Garza 2014; Darbouze 2021; Dougé-Prosper 2021), to which Ilionor Louis, my colleague at the Faculté d'Ethnologie and director of Sant Egalite, added, poverty is also state violence, a violation of our rights. The activist collective Sèk Gramsci's commemoration was, as per their usual, street theatre. The title of their performance highlights the many faces of the same disaster: *mòd leta* (modes of the state or governance strategies, but also a play on words, since *mò* means the state's "dead"). The performance began minutes after 4 p.m., when activist professor Janil Lwijis was pronounced dead in General Hospital after being assassinated, and continued through 4:53, when Goudougoudou struck. The culprit in both was state violence, engineered and directed by the neoliberal troika of International Monetary Fund, World Bank, and Interamerican Development Bank. Performers poked fun at a pastor profiteering from the "act of God" and later making unwanted advances on a female congregant. Characteristically not shying away from current commentary, Sèk Gramsci denounced the current government of Jovenel Moïse for being in league with both gangs and the UN military to kill the population in order to quell dissent, including the massacre of November 2018 in a popular neighborhood of Lasalin and the high-profile murder of three journalists – and this is before other high profile murders, including a week before the assassination of Moïse himself.

Several analysts noted a continuity in the oppression faced by Haiti's poor majority as well as in organized protests. Referring to the nine-week *peyi lòk*—the "lockdown" or general strike—in September, MOLEGHAF's Guy Lauore Rosenez, as well as other activists such as Guy Numa of the coalition Konbit and anthropologist Mamyrah Dougé Prosper, placed the mobilization in the context of a long-term struggle and current outcroppings of the 6 July 2018 uprising. Rosenez called upon the resistance of the ancestors, saying that the tenth anniversary of the earthquake should be the second Bwa Kayiman, the Vodou ceremony that set the Haitian Revolution aflame on 14 August 1791. Oxygène, using the opportunity of the earthquake for reflection about the impasse of the popular movement, said activists should add the question #KòtKòbCIRHla?—that is, where is the money from the Interim Haiti Reconstruction Commission?—to activists' quiver.

Dignity and humanity rose to the top of activists' demands, from the *Amouni* text to formal presentations to commentary from audience members. The president's motorcade of over eighty vehicles zooming from Titanyen to pay homage to the mass grave—leaving behind trails of dust residents had to sweep up—didn't erase the everyday practice of state dehumanization for many Kanaran residents like KOD-15 coordinator

Laguerre. Speaking to candidates' instrumentalizing the belated visibility of Kanaran and its now 250,000 residents, Rosedite concluded, *lè nou fin vote, nou pa moun ankò* (when we're done voting, we cease being people). The audience erupted in a hearty *ayibobo* (amen): We're not sacks. We are people. "For the state, there are no citizens here."

Despite this structural violence, the tone of the conversation, both prepared remarks and comments from participants, was defiant. People are *degaje*, getting by, and several spoke of a new opportunity. Collette Lespinasse applauded Kanaran residents for taking initiative and showing what Haitian people can do when they take the lead: "We don't need foreigners." Speaking back to the discourse of Kanaran being the *pitit san papa leta ak ONG* (bastard child of the State and NGOs), UEH professor Odonel Pierre-Louis also drew inspiration from Kanaran residents for *fè papa two renmen w* (making papa so proud that he claims you). Sabine Lamour, sociology professor, feminist, and director of Solidarity of Haitian Women (SOFA), spoke of the ongoing struggle by Haitian feminist organizations. Rather than using the language of "waves," which erases Haitian women's history of struggle against imperialism and inhumanity since 1915, the commencement of the US occupation. Lamour proposes *sekous*: ripples, shocks, or shaking. Rather than mourning, Lamour encourages activism: *Nan aksyon nou, chak jou nap fè dèy la* (In our actions, every day we honor the dead).

Toward a Caribbean Epistemology of Disaster

Disaster scholarship in the US and other areas within the global north is dominated by political ecology. While this paradigm is essential to unpacking the nexus of geography and political economy in the natural and built environments, and to divorcing hazards from disasters, the lived experience, response, and analysis of Haitian people demand more. Insights from Haitian artists and literary figures tap into the deep wisdom of Vodou and its resistance to slavery. Building on recent scholarship—in this series—on "repeating disasters" (Hoffman and Barrios 2019), insights of Caribbean literary theory offer useful centering of the fragmented experience of (post)plantation societies, such as Antonio Benítez-Rojo's (Benítez-Rojo 1997) concept of "repeating island," and the Haitian literary and artistic genre of spiralism (Glover 2010). Indeed, many other brilliant essays in this present collection make the case for the importance of bringing postcolonial theory to the study of disasters.

The Caribbean was the birthplace of plantation slavery and global capitalism (McKittrick 2013). This violence and dehumanization engendered unequal exchange that still hampers the region. The Caribbean is disproportionately beset by hazards: the word "hurricane" is a transliteration of a Taino concept long predating colonization (Moreira 2010; Ortiz 2010; Ramos Guadalupe 2010). Currently, the Caribbean disproportionately pays for warming sea temperatures (Taylor et al. 2012). Seen from the Caribbean, climate change is a violent continuation of slavery and displacement (Sheller 2020). Local folk theories long disaggregated "hazards" from "disasters," and community mutual aid and survival, adaptations to slavery, are precursors to "resilience"—in all its contradictions—long before it became popularized.

Haiti's experience and Haitian people's analyses push at the edges of received scholarship on disasters. From whose point of view do events become "disasters," and what is the "disaster" itself? A typical disaster narrative focuses media, and therefore philanthropic and agency, attention on the disaster event, iconically captured in the photo op. Douz Janvye was the archetypical photo op: testifying to how much money media agencies made off of images of the suffering of Haitian bodies, Haitian photographer Daniel Morel received a settlement in his lawsuit of $3 million. A generation of political ecology–oriented disaster social science has argued for moving away from events and toward process to understand disasters. The experience, lived realities, and analyses of people in Haiti and the Caribbean go further: the disaster is not merely impacted by global capitalism but the violence inherent to global racial capitalism is itself the disaster.

Mark Schuller is Presidential Research Professor of anthropology and nonprofit and NGO studies at Northern Illinois University and affiliate at the Faculté d'Ethnologie, l'Université d'État d'Haïti. Supported by the National Science Foundation Senior and CAREER Grant, the Bellagio Center, and others, Schuller's research on NGOs, globalization, disasters, and gender in Haiti has been published in fifty peer-reviewed articles or book chapters as well as in public media. He authored or coedited eight books, including *Humanity's Last Stand: Confronting Global Catastrophe* (Rutgers, 2021). Recipient of the Margaret Mead Award, the Anthropology in Media Award, and the Haitian Studies Association's Award for Excellence, he is active in several solidarity efforts.

Notes

The author would first like to thank the activists, scholars, neighbors, colleagues, students, and organic intellectuals in Haiti for the inspiration and wisdom. Also I would like to thank the organizers of Florida State University's Winthrop-King institute's conference, "From Katrina to Michael" for the invitation as keynote, and the participants for the productive and engaged conversation and critique. Especially acknowledged are volume editors Vincent Joos, Martin Munro and John Ribó. Feedback from NIU writing group Dana Bardolph and Micah Morton was invaluable, as well as anonymous reviewers. This research was made possible by a grant from the National Science Foundation Early Career program, grant# 1455142, and by Senior Research Grant # 1122704. The views expressed in this piece are solely the author's and do not necessarily reflect those of the NSF.

1. See also Braziel, in this volume, for a discussion of necrocapitalism.
2. See Mark Schuller, "Humanitarian Occupation in Haiti," North American Congress on Latin America website, 28 July 2015, https://nacla.org/news/2015/07/28/humanitarian-occupation-haiti.
3. Derek Walcott's Nobel Prize for Literature speech on December 7, 1992, was subtitled "Fragments of Epic Memory," also the main title of a 2021–22 exhibit at the Art Gallery of Ontario. See https://www.nobelprize.org/prizes/literature/1992/walcott/lecture/ and https://ago.ca/exhibitions/fragments-epic-memory.
4. Jonathan Katz, "The King and Queen of Haiti," *Politico Magazine*, 4 May 2015, https://www.politico.com/magazine/story/2015/05/clinton-foundation-haiti-117368/.
5. See also Ansel Herz and Kim Ives, "WikiLeaks Haiti: The Post-Quake 'Gold Rush' for Reconstruction Contracts," *The Nation*, 15 June 2011, https://www.thenation.com/article/archive/wikileaks-haiti-post-quake-gold-rush-reconstruction-contracts/; and Isabel Macdonald and Isabeau Doucet, "The Shelters That Clinton Build," *The Nation*, 11 July 2011, https://www.thenation.com/article/archive/shelters-clinton-built/.
6. As part of a larger commitment to decolonize research on Haiti, place names are referred to in Haitian Creole (Kreyòl)
7. Haitian activists decried the other "genetically modified" organisms when it was discovered that Monsanto seized upon the disaster to make a stealth donation of GMO seeds.
8. National Network for the Defense of Human Rights, "The Events in La Saline: From Power Struggle Between Armed Gangs to State-Sanctioned Massacre," 1 December 2018, https://web.rnddh.org/wp-content/uploads/2018/12/10-Rap-La-Saline-1Dec2018-Ang1.pdf.

References

Agier, Michel. 2003. "La Main Gauche de l'Empire: Ordre et désordres de l'humanitaire." *Multitudes* 11(1): 67–77.

Ayiti Kale Je. 2010. "Cash for . . . What? Argent contre . . . Quoi? Dinero para . . . Que?" Haiti Grassroots Watch. 9 November, http://haitigrassrootswatch.squarespace.com/journal/2010/11/8/cash-for-what-argent-contre-quoi-dinero-para-que.html.

Baguidy, Wisner. 2020. "Le séisme du 12 janvier 2010, les ONG-États et l'action humanitaire en Haïti : Une analyse de leurs impacts socio-culturels au Vilaj Abita et à MODSOL (Léogâne)." maitrise, Anthropologie Sociale, Faculté d'Ethnologie, Université d'État d'Haïti.

Bastien, Rémy. 1961. "Haitian Rural Family Organization." *Social and Economic Studies* 10(4): 478–510.
Bengtsson, Linus, Xin Lu, Anna Thorson, Richard Garfield, and Johan von Schreeb. 2011. "Improved Response to Disasters and Outbreaks by Tracking Population Movements with Mobile Phone Network Data: A Post-Earthquake Geospatial Study in Haiti." *PLOS Medicine* 8(8), e1001083. doi:10.1371/journal.pmed.1001083.
Benítez-Rojo, Antonio. 1997. *The Repeating Island*, translated by James E. Maraniss. Durham, NC: Duke University Press.
Bergan, Renée, and Mark Schuller. 2009. *Poto Mitan: Haitian Women, Pillars of the Global Economy*. Watertown, MA: Documentary Educational Resources.
Clarke, Edith. 1957. *My Mother Who Fathered Me: A Study of the Family in Three Selected Communities in Jamaica*. New York: G. Allen & Unwin.
d'Adesky, Anne-Christine, and Poto Fanm+Fi. 2012. *Beyond Shock—Charting the Landscape of Sexual Violence in Post-quake Haiti: Progress, Challenges, and Emerging Trends, 2010–2012*. Foreword by Edwidge Danticat and photo essay by Nadia Todres. San Francisco and Port-au-Prince: Poto Fanm+Fi Initiative.
Danticat, Edwidge. 2010. "A Little While." *The New Yorker*, 1 February, https://www.newyorker.com/magazine/2010/02/01/a-little-while.
Darbouze, James. 2021. "Trapped in the Imperial Grip." *NACLA Report on the Americas* 53(1): 37–42.
Davis, Angela Yvonne. 1983. "The Legacy of Slavery: Standards of a New Womanhood." In *Women, Race and Class*, 3–29. New York: Vintage.
Desir, Charlene. 2011. "Diasporic Lakou: A Haitian Academic Explores Her Path to Haiti Pre- and Post-Earthquake." *Harvard Educational Review* 81(2): 278–95.
DeWind, Josh, and David H. Kinley III. 1988. *Aiding Migration: The Impact of International Development Assistance on Haiti, International Studies in Migration*. Boulder, CO: Westview Press.
Dougé-Prosper, Mamyrah. 2021. "An Island in the Chain." *NACLA Report on the Americas* 53(1): 30–36.
Dubuisson, Darlène. 2021. "'We Know How to Work Together': Konbit, Protest, and the Rejection of INGO Bureaucratic Dominance." *Journal of Haitian Studies* 26(2): 53–80.
Dupain, Etant. 2012. "New Threats of Eviction After One Death in a Port-au-Prince Camp." In *Tectonic Shifts: Haiti since the Earthquake*, ed. Mark Schuller and Pablo Morales, 147–48. Sterling, VA: Kumarian Press.
Dupuy, Alex. 2005. "Globalization, the World Bank, and the Haitian Economy." In *Contemporary Caribbean Cultures and Societies in a Global Context*, ed. Franklin Knight and Teresita Martinez-Vergne, 43–70. Chapel Hill: University of North Carolina Press.
Étienne, Sauveur Pierre. 1997. *Haiti: L'Invasion des ONG*. Port-au-Prince, Haiti: Centre de Recherche Sociale et de Formation Economique pour le Développement.
Ferguson, James. 2005. "Anthropology and Its Evil Twin: 'Development' in the Constitution of a Discipline." In *The Anthropology of Development and Globalization: From Classical Political Economy to Contemporary Neoliberalism*, ed. Marc Edelman and Angelique Haugerud, 140–53. Malden, MA: Blackwell Publishing.
Garza, Alicia. 2014. "A Herstory of the #BlackLivesMatter Movement by Alicia Garza." *The Feminist Wire*. 7 October, https://thefeministwire.com/2014/10/blacklivesmatter-2/.

Glover, Kaiama L. 2010. *Haiti Unbound: A Spiralist Challenge to the Postcolonial Canon.* Liverpool: Liverpool University Press.
Gramsci, Antonio. 1971. *Selections from the Prison Notebooks of Antonio Gramsci,* ed. and trans. Quintin Hoare and Geoffrey Nowell Smith. New York: International Publishers.
Hartman, Saidiya V. 1996. "Seduction and the Ruses of Power." *Callaloo* 19(2): 537–60.
Hoffman, Susanna, and Roberto Barrios, eds. 2019. *Disaster Upon Disaster: Exploring the Gap between Knowledge, Policy and Practice.* New York: Berghahn Books.
Jean-Baptiste, Chenet. 2012. "Haiti's Earthquake: A Further Insult to Peasants' Lives." In *Tectonic Shifts: Haiti since the Earthquake,* ed. Mark Schuller and Pablo Morales, 97-100. Sterling, VA: Kumarian Press.
Kivland, Chelsey. 2020. *Street Sovereigns: Young Men and the Makeshift State in Urban Haiti.* Ithaca, NY: Cornell University Press.
Klarreich, Kathie, and Linda Polman. 2012. "The NGO Republic of Haiti." *The Nation,* November 19.
Klein, Naomi. 2007. *The Shock Doctrine: The Rise of Disaster Capitalism.* New York: Metropolitan Books.
Kristoff, Madeline, and Liz Panarelli. 2010. *Haiti: The Republic of NGOs?* Washington, DC: US Institute of Peace.
Laguerre, Michel. 1973. "The Place of Voodoo in the Social Structure of Haiti." *Caribbean Quarterly* 19(3): 36–50.
Lahens, Yanick. 2010. *Failles.* Paris: Sabine Wespieser.
Louis, Ilionor. 2013. *Des Bidonvilles aux Camps: Conditions de Vie à Canaan, à Corail Cesse-Lesse, et à la Piste de l'Ancienne Aviation de Port-au-Prince.* Port-au-Prince, Haiti: Faculté d'Ethnologie.
Lwijis, Janil. 2009. *ONG: Ki gouvènman ou ye?* Pòtoprens, Haiti: Asosyasyon Inivèsite ak Inivèsitèz Desalinyèn—ASID.
Mauss, Marcel. 1990. *The Gift: The Form and Reason for Exchange in Archaic Societies.* London: Routledge.
Mbembe, Achille. 2003. "Necropolitics," trans. Libby Meintjes. *Public Culture* 15(1): 11–40.
McKittrick, Katherine. 2013. "Plantation Futures." *Small Axe* 17(3): 1–15.
Minn, Pierre. 2016. "Components of a Moral Economy: Interest, Credit, and Debt in Haiti's Transnational Health Care System." *American Anthropologist* 118(1): 78–90.
Montas-Dominique, Michèle. 2011. "Sim Pa Rele (If I Don't Shout)." In *Haiti after the Earthquake,* ed. Paul Farmer, 259–72. Philadelphia: Public Affairs.
Moreira, Lilliam. 2010. "El huracán de don Fernando Ortiz y su trascendencia actual." *Catauro: Revista Cubana de Antropología* 12(22): 43–48.
Muggah, Robert. 2011. "Security from the Bottom Up in Haiti: Before and after the Quake." Small Arms Survey. https://www.slideshare.net/CivMilCoE/robert-muggah.
Nelzy, Sandy. 2013. "The Impact of NGOs in Saint-Louis de Gonzague Camp, Haiti." *Practicing Anthropology* 35(3): 20–22.
N'Zengou-Tayo, Marie-José. 1998. "Fanm Se Poto Mitan: Haitian Women, the Pillar of Society." *Feminist Review* 59: 118–42.
Olivier, Djems. 2020. "Territoires de la violence, territoires des ONG : quelles (in)cohérences" Ph D, Géographie, Université Paris 8.
———. 2021. "The Anatomy of Haiti's Armed Gangs." *NACLA Report on the Americas* 53 (1): 81–85.

Ortiz, Fernando. 2010. "El huracán, los conquistadores y los indios." *Catauro: Revista Cubana de Antropología* 12(22): 147–77.
Peck, Raoul. 2013. *Assistance Mortelle (Fatal Assistance)*. Arte France.
Ramos Guadalupe, Luis Enrique. 2010. "Apuntes históricos en torno a la ciclonología cubana." *Catauro: Revista Cubana de Antropología* 12(22): 23–37.
Schuller, Mark. 2008. "'Haiti Is Finished!' Haiti's End of History Meets the Ends of Capitalism." In *Capitalizing on Catastrophe: Neoliberal Strategies in Disaster Reconstruction*, ed. Nandini Gunewardena and Mark Schuller, 191–214. Lanham, Md.: Alta Mira Press.
———. 2012a. "Genetically Modified Organizations? Understanding and Supporting Local Civil Society in Urban Haiti." *Journal of Haitian Studies* 18(1): 50–73.
———. 2012b. *Killing with Kindness: Haiti, International Aid and NGOs*, foreword by Paul Farmer. New Brunswick, NJ: Rutgers University Press.
———. 2012c. *Homeward Bound? Assessing Progress of Relocation from Haiti's IDP Camps*. Northern Illinois University and Faculté d'Ethnologie (DeKalb and Port-au-Prince).
———. 2016a. *Humanitarian Aftershocks in Haiti*. New Brunswick, NJ: Rutgers University Press.
———. 2016b. "The Tremors Felt Round the World: Haiti's Earthquake as Global Imagined Community." In *Contextualizing Disaster*, ed. Gregory V Button and Mark Schuller, 66–88. New York: Berghahn Books.
———. 2018. "Fè ONG: Yon Nouvo Gramè ONG." *Chantiers* 4: 231–44.
Schuller, Mark, and Tania Levey. 2014. "Kabrit Ki Gen Twop Met: Understanding Gaps in WASH Services in Haiti's IDP Camps." *Disasters* 38(S1): S1–S24.
Sharpe, Christina. 2010. *Monstrous Intimacies: Making Post-Slavery Subjects*. Durham, NC: Duke University Press.
Sheller, Mimi. 2020. *Island Futures: Caribbean Survival in the Anthropocene*. Durham, NC: Duke University Press.
Spillers, Hortence J. 1987. "Mama's Baby, Papa's Maybe: An American Grammar Book." *Diacritics* 17(2): 64–81.
Steinke, Andrea. 2012. "Republik der NGOs" [Republic of NGOs]. *Analyse und Kritik* 568: https://archiv.akweb.de/ak_s/ak568/16.htm.
Taylor, Michael A., Tannecia S. Stephenson, A. Anthony Chen, and Kimberly A. Stephenson. 2012. "Climate Change and the Caribbean." *Caribbean Studies* 40(2): 169–200.
Thomas, Frédéric. 2013. *L'échec humanitaire: Le cas haïtien*. Bruxelles: Couleur livres.
Trouillot, Michel-Rolph. 1990. "The Odd and the Ordinary: Haiti, the Caribbean, and the World." *Cimarrón: New Perspectives on the Caribbean* 2 (3): 3-12.
Ulysse, Gina Athena. 2010. "Why Representations of Haiti Matter Now More Than Ever." *NACLA Report on the Americas* 43 (5): 37-41.
———. 2011. *Fascinating! Her Resilience*. Middletown, CT: Wesleyan University Center for the Arts.
Victor, Gary. 2010. *Le Sang et la Mer*. La Roque d'Anthéron, France: Vents d'Ailleurs.

CHAPTER 2

After the Storm
Hurricane Matthew, Haiti, and Disaster's Longue Durée

LAURA WAGNER

"That night, the wind began to blow. All night, Claudine was calling me [from Port-au-Prince], telling us to get out of there, to be careful. When she hung up, she told me she'd call me at three in the morning. But by three o'clock, there was no communication. All the antennas had come down." My friend Claudine's father, St. Neret, described the night that Hurricane Matthew struck his home, in the seaside mountains of Haiti's Grand'Anse department, on 4 October 2016. He, his wife Olène, their six-year-old daughter Ashkaïna, and Olène's preteen daughters took shelter in their small wooden home.

> The wind was blowing. I heard the grapefruit tree break in half, but no one could even stick their head out to see. By four in the morning, the house started to come apart. The sheet metal peeled away from the roof one by one. Olène started to cry. She was holding onto Ashkaïna, and the other girls were hiding under the table. I took Ashkaïna, I shielded her behind my back, and I stood in the corner, so that if a piece of wood or sheet metal came at us, it would hit me instead. I made her stand behind my back, and I stood in front of her. I told Olène, "Stop crying, you're an adult, you have to stay strong for the children. You have to resign yourself. Everyone knows it's either life or death. So resign yourself."

After a few hours, they thought the worst was over. The wind had calmed, and St. Neret ventured out to check on his mule. But it was only the eye of the Category 4 storm passing over them. While he was outside, the wind picked up again, and he hurried back to his family. They cowered under the beds and tables as the house flew apart. "Even the dogs were under the table," St. Neret recalled. "A piece of meat had fallen on the ground, and the dogs didn't care. When I saw that, that's when I knew we were going to die." They fled, along with perhaps fifty neighbors, to caves in the nearby mountains.

"While we were sitting in the cave, me and Ashkaïna, she turned to me and said, 'Papa, we're going to escape. The time for us to die has passed.'"

"I said, 'That's right, my child. We're going to escape. We're not going to die. We're not going to die yet.'"

"Then she asked, 'Papa, can't we go to Port-au-Prince?'"

"I said, 'No, we can't go to Port-au-Prince. All the roads are cut off and there's no way through.'"

"She asked, 'Can't we walk?'"

"I said, 'Do you think you can walk that far?'"

"And she said, 'You can carry me on your back.'"

For a small child, the two hundred miles did not seem so insurmountable. They spent the next three days in the cave.

For days, I had watched as Matthew crept toward Haiti, a great white spiral on a satellite feed, as big as the Caribbean itself. It was heading straight for Haiti's southern peninsula. I called Claudine, and she called everyone back home. "Tell everyone this isn't like the other hurricanes they've lived through," I'd told her. "This is going to be really, really bad."

Our lives had become entwined because of another disaster, nearly seven years earlier: the earthquake of 12 January 2010. Claudine's aunt Melise lived and worked in the house where I had rented a room. She was a household worker, a migrant from the Grand'Anse, who had come to Port-au-Prince in search of a better life for her family. Melise, her daughter, and Claudine lived together in a room off the downstairs kitchen. When the house collapsed in the quake, Melise was upstairs folding laundry. She was crushed to death in a house that was not her own, in a city that was not her home.

I was buried in the rubble of the same house, and rescued later that night by two gentlemen, Prenel and Bòs Jhon, both of whom, like Melise, had worked for my landlady. Prenel hailed from the same community in the Grand'Anse as Melise. Because it is by sheer luck that I am here while Melise is not, and because I owe my life to someone from there, I am beholden to Melise's community, and that is why I watched, with a sickening sense of powerlessness, as Hurricane Matthew gathered strength and bore down on southwestern Haiti.

Andeyò

In Haiti, they call migrants from the countryside—such as Melise—*moun andeyò*. To be andeyò, from the French *en dehors*, is literally to be outside. The *peyi andeyò* is the outside country, the land beyond the city (*lavil*), specifically beyond Port-au-Prince. To be a moun andeyò is to be a person from the outside land. An outsider. But andeyò is not merely a geographical designation. It also means political, social, and economic exclusion.

On 5 October, one day after the storm, Haitian artist and cartoonist Ralph Penel Pierre created a poignant image of a broken Haiti, the southern peninsula disconnected from the rest of the country. The southern peninsula is an arm reaching out in desperation, while four hands extend from the rest of Haiti, desiring but unable to help. Hurricane Matthew laid bare the tenuous infrastructure that had held Haiti together, if just barely. With the bridge washed away and cell phone towers down, southern Haiti was cut off. For days, people in Port-au-Prince remained in a holding pattern, awaiting news from their loved ones—just as their families in the Grand'Anse had done years before, after the quake.

At first, there was so little news about conditions in the southern peninsula. I searched social media for any information I could find, sifting through some fake news and many white saviors, some of whom were already bandying about one of the words I hate the most: *resilience*. Lauding the Haitian people for their so-called resilience implies that Black bodies, minds, and souls can take more suffering and brutality than other people can.

A US missionary posted photos on Facebook that showed women with their breasts exposed and an adolescent boy wearing no pants. In one image, several people run toward the camera, including a child in motion, one foot on the ground. Someone has commented, "The smiling amputee reminds me of the earthquake. They have been through so much and still they rejoice in any gesture."

Under that, another person has replied, "I think his leg is behind him. I don't think he's an amputee."

After the storm hit, CNN reported: "Haiti had only just begun rebuilding from a devastating earthquake six years ago when Hurricane Matthew tore through the small Caribbean nation."[1]

But the far south of Haiti—the area struck hardest by Hurricane Matthew—was not physically hit by the earthquake, while Port-au-Prince, in turn, was affected only minimally by the hurricane. The earthquake was mostly an urban disaster, while the hurricane swept away small homes and *lakou* (family compounds), livestock, and crops. Yet to most international news outlets, Haiti might as well not have regions.

This is the standard media narrative: Haiti, and Haitian people, nonspecific and undifferentiated, are inherently doomed. There were fundamental, specific differences between the 2010 earthquake and Hurricane Matthew. At the same time, the two catastrophes are connected through historical and social patterns of displacement and exclusion. The earthquake was a disaster because it hit Port-au-Prince, the capital of an overcentralized country, filled with people from the countryside seeking a better life, forced by poverty and circumstance to live in precarious housing. Hurricane Matthew was a disaster because it hit areas far from Port-au-Prince: far from the capital, far from the aid apparatus and infrastructure, for Haiti is at once "the republic of NGOs," where nongovernmental organizations have taken over the role of the state, and "the republic of Port-au-Prince," where almost all governance and services are concentrated in the capital. In other words, the earthquake and the hurricane both came down to centralization and exclusion.

There are valences of andeyò. There are outsiders, and then there are *outsiders*. Migrants to Port-au-Prince refer to their home communities as simply *pwovens* (the countryside) or *andeyò*, as though the only thing you need to know about the places from which they hail is that they are not the capital. They speak of home in metonyms: anyone from Grand'Anse becomes *moun Jeremi*, people from the main regional city of Jérémie, and, if asked for more specificity, people like Claudine's family, who come from the communal sections, refer to themselves in terms of the nearest town. (In their case, the town is Abricots.) Most people have never heard of their true homes anyway.

These concentric valences of outsiderness are also valences of political and social exclusion, valences of vulnerability. Outsiderness and vulnerability are inextricable, and they underlie most ordinary injustices and ordinary preventable deaths: the citizen who must walk two hours to vote for candidates that will not represent their interests, the mother who dies in labor because she cannot get to the clinic in the nearest town in time, the child who dies of a burst appendix, or any ordinary infection that goes to sepsis.

Hurricane Matthew's devastation, and the response to it, corresponded to these layers of exclusion. People in cities or towns are more likely to have cement roofs that can withstand hurricane-force winds. People in cities or towns were more able to access posthurricane aid—whether food or tarps—than people living in the distant communal sections. To be andeyò is to be beyond any safety net; it is to exist in a chronic state of precarity.

There was no celebrity telethon after Hurricane Matthew, no "We Are the World," no grand (if ultimately empty) gestures of international solidarity, as there had been after the earthquake. Why not? Because no one saw the earthquake coming. Because high death counts at the direct moment of impact matter more than indirect deaths from hunger, disease, or poverty in the long aftermath. The earthquake hit a capital city, where a handful of foreign journalists already lived, which allowed international media coverage to begin immediately and surge once the parachuters hit the tarmac. Because the earthquake leveled schools, government ministries, hotels, and the UN headquarters, killing rich and poor alike, and foreigners too.

Hurricane Matthew was the sort of disaster outsiders expect in Haiti. Its effects were harder to immediately discern, because the most affected areas were hard to reach, and even if you did, maybe the devastation didn't look like much, unless you knew what the Grand'Anse looked like before the storm. You wouldn't know that the Grand'Anse was one of the most fertile parts of the country. After all, Haiti is notoriously denuded, eroded, and poor.

Return

In December 2016, two and a half months after the storm, I went home with Claudine and her cousin Bazelet. As we traveled from Port-au-Prince along the southern peninsula on a crowded bus, the landscape changed. Palm trees stood lopsided, their fronds gone from the direction the wind had blown. As we headed west, they were bald, like great Q-tips.

Even further west, they were ripped out, flat on the ground. The Grand'Anse was unrecognizable. Houses that didn't used to be visible through the trees now stood out from miles away. Sometimes they weren't really houses at all, but improvised constructions of tarp, sheet metal, and straw mats. It looked like Port-au-Prince in 2010, a sea of blue and grey tarps, each branded with the name of the agency that provided them, as if to continually remind the grateful recipient of their good fortune.

Before the storm, everyone used to relax in the shade of the enormous mango tree in Claudine's family's lakou, where the air felt fresh, even on the hottest days—sitting on the exposed roots, as high as benches, or leaning a chair against the trunk, or stretching out on a sisal mat. Hurricane Matthew stripped the tree bare, and there was nowhere to hide from the midday sun. When St. Neret wasn't in his fields, trying to plant and recover what he could, when Olène wasn't cooking over the fire in the makeshift outdoor kitchen they'd built after Matthew washed away their old one, they took refuge inside the small house. The roof had been swept away but they'd covered the house with tarps, rocks, and pieces of wood. It was the only place that offered some relief from the sun.

But in the evenings, when the sun went down and the air grew cooler, we would gather in the lakou to eat, and things felt almost like they did before Matthew. The trees had been uprooted and destroyed, too, so there was no tonmtonm, pounded breadfruit eaten with okra sauce, for those first few months. We ate food aid, or *manje sinistre*: US-grown white rice, giant USAID cans of cooking oil, and lentils. When the sea wasn't rough, people could go fishing, so at least there was fresh fish and *brigo*, sea snails. Because limes were expensive and scarce, Claudine's stepmother, Olène, used a green plant with little pods to give food a sour, acidic taste. "Do you know this plant?" she asked me. I shook my head. "It's called *bleng bleng*. It's what we used a long time ago. It's what we use now when we don't have limes or vinegar."

We'd sit in the lakou and chat, and tell stories and jokes. Claudine would text with her boyfriend back in Port-au-Prince, scour the cooking pots, and throw scraps of fish to their three dogs, and sometimes to Claudine's grandfather's dog too, a handsome black-and-brown fellow with eyebrows and a white-tipped tail, which he holds proudly erect as he marches around the lakou. His name is Ipokrit, "Hypocrite."

Patterns of everyday life, like the landscape itself, were turned on their heads. Tonmtonm, long a staple, had become a rarity, a special occasion food. In the months after the storm, breadfruit could only be bought in Port-au-Prince at a steep price and brought back to Jérémie. "Breadfruit is what maintained the people of Grand'Anse," Melise's cousin Samuel explained to me. "Now we don't know in what year we'll ever see breadfruit again."

"The hurricane destroyed everything we had," Samuel continued. "Now we are living like animals, in the open air, in the rain. All of our livestock—goats, cows, horses, mules, pigs, chickens—they all died." If people manage to buy seeds, plants, or livestock to replace what they lost in the hurricane, the treeless landscape leaves them little shade to plant those seeds or tie up their livestock. "It's too much sun," Samuel said, "they all burn up."

He went on. "I don't know how to read. I can't go sit in an office. This is my work." He showed me his well-used machete, caked with red earth. He held it in his calloused hands and said, "I am a farmer. That is how I live. And it's all lost. . . . All the yams are lost. Only the plantain trees have started to grow again. After the hurricane, I tried to plant beans, but the sun was too much and they were all lost, too. Even the bananas, if they get too much sun, will die. They'll all die."

Before Matthew struck, there had been a bumper crop. "This year, it was as though the breadfruit would never end," Olène recalled wistfully, sitting on a straw mat on her porch as night fell. The sky was wider, with the tree cover gone. With no ambient light beyond the faint glow of a flashlight, it sparkled with stars. She took a discreet pinch of powdered tobacco and sniffed, then blew her nose. "Breadfruit, coconuts. Everyone ate so well."

The coconut trees that allowed Claudine's father to provide for his family and send his children to school were destroyed. The chickens and goats all perished and were scavenged by dogs. If it weren't for *manje sinistre* and remittances from abroad, people would have starved. Friends from remote areas of the Grand'Anse report that their families never received any *manje sinistre* at all. Even for those who receive them, the distribution of aid vouchers is rarely equitable; in many cases, the vouchers distributed by the municipal government fall into the hands of powerful people, who give them to their supporters, families, and friends. But even when everyone knows that the game is rigged, even when everyone knows that food aid undercuts domestic production, even when people suspect that the NGOs are out for profit, no one can extricate themselves from the aid economy.

"For those of us of a certain age—me, I was born in 1970—we lost everything we are used to, everything we lived off of," Samuel said matter-of-factly. "I might die and never see them again. Maybe my children, down the road, will be alive when the trees sprout again."

"Mwatye sa a mezire pou tout moun"

"Matthew" is not a familiar name to most people in that part of rural Haiti. In Claudine's hometown, they turned the word into something more common: *Mwatye*.

A *mwatye* is a small old-fashioned glass Coca-Cola bottle, which people use to measure out cooking oil or *kleren* (high-proof sugarcane liquor) in the public markets. They called the hurricane Mwatye, and people joked, "Mwatye sa a mezire pou tout moun. Tout moun jwenn" (That mwatye contained enough for everybody. Everybody got some). The joke had a stinging core of social commentary: Mwatye was an equalizing force that destroyed everything in sight.

Bazelet took me to meet one of their neighbors, a fisherman named Michel and his wife Marie. Michel cradled his infant son on his lap, and described how he lost his dugout canoe—his livelihood—in the storm. "I would rather have lost my house than my *kanòt*," he sighed. He lost both.

"We thought we wouldn't live," Michel continued. "We had no hope that we would survive. It started around eight in the evening, and it got stronger and stronger all night. By five in the morning, it was pounding us over and over, it was destroying all the houses. And we thought we wouldn't survive. We knew a hurricane was coming, but we never imagined it would be that strong."

"I always say it was God. Why? You see where that mango tree is? It was uprooted, but it didn't fall on the house. You see that breadfruit tree?" he gestured. "It was uprooted, but it didn't fall on the house. If that wasn't God's power at work, then what was it?"

What house? I thought to myself, but didn't say anything. Throughout the community, I'd seen how the hurricane had ripped away sheet-metal roofs, leaving the wooden frames behind, but in Michel's case, the walls crumbled completely, leaving the low metal roof behind on the ground. They made a hole to serve as a door and stretched a USAID tarp over the top, and that is where their family lived.

"I've got a buddy," Michel continued. "That night, when the wind really started to blow, and he heard the trees cracking, they were falling on the roof—boom!—he said, 'Mezanmi, what's going on?' And he opened the door, he looked outside, and he saw a fire coming down on him, and—bang!—he shut the door. He said he didn't know if anyone else saw it, but there really was a fire in there. That's why so many of the trees burned. They say there really was fire in it. I saw other trees that were all blackened, every one of them. There was a fire in the storm, there was a product in it that devoured things. They say it's something the *blan* sent, or else it was God." In Haiti, blan means foreigners of any color.

"Blan sent the hurricane?" I asked.

"Well, that's what some people say. They say blan can do that, but then other people say it can't have been the blan, because why would they send the hurricane and then rush in to bring us food?"

Bazelet laughed. "Well, that's good logic! If the blan really wanted to kill us, I don't think they'd rush with food for us to eat!"

Michel nodded. "That's what I always tell people. If the blan had done this, if they had sent this hurricane to kill us, they wouldn't then get on airplanes to bring us food. I always say: blan wouldn't hate me so much that they'd send this hurricane."

He does not argue that blan couldn't intentionally create a hurricane that could rip through the entire Caribbean. He asks instead why would they *bother* to do that, only to come help afterward. Blan have the power to destroy or to save.

"If it weren't for the blan, we would all have gone mad, we all would have died," interjected Michel's wife, Marie. "Our only hope lies with the blan."

"Aprè Bondye se blan," Michel declared, his baby son babbling on his knees, as we looked out over the sea where he used to fish, and the wind whipped over the hillside where his house used to be. "Foreigners are next to God."

Rebuilding

We can't talk about the Haiti earthquake without talking about poverty, we can't talk about poverty without talking about power, and we can't talk about power without talking about slavery, imperialism, and colonization. If you ask why the hurricane or the earthquake were disasters, I'd start with Columbus. All the seemingly disparate "bad things" that have "happened" to Haiti in the past ten years—the earthquake, hurricanes, epidemics, political upheaval—are connected and cumulative, and they all come down to power. The exceptional moment of crisis is inseparable from ordinary vulnerability.

Disasters lay bare the vulnerabilities in a society. Disasters make places more susceptible to other disasters, like a house with a cracked and crumbling foundation. What does recovery mean when the disaster never ends? When an earthquake kills a breadwinner and the family can no longer afford hospital fees, when a hurricane washes away a year's worth of crops or fills a basement with toxic black mold, when the power stays off for weeks and insulin goes bad, how do you count the dead? Disasters are caused by poverty and they worsen poverty, and poverty kills people every day. Ordinary deaths by malaria, by hypertension, in childbirth—after the rest of the world has moved on from the initial crisis. Disasters are always political. But so, too, are ordinary deaths.

Disasters can also reveal the decency that lies within individuals and in societies. Ordinary acts of solidarity and reciprocity are transformed, by the precarity of life, into political acts of survival. I witnessed that decency in the wake of the earthquake. I owe my life to it.

But that grassroots solidarity begins to fray when states and other institutions intervene. On the night of 12 January 2010, the rupture was so unmendable, the devastation so complete, I thought it certain that things would change. Looking back, that sense of certainty appears foolish. It now seems inevitable that the aid response itself would be a disaster, and that Haiti would continue to be destroyed, from within and from beyond, by the same forces that have been devouring it for centuries.

After Hurricane Matthew, just as after the earthquake, people came together to save what could be saved.

My own survival was not a question of luck. The two men who saved my life, both of them migrants from the countryside, had been prepared by a lifetime of having to ensure their own survival. Beyond the reach of the centralized state, beyond the scope of the centralized NGO apparatus, outside of what most outsider observers would term "civil society," it was those very strategies of survival, collaboration, mutual aid, and reciprocity—the traditions of *konbit* (cooperative communal labor) and other forms of grassroots organization—that allowed people to survive the storm, and, however haltingly, to begin to recover.

Days before we had news of our friends living on the southern peninsula, my friend and colleague Vincent Joos and I launched a GoFundMe campaign. It was the ordinary thing to do. Countless Haitian people in the diaspora and in Port-au-Prince likewise raised money and collected goods, seeds, plants, and livestock for people in the south. Everyone knew that institutional humanitarian aid, whatever form it took, would be unequal to the scale of the disaster. We were astonished to raise more than $20,000 through word of mouth on social media. If Vincent and I were particularly successful, it was because we had established reputations as (foreign) scholars who had published about Haiti: credibility through whiteness, credibility through Googleability. We split the money. Vincent sent his portion to friends in Chambellan and I sent mine to Claudine. Within a week of the hurricane, Claudine and Bazelet brought food from Port-au-Prince, days before any other food aid reached that area.

On later trips they brought sand, sheet metal, rebar, and other building materials, and Bazelet, who was studying civil engineering, helped his family build stronger, more hurricane-proof homes.

The humanitarian question is not whether intervening is good or bad. Intervening is not a choice, neither for foreigners who have developed relationships in Haiti, nor for Haitian people who have left to seek a better life abroad. We know that individual acts of charity or patronage are no substitute for governance, but they are also an obligation. We act because we must, even though we know that such interventions do not fix the underlying problem and are no substitute for justice. There will be more crises, more emergencies, more losses. Having the right connections can temporarily transcend the pervasive forces of structural violence, sometimes. We do not need to wonder what happens every day to people who do not have powerful contacts and advocates.

In January 2017, I watched as the men and boys formed a *konbit* each day to haul heavy coral rocks up from the ocean's edge, to create the foundations of the new houses they were building. Even the six-year-old nicknamed Baby Jhon participated, carrying a rock balanced on a *twokèt* on his head, holding it with both hands. When they grew tired, the men would sit in Claudine's family's lakou and pass around a bottle of kleren.

"Don't give any to Baby Jhon!" Claudine admonished.

"E pa gason li ye? Isn't he a man too? He participated in the corvée," Samuel replied. Then, chastened, he added, "We'll just give him a capful."

They passed me the bottle too, though I protested that I had carried no rocks, and Samuel wiped his brow. He told me, "Lolo, we suffered so much in the storm, that storm Mwatye. Many people thought they wouldn't survive, because after the storm, they didn't know where to go. There was nothing left. There was nothing left. But Laura, let me explain something to you."

"You see, when Claudine came, she brought food for us. . . . The food you sent for us was the first food that saved us. And that's what gave me *libète m, egalite m, fratènite m* [my liberty, my equality, my brotherhood]. Without Claudine, I would never have gotten that food, because she divided the food up among all of us. That food saved me. And I salute Claudine's aunt who died too, Melise. I say to Melise: thank you. Claudine has taken Melise's place. I salute Melise, in death."

Melise's family still feels Melise's absence, but more than that, they feel her presence, the abiding effects of her life. She is still there. She is still taking care of her siblings and her village, as she did in life, when she sent a portion of her wages home each month. The relationships she made and nurtured, within her own family and beyond it, last beyond her death. I thought of the earthquake and the storm—two disasters seven years apart; two regions, one *lavil* and the other *andeyò*. I thought of everything that binds us together. I thought about the crisis that never seems to end. Melise, too, lingers. Her life, too, never ends.

Postscript: God Loves the Grand'Anse

Fifteen months after the storm, when I visited again, I was astonished to see how the Grand'Anse recovered. A year earlier, it had looked like a desert. By 2018, it was green, filled with banana trees. In a country that so many observers easily label eroded, deforested, and barren, the land revealed itself to be alive.

The rebirth was miraculous because of the fragility and precariousness that lie hidden beneath the bounty. To be andeyò is to be subject to the winds of fate.

People harvested plantains, yams, manioc, even some breadfruit. Coconuts, cacao, and coffee—cash crops—will take longer to regenerate. But there were unforeseen gifts, which appear as miracles: papaya trees, laden with heavy fruit, grow where there were no papaya trees before. *Maskreti*—castor oil beans, used to make profitable oil—grow where there were no maskreti before.

They say the hurricane winds brought the papaya and the maskreti. They say, "This is nature's response to manje sinistre." They say, "God loves the Grand'Anse."

Laura Wagner holds a PhD in cultural anthropology. Her ethnographic research focused on displacement, humanitarian aid, and everyday life in the aftermath of the 2010 earthquake in Haiti. From 2015 to 2019, she was the project archivist for the Radio Haiti Archive at the David M. Rubenstein Rare Book & Manuscript Library at Duke University. She is also the author of *Hold Tight, Don't Let Go*, a young adult novel about the earthquake, which was published by Abrams/Amulet in 2015. She is currently writing a book-length monograph about Radio Haïti-Inter.

Note

1. Park, Madison, Angela Dewan, and Chandrika Narayan. "Haiti: Hurricane Matthew Leaves Hundreds Dead." CNN, October 7, 2016. https://www.cnn.com/2016/10/07/americas/haiti-hurricane-matthew.

CHAPTER 3

Malediksyon
(Neo)colonial Development, Disasters, and Countercapitalism in Northeastern Haiti

VINCENT JOOS

Caracol is a small coastal town of northeastern Haiti where, before the opening of a large industrial park in 2011, people fished, harvested salt, cultivated produce, and raised cattle. While the industrial park did not immediately affect fishing and salt harvesting, the coming of new factories brought an abrupt end to many farming activities in the area. People of this region often referred to Caracol as the breadbasket of northeastern Haiti. Before 2011, more than four hundred families grew produce that allowed them to be self-sufficient and even to generate income with the sale of their surpluses. As one farmer told me during my fieldwork there, "We grew plantains, peas (*gwo pwa*), corn, cassava (*maniok*). This allowed us to make a living, to have money to send our children to school, to buy an animal if we needed to.... We were able to get the money we needed to live." Since the demonstrations against the high price of food in 2008, the Haitian state and its international partners made reviving the country's agriculture one of their main priorities. Yet, after the 2010 earthquake that ravaged the Port-au-Prince region, the Haitian state and its international partners harmed the country's agriculture by using recovery funds to create free-trade zones and industrial parks outside the disaster zone. To make room for these projects, the Haitian state evicted peasant farmers from fertile lands and thereby accentuated food insecurity in the country. Boosting the industrial sector was supposed to uplift the Haitian economy and to generate growth that, in turn, would fund the recovery. Ten years after the earthquake, it is clear that the plan to rebuild Haiti through industrial development failed spectacularly.

The story of Caracol is not unique. It follows the well-worn pattern of development through industrialization that has ravaged Indigenous communities throughout the Americas. Pipelines destroying Native American lands, dams displacing Indigenous people in the Amazon Forest, or oil wells polluting and harming communities throughout Ecuador are just a few examples of industrial practices that lead to ecological and social crisis. However, the story of Caracol stands out as an origin story of extractive economies and sheds light on the colonial origins of current neoliberal development frameworks. It is in this region that Christopher Columbus's largest ship, the Santa Maria, sank in 1492. It is also in this region that Columbus ordered thirty-nine of his sailors to build La Navidad, the first fortified colonial village in the Americas. The sailors were tasked with exploring the region and finding gold. While archaeologists are still trying to locate both the wreck of the Santa Maria and the village of La Navidad, naval historian Samuel Morison claimed that the ship sank in Caracol Bay and that sailors used its remains to build a fortified village within an existing Taíno community located in today's town of Caracol (1940). Even if this information is perhaps not exact, many locals I talked with recall this narrative to frame the long history of industrial land grabs and violence in their region. The 2011 construction of the industrial park on the most fertile land of Caracol is anchored in such a colonial narrative. As Milostène Castin, a local activist who fights against peasant evictions and ecological devastation in northeastern Haiti, told me on 6 June 2019 during an interview, "Caracol is of the utmost historical importance. It is where Columbus and his men first settled." After a pause, with a hint of sarcasm, he added, "se tankou yon malediksyon—it is like a curse."

In this chapter, I sketch a short and simplified history of plantation and industrial ventures in the Caracol region to understand how the repetition of (neo)colonial genocide, forced labor, and resource extraction shaped and destabilized northeastern Haiti. Often times, the narrative of a curse is used by Western journalists to describe Haiti's seemingly unstoppable spiral of disasters, as if the island were subject to supernatural forces (Duval 2021). Castin does not state that the country is cursed but that a process looking "like" (*tankou*) a curse is affecting the island. The curse he is talking about is not supernatural but a recurring feature of Haiti's reality. In this sense, *malediksyon*—malediction, or curse—points to a recurring pattern of colonial violence while also entailing forms of condemnation and excommunication forged by colonial powers. Malediksyon means at once othering, punishing, and excluding. Its mechanisms are not occult but visible in the economic and industrial history of the island. Such a reckoning implies that these patterns can change and be reversed.

Accounts of Columbus disembarking in Caracol are not only regional folklore but also a way to point to the recurrent destructive industrial intrusions in northeastern Haiti and the narratives that keep these repetitions going unabated. When Columbus first saw Indigenous people in the Caribbean on 11 October 1492, he placed them outside of civilization, and portrayed them as subhumans that could be Christianized and enslaved. As he stated in his journal, Indigenous people "appeared to me to be a race of people very poor in everything. They go as naked as when their mothers bore them. . . . Their hair is short and coarse, almost like the hairs of a horse's tail. . . . They should be good servants and intelligent, for I observed that they quickly took in what was said to them, and I believe that they would easily be made Christians, as it appeared to me that they had no religion" (Dunn and Kelley 1989: 69). The same mechanism—the blank-slate narrative—remains a key part of the neocolonial malediksyon that plagues Haiti today. Columbus considered the Caribbean to be a virgin place and Indigenous people to be humans without history or religion. He also stated that they were "poor in everything," hence comparing them and making them inferior to Europeans, both from a material and religious standpoint, and framing the island as a place with people in need of external help. I argue that narratives casting Caracol as a blank slate and as a poor region in need of development have formed, since the beginning of colonization in the Americas, a structural matrix that enables the repetition of man-made and "natural" disasters in northeastern Haiti.[1]

Indigenous people, and later enslaved persons, always fought back against colonization and proposed viable countermodels of social and economic organization. It is in this overexploited region that the Haitian revolution (1791–1804) and many peasant-led rebellions started. Northeastern Haiti is one of the key places where a powerful countercolonial system enabling a majority of Haitians to live autonomously since 1804 was forged.[2] The Cap Haitian region writ large has long been a battlefield for colonial settlers and postcolonial developers who are not only trying to revive the plantation system but who were and are actively engaged in suppressing countercapitalist resistance and silencing a long and fruitful maroon history. As the historian Johnhenry Gonzalez argues, a majority of Haitians refused the return of the plantation economy imposed by state leaders after the 1804 independence and formed a "maroon nation" (2019). They forged small autarkic societies and created farming systems that enabled them to be self-sufficient and to engage in the global market on their own terms. Since 1804, developers of all kinds—from Haitian state leaders and business elites to US occupiers—have fought against these autonomous communities and tried to dismantle peasant farming as it was deemed to be "backwards." Haitians living in the countryside have long been defined as second-class citizens in their own country and have been the target of many US sponsored military operations meant to suppress subsistence agriculture and Vodou religion (Castor 1978). The curse Castin talked about is here read as a *structural* pattern that generates cycles of conflicts between Haitian peasants and so-called developers.

Following Columbus's remarks on Indigenous people's supposed lack of religion, I take the idea of malediksyon further. The people who farmed small plots of land after the revolution not only did so as a reaction against the plantation economy. Peasant farming developed around polycultural practices developed by enslaved people who cultivated small plots of land on plantations and in maroon communities. These practices are inseparable from cosmologies and epistemologies where the spiritual and physical well-being of humans is a result of respectful relations with the environments that surround them. In Vodou thought, for instance, trees can be the dwelling of *lwa* (deities) or *zansèt* (ancestors) (Bulamah 2018). Cutting a tree down, as I was told many times by Vodou practitioners and nonpractioners alike, can bring misery and disease on humans. As Haitian novelist Jacques Stephen Alexis wrote in *Les Arbres Musiciens*, spirits and deities "live in the earth, in the rivers, under the sea, in the waters of lakes" (1957, 346). Deforesting an area to mine for gold or copper, or bulldozing farms and fields to establish an industrial park, are not just plain ecological destruction but also spiritual uprooting (*déchoukaj*). Castin noted several times, during our conversations, that social and environmental elements could not be dissociated in Haitian peasant struggles. He refers here to what Mimi Sheller calls "arboreal landscapes of power and resistance"—spaces where "social relations of power, resistance, and oppositional culture building are inscribed into living landscapes of farming, dwelling, and cultivation" (2012: 187). As such, arboreal landscapes offer a Haitian countercosmology and counterecology that could serve as an antidote to the malediksyon. Of course, from a material viewpoint, the bulldozing of farms renders people homeless. However, I argue that we can read more in Castin's words: malediksyon happens when economies treating nature as separated from human communities lead to the desecration of spiritual, human, and natural dwellings. Not surprisingly, major industrial ventures are often accompanied with anti-Vodou campaigns. What happens when an industrial park or a plantation replaces hundreds of small farms and fields is far more than the transformation of an environment: each (neo)colonial venture in northeastern Haiti is an active attempt to erase local histories, epistemologies, and cosmologies that sustain independent peasant farming. To put it bluntly, Caracol is a space where capitalists actively combat and suffocate viable countercapitalist economies. Treating Hispaniola, and later Saint Domingue and Haiti, as a blank slate where people need to be uplifted from poverty by external interventions is at the heart of the structural and spiritual curse that continues to destabilize Caracol today. And again, this is not a supernatural curse but an infrastructural and superstructural one. In the aftermath of the 2010 earthquake, the blank-slate mentality, to use William Easterly's concept, fosters disaster vulnerability by displacing people and preventing them from growing food (2014).

Narratives stating that Haitians cannot govern themselves and cannot take care of their country have flooded newspapers since its independence in 1804. Political instability and lack of leadership were the main reasons given by the US government for the invasion of the island in 1915. Of course, in the larger context of the banana wars, it is clear that the US had its own strategic and economic interests in mind when it imposed military rule in Haiti. If it is true that competing economic interests and political discord destabilized the export economy of the country in the nineteenth and early twentieth centuries, a majority of Haitians have managed to live self-sufficiently since 1804 (Barthélémy 1990; Gonzalez 2019). As the geographer Georges Anglade has shown, Haitian peasant farmers created a strong and decentralized market system that reduced their reliance on exports to generate incomes (1982). Yet, because the Haitian state had to reimburse enormous and immoral debts, the country almost never modernized its infrastructure and remained tied to foreign powers that used cannonball diplomacy to make sure the Haitian state paid what it supposedly owned them (Dubois 2012).[3] Even if a majority of Haitians lived decent lives, the US invaded their country by arguing that political instability plagued the island. The US also wanted to make sure that the Haitian state paid its foreign debts: developing the industrial sector of the country while handling its budget and economic policies was supposed to be the solution to this problem. What happened was a US takeover of lands and export industries that only benefited US corporations and a handful of wealthy Haitians. The US occupation developed the centralization of all economic and administrative activities in Port-au-Prince, suffocated the province's economy, and implemented structural adjustments that created an almost tax-free environment for foreign corporations while displacing the tax burden onto the back of peasant farmers (Castor 1978). In brief, the US developed disaster vulnerability and economic instability for a majority of Haitians. These destructive probusiness policies went on, even after the US left the country in 1947 (Dupuy 1989; Fatton 2014).

Probusiness policies such as low taxes for corporations and high taxes for Haitian workers, low import tariffs, absence of budgets for provinces, and austerity when it comes to the welfare elements of the state such as health and education are the hallmarks of most governments that took control of the island after the long US occupation (1915–47). The Duvalier dictatorships (1957–86) only reinforced the patterns put in place during the occupation by continuing to deny provinces financial and administrative autonomy and by concentrating administrative and economic power in the capital. International allies along with international financial institutions (IFIs) such as the International Monetary Fund or the Inter-American Development Bank backed and funded corrupt governments and turned a blind eye to the most brutal aspects of the Duvalier dictatorships. These policies transformed Haiti into a small-scale "supplier of garments, dolls, magnetic tapes, and electronic equipment" (Trouillot 1990: 202), and the swift and violent slaughter of Haitian pigs broke the economic back of the Haitian peasantry. As Mark Schuller writes, "responding to an outbreak of swine fever, the U.S. government killed off Haitian pigs, de-facto bank accounts, replacing them with high-maintenance pink U.S. pigs, amounting to Haiti's 'great stock market crash'" (2007: 150). This series of man-made economic disasters, along with accrued political repression, triggered massive migration movements and led to the ousting of Jean-Claude Duvalier in February 1986. After almost thirty years of violent dictatorship and constant economic sabotage, Haitians lived in a country devoid of public services and basic infrastructure. Again, these failures are not due to a curse but to clear and simple man-made and internationally sponsored sabotage.

This history is well known, yet, after the devastating earthquake that took the lives of more than three hundred thousand people in the Port-au-Prince region on 12 January 2010, the same economic recipes made a forceful comeback. Touted by Bill Clinton and the economist Paul Collier, the "Building Back Better Plan" of the US was based on the development of the industrial sector. Developing the garment industries would generate economic growth that, in turn, would generate the funds required for the reconstruction of the country. Hence, instead of rebuilding the Port-au-Prince region after the quake, the Haitian state and its powerful international allies funded the creation of free-trade zones and industrial parks. It was not the first time that the idea of developing the garment industry and transforming Haiti into a "little Taiwan" had been implemented. From 1970 to 1980, assembly industries became a key sector in Haiti's economy, and they employed 80 percent of the industrial workforce (Péan 1987). They functioned on an enclave model: international manufacturers in Haiti benefited from tax and tariff exemptions and paid no taxes on materials and machineries imported for goods production. The resulting sweat shops paid their workers very low salaries and often subtracted extra money from employee paychecks for unreasonable expenses. This same model is pervasive in Haiti today. We see roughly the same system of shaving salaries in industrial parks in contemporary Haiti.

Even though the assembly industry mostly generates poverty and ecological destruction, the Haitian state and its partners—in this case USAID and the Interamerican Development Bank—argued that transforming northeastern Haiti into an industrial center would heal the wounds of the Port-au-Prince region (Lucien 2018). In 2011, this industrial center, which was intended to catalyze the creation of the Northern Economic Corridor, emerged in Caracol in the form of a 617-acre industrial park. This was the costliest postearthquake project and the centerpiece of the "new" economic plans for Haiti. Because Haitian administrators were mostly bypassed, the construction of the park was swift. Similarly to what happened in the American Wild West, developers invaded and destroyed Caracol as if it were a blank slate devoid of history and human activity. The project was well funded: Sae-A Co. Ltd. invested $78 million to buy equipment and promised to hire twenty thousand workers (Shamsie 2019). The IDB provided $200.5 million for the construction of buildings, roads, and a water treatment plant while the US government funded a $98-million electrical power plant. The main garment producer that moved to Caracol at this time and created thirteen thousand jobs between 2012 and 2019 was Sae-A, a large Korea-based multinational apparel production company. When Daniel Cho, president of the Haiti subsidiary of Sae-A, arrived at the park's construction site in early 2012, he said, "You can see. Nothing is here. This area is like a white paper, and we can draw on it" (quoted in Sontag 2012). Cho's words crudely reflect what economist William Easterly calls the blank-slate mentality, namely the tendency to "ignore history and to see each poor society as infinitely malleable for the development expert to apply his technical solutions" (2014: 25). Sae-A supplies US retailers such as Walmart and Kohl's and has played a major role in the industrial development of several Latin American countries.

Of course, Caracol was not and is not a blank slate or piece of white paper. But the blank-slate narrative is a common tool that developers of all stripes have used to transform the Caracol region many times before (Lucien 2018). In the case of the Caracol Industrial Park (CIP), in order to make room for the project, an estimated 366 families were displaced from their land (Chérestal 2015). The CIP also negatively impacted "720 agricultural workers and thousands of resellers, food processors and pastoralists, as well as rural community members who relied on the agricultural production of the land for food and livelihood or used it to access water" (3). Actually, a more recent report explains that the CIP exacerbated food insecurity in the region by actually displacing 442 families (Kolektif Péizan 2017). Although some farmers received small financial compensations for their lost land, the money did not make up for their lost livelihoods.

During the fieldwork I conducted intermittently between 2015 and 2019, I observed that the CIP failed to increase quality of life for most people who live in northeastern Haiti (Joos 2021a). The park's employees, and Sae-A's workers in particular, receive meager wages for the hard work they perform in overheated factories. My interlocutors resented that managerial positions were given to people from Guatemala and Korea while Haitians were only offered menial, low-paid jobs. Although the park was supposed to create 60,000 jobs in five years, only about 35,000 people worked in the Haitian apparel industry as of 2018, and approximately 9,000 people worked in Caracol (Haiti Libre 2018). In 2019, fewer than 15,000 people worked in the CIP. As you will hear below from people who worked at the CIP, it destroyed not only the livelihoods of peasant farmers but also the complex cultural, social, religious, and economic systems that enabled them to thrive in their homeland. Farms and livelihoods were crushed but value systems in the area, where deep relations between humans and their environment sustain a fragile but vital social and environmental equilibrium, were also deeply disrupted.

Although evicting farmers from their land and crushing their livelihoods is not new in the region, the situation with the CIP did present a novel development: for the first time in the region's history, the Haitian state and IFIs negotiated with the people they displaced. The IDB even created a compensation plan and offered packages to displaced farmers. In addition, state officials went to Caracol to "educate" people about the benefits of the CIP; information sessions held by state representatives from Port-au-Prince took place before the park was constructed (Shamsie 2014). However, as my informants made clear, the state's compensation efforts were mostly empty promises intended to calm the local population. The promises, backed by the IDB, were not fully kept. And the compensations that did occur opened new fault lines in the Caracol community.

Alain Petit-Frère is a farmer who had a large plot of land and who employed up to twelve people during harvest season. I first met him when my friend Francis introduced us in 2015, but we reconnected during my fieldwork in 2019. When I asked him about the money he received from the IDB when he lost his land in 2011, his answer was blunt: "Compensation? They gave us a little bit of shit money. A little bit of shit money" (Yon ti kaka kob yo ban nou. Yon ti kaka kob). Farmers displaced by the CIP never received what the IDB and the Haitian government promised them. To this day, the IDB website states that "the 366 people who used to farm that state-owned land on which the industrial park is being developed have received a total $1.2 million in compensation (about $3,500 per household, or five times the Haitian per capita income). All were offered access to a nearby plot with similar characteristics that will be improved with irrigation. Those [who] expressed interest in learning a new trade were offered job training. In addition, the elderly and more socially vulnerable received housing assistance" (IDB 2012).

I had printed this document when I met with Alain Petit-Frère in the front yard of his house in Quartier Morin in March 2019, when I resumed my inquiries about the CIP. When I translated this part to Alain, he explained that he and the people he knew only received "yon ti kaka kob" (a little bit of shit money), and that 442 families were affected and not 366 as the IDB website claimed. He also said that, to his knowledge, no one in the area had ever received land with similar characteristics to the plots they had lost. "What they don't understand," he said, "is that the Tè Chabè was the best land around here. Even during times of drought, we would be able to produce food. I mainly cultivated peas. I had two harvests a year! I sold these peas to people from Cap Haitian. Not only was I able to make a living and to send my children to school, I also employed many people." With anger in his voice, he added, "Development! Well, I know how to make development!" As he made clear, the way he produced food before his land was taken was ecologically and economically sustainable. He pulled a notebook from a backpack he had brought from his house and showed us numbers: the salaries he paid to temporary workers and the benefits he generated by selling produce were indeed impressive. He repeatedly noted that Caracol was not a poor town before the CIP; it was a place where people could make a living by fishing or by growing food. Very few people in the area actually supported the project. Alain Petit-Frère certainly did not.

Eventually, though, the Haitian government ceased the compensations, which were supposed to be disbursed over a five-year period. At that point, communication between displaced people and the government broke down. "The government disappeared," Alain said, "and that ti kaka kob (little bit of shit money) too!" As another displaced farmer said to me during a conversation, "In 2014, we formed a new organization named the Komite Tè Chabè (Kolektif Peyizan Viktim Tè Chabè—the Peasant Collective of the Chabè Land Eviction Victims). Since we couldn't reach anyone, we asked Castin, one of the organization's founders, to reach out to someone, a lawyer from the US. That way, we were able to contact the IDB. They started to investigate and investigate, and in the meantime, we didn't receive anything. What we received before wasn't enough, they cannot replace the land that gave us food. It's been five years we are mobilized."

Milostène Castin is a longtime grassroots activist who founded the Action pour la Reforestation et la Défense de l'Environnement (AREDE), an organization created in 2004 to fight deforestation, protect biodiversity, and defend people against land grabs. In 2013, Castin started meeting with peasant farmers displaced by the CIP and meticulously studying the compensation process that unfolded between 2011 and 2014. By talking with people and comparing their compensation amounts with what was promised in state documents, he discovered a great deal of irregularities in the process. Castin's administrative work was impressive and precise. He amassed every official document he could find and tracked public statements from key project stakeholders to describe the discrepancies between what they promised and what happened on the ground. By doing so, he was able to take the case to the Independent Consultation and Investigation Mechanism (MICI) of the IDB. I met with him again in Trou du Nord on a morning in June 2019. For two hours, we sat and talked under a tree in the backyard of a house that belonged to one of his friends. I took notes during our discussion and will reproduce excerpts of them here.

Castin first explained that he was currently fighting on two fronts—he demanded environmental and socioeconomic accountability from the IDB. He said:

> The IDB has given the Haitian state some funds to compensate the peasants who were displaced from their land, but the distribution of these funds was not well organized and, at times, clearly fraudulent. I had witnessed people expelled from the land they cultivated in Limonade, when Moïse [Jovenel Moïse, the actual president of Haiti] built Agritrans. Many farmers were just chased away from the places they had lived [in] and worked for a long time. It happened in Ouanaminthe in 2002 as well, when the government built an industrial park. I saw hundreds of peasant farmers disposed from their lands. This good, fertile land is replaced by factories that produce CO_2 and that potentially pollute surrounding waters. When I started to talk with the farmers in Caracol, I felt we should organize and fight back, and we did.

Agritrans was the first banana plantation in Haiti to be located in a free-trade zone. After the quake, Moïse, a close ally to then-President Martelly, received the help of the state to displace more than a thousand farmers from the Limonade area. People lost their livelihoods without receiving any kind of compensation. As the geographer Jennifer Vansteenkiste has aptly shown through her fieldwork in Limonade, the brutal displacement of peasant farmers who were self-sufficient before the earthquake contributed to a major food crisis in the region and to social instability. As she notes, land and trees are not replaceable; they are part of people's cosmology (2016). For many people in the Cap region, trees are sacred. Vodou deities—*lwa*, often called *zanj* in northern Haiti—inhabit the trees and form an essential element of people's physical and social worlds (Bulamah 2018). As Vansteenkiste notes, "the loss of large trees such as mangos through land conversions is equivalent to dechouké, or the uprooting, of the Haitian belief system" (2016: 22). The loss of arboreal landscapes means the loss of spaces imbued with the history and cosmology of peasant farmers, spaces that allow many Haitians to maintain social and economic stability in their communities.

The northeastern region of Haiti, as Castin explained, has a violent history of land grabs. He said, "It started in 1927 with the Dauphin Plantation in Fort-Liberté, not far from Caracol. It was during the US occupation. American businesses took over the fertile lands of the region to produce sisal [a fibrous plant used to produce textiles.] The American army displaced thousands of farmers, forced them to work for little money in the sisal fields, or forced them to migrate to Cuba or the Dominican Republic, so they would work on sugar plantations. I think the sisal plantation lasted until the early 70s." As geographer Georges Eddy Lucien (2018) details, Andre De Coppet, a wealthy Wall Street financier, started the Dauphin Plantation in 1926 with the help of the US military. To make space for the textile factories, the settlements of American workers, and the sisal plantations, the American army violently evicted peasants from their small farms and burned down the buildings, woods, and fields that stood in their way. Indeed, according to Suzy Castor, Americans displaced fifty thousand peasants to make room for this plantation, which she called a "classic colonial enclave" (quoted in Naimou 2015: 244). As Lucien puts it, the Haitian puppet government and its military and corporate allies tore away large swaths of land from the peasantry through newly invented legal means and violent action, and, in the process, created a de facto mobile, homeless workforce that moves between factories and plantations in order to receive meager salaries (2018).

After US Marines invaded and destroyed the region, it fell into a period of decay and hopelessness. Robert Pettigrew, the Dauphin Plantation manager in the 1940s, described the enterprise when he said, "This is the story of a small corner of the Republic of Haiti and the development of a truly remarkable enterprise that revived it from the decay and hopelessness into which it had sunk through neglect, strife and ineptitude over the years since it flourished as a part of France's richest American colony" (1958, 7). Pettigrew's words echo Christopher Columbus's first impressions of Hispaniola as a territory peopled by indolent, areligious communities. This narrative strategy, depicting Indigenous people as inept and negligent, allows for the erasure of their world.

However, the Dauphin Plantation slowly declined. Once De Coppet passed away, American entrepreneurs bought it in 1953. The Dauphin Plantation closed in the early 1970s when the price of sisal declined. Even though US companies eventually left the region in the 1970s, state-owned companies continued to use the land in Caracol and in Fort-Liberté to grow sugar and sisal until 1986. "Moreover," Castin continued, "the site where the CIP is built is sacred for us Haitian peasants. . . . It's called Tè Chabè. Until 1986 and the fall of the Duvalier dictatorship, plantations of sisal and sugar occupied this land. Once the dictator was out, people reclaimed this land, because it was ours. It is officially state-owned, but Haitian peasants have historically reclaimed state-owned land for themselves. Tè Chabè is where American occupants buried Charlemagne Péralte, a revolutionary leader who fought against the occupation. When they bulldozed our fields, they also erased our history." Castin paused and then said: "Péralte is a hero, but we cannot fight like him today. We cannot afford to fight a violent struggle. I am a revolutionary, but I use pacific and legal means to reach my goals."

Tè Chabè was a concentration camp during the American occupation. In 1918, Charlemagne Péralte led a rebellion against the American occupiers who had maintained a forced-labor system called the corvée in the north (Bellegarde 1937: 270; Anglade 1977, 29). Moreover, peasant farmers protested the massive displacements caused by the US corporate invasion of their land (Castor 1978). Péralte led an army of more than five thousand peasant farmers (*les Cacos*) in guerilla warfare against the American occupiers. According to the scholar Jerry Philogène, "After years of resisting the U.S. occupying forces, Péralte was captured and killed on October 31, 1919, by two U.S. marines, Herman Henry Hanneken and William Robert Button, who infiltrated his camp disguised in blackface" (2015: 109). Caco rebels and displaced farmers were then imprisoned and sent to the Cap Haitian prison or to the Tè Chabè concentration camp. Haitian historian Dantès Bellegarde has written that 5,475 prisoners died in the Tè Chabè camp. American authorities dismissed this massacre and stated that repressing Haitian "brigandage" evidently entailed the loss of Haitian lives (1937: 56–57). Péralte's body was buried in a concrete cast to prevent his followers from exhuming the body or resurrecting it (Philogène 2015: 112).

Before that point, however, the US army publicly displayed Péralte's body in Grand Rivière, so local Haitian officials and people who knew Péralte could verify his death. An anonymous US Marine photographed Péralte's body, which was tied to a door and partly covered in white cloth. The US army then disseminated the image by airplane throughout the countryside as a warning to Caco rebels. However, this image, which unintentionally evokes a crucifixion, became a symbol of resistance for the Haitian peasantry. The Cacos refused to back down and led a second war against the US army that ended in 1920. Across the country, Péralte became a symbol of resistance, a symbol of the Haitian peasants' willingness to fight to preserve their autonomy, their lands, and their livelihoods. As Yveline Alexis recently showed, the struggles of Péralte and of the Cacos remain an important symbol and provide a crucial framework for activists who are currently fighting for Haiti's sovereignty (2021).

When they built the CIP on a site deemed sacred by many people who live in Caracol and who worked the fertile lands of Tè Chabè, the Haitian government and the Clinton Foundation–USAID assemblage may not have intended to erase this history. However, they bulldozed one of the last strongholds of the Haitian peasantry and built factories on land where people had fought against the brutal return of the plantation system, and local Haitians considered these acts an affront. In 2015, as I sat with my friends Pierre and Tony Valcin in front of their home in Bodmè Limonade, they explained why land and trees were dear to them. "Bodmè is a pilgrimage site for Vodouyzan," Pierre said. "Here trees are very important. When you cut a big tree, like a mapou tree, it makes you sick. Gods live in trees (gen zanj nan chak pyebwa)." Farmers in other parts of Haiti told me the same thing, and ample scholarship has shown the spiritual and historical importance of trees to Vodou practitioners (Bellande 2015; Bulamah 2018). Many of the zanj or lwa with which people interact are ancestors who have returned in spiritual form. Bulldozing Tè Chabè is, in the words of Jennifer Vansteenkiste, a déchoukaj—an uprooting of the peasants' cosmology, value systems, and social cohesion. It is also an indirect form of silencing history that has long been practiced by the Haitian Creole state (2016).

For the people of Caracol, the fact that the CIP was built on a former concentration camp was a catalyst for action. The farmers I met were related to people who had died in the not-so-distant Caco wars. As Roger Gaillard has shown in his brilliant oral history of the American occupation, narratives pertaining to the ruthless reimposition of the plantation system by the United States never left the Haitian collective memory (1982). Most of the people I met in Caracol were angered by the loss of their sacred land, their history, and their livelihoods.

Caracol, and Haiti, are not blank slates ripe for modern development. As the people I met in Caracol made clear, a strong and viable agricultural economy existed right where the site of the CIP stands today. People know full well that the malediksyon Castin mentioned is not a supernatural curse triggered, as televangelist Pat Robertson famously said after the 2010 quake, by people practicing "voodoo" and engaging in a "pact with the devil." Such narratives exist in secular form as well, even though disguised as expertly written economic studies (Lundahl 2013).[4] However, there is a dire need to value true Vodou economics, and more broadly, peasant environmental and social practices. Exchanges based on reciprocity, collectively organized work, and subsistence farming in rural Haiti are anchored in a larger relational frame where nature is not a backdrop to human activity but a fully agentic force that shapes people's ties to human and nonhuman communities. As Alex Bellande demonstrated in his brilliant study of the Haitian environment (2015), peasant farmers are not responsible for the environmental foes of the country, nor do they push its economy backwards. To the contrary, listening to peasant leaders would reinforce sustainable fishing and agricultural practices and reinforce food security. It would generate economic growth, this time not for foreign corporation but for families like the one of Alain Petit-Frère. Haiti is not a cursed country. The malediksyon plaguing it today has nothing to do with some devilish pact or so-called backwards economic practices. To the contrary, the blank-slate narrative of industrial developers and the policies, destruction, and uprooting it generates is the central mechanism that forms a structure enabling the repetition of disasters. Hence, the curse can be stopped if we uproot (neo)colonial development practices from Haiti and if the needs, desires, and savoir faire of Haitians form the basis for new political horizons.

Vincent Joos is an assistant professor of anthropology and global French studies at Florida State University. His work has appeared in *Economic Anthropology, Transforming Anthropology, Vibrant,* and *World Politics Review*. His work focuses on postdisaster reconstruction in the Caribbean. He recently published his first book, *Urban Dwellings, Haitian Citizenships: Housing, Memory, and Daily Life in Haiti* (Rutgers University Press, 2021).

Notes

1. Fuller historical accounts of these repetitions can be found in Alex Dupuy (1989), Georges Eddy Lucien (2018), and Vincent Joos (2021b).
2. The Bois-Caïman ceremony led by Dutty Boukman and Cecile Fatiman on 14 August 1791 stands as the beginning of the revolution. In this political and religious meeting, Vodou practices brought together various ethnic groups into one common struggle. It was during this ceremony that Dutty Boukman called for a general insurrection. The Indigenous Army made of formerly enslaved people liberated Haiti from French colonialism. The country became independent on 1 January 1804.
3. In 1825, France imposed a debt on Haiti in exchange for its recognition of Haiti as a nation. The debt was meant to reimburse the planters who had lost properties during the revolution. The payment of this debt was a major burden and represented an enormous part of the Haitian state's budget until it was fully paid in 1947. For a fuller account, see Dubois 2012.
4. The Swedish economist Mats Lundahl, who wrote extensively about the Haitian economy, relentlessly vilifies what he calls "voodoo" and depicts it as a force that impedes social and economic change. Spelling Vodou as "voodoo" is in itself a mark of disdain, since "voodoo," when applied to Haiti, is a mock term for Vodou religious practices.

References

Alexis, Jacques Stephen. 1957. *Les Arbres Musiciens*. Paris: Gallimard.
Alexis, Yveline. 2021. *Haiti Fights Back: The Life and Legacy of Charlemagne Péralte*. New Brunswick, NJ: Rutgers University Press.
Anglade, Georges. 1977. *Mon Pays d'Haïti*. Québec : Presses de l'Université du Québec, Editions de l'Action Sociale.
1982. *Atlas critique d'Haïti*. Montreal: Groupe d'etudes et de recherches critiques d'espace, Departement de geographie, Universite du Quebec a Montreal; Centre de recherches caraibes de l'Universite de Montreal.
Barthélémy, Gerard. 1990. *L'univers rural haïtien: le pays en dehors*. Paris: L'Harmattan.
Bellande, Alex. 2015. *Haiti Déforestée, Paysages Remodelés*. Montreal: CIDIHCA.
Bellegarde, Dantès. 1937. *L'Occupation américaine d'Haïti*. Montreal: Editions Beauchemin.
Bulamah, Rodrigo. 2018. "Ruínas circulares: Vida e história no norte do Haiti." Tese (doutorado)—Universidade Estadual de Campinas, Instituto de Filosofia e Ciências Humanas, https://www.ifch.unicamp.br/ifch/ruinas-circulares-vida-historia-norte-haiti
Castor, Suzy. 1978. *La Ocupación Norteamericana de Haití y sus Consecuencias, 1915–1934*. Havana, Cuba: Casa de las Americas.
Chérestal, Kysseline Jean-Mary. 2015. "Building Back Better? The Caracol Industrial Park and Post-earthquake Aid to Haiti." Washington, DC: ActionAid, https://www.actionaidusa.org/publications/building-back-better-caracol-industrial-park-post-earthquake-aid-haiti/
Dubois, Laurent. 2012. *Haiti: The Aftershocks of History*. New York: Macmillan.
Dupuy, Alex. 1989. *Haiti in the World Economy: Class, Race, and Underdevelopment since 1700*. Boulder, CO: Westview Press.
Dunn, Oliver, and James Kelley. 1989. *The Diario of Christopher Columbus's First Voyage to America, 1492–1493*. Norman, OK: University of Oklahoma Press.
Duval, Frantz. 2021. "Haïti n'est pas un pays maudit!" Courrier International, 20 August, https://www.courrierinternational.com/article/interview-non-haiti-nest-pas-un-pays-maudit
Easterly, William 2014. *The Tyranny of Experts: Economists, Dictators, and the Forgotten Rights of the Poor*. New York: Basic Books.
Fatton, Robert. 2014. *Haiti: Trapped in the Outer Periphery*. Boulder, CO: Lynne Rienner Publishers.
Gaillard, Roger. 1982. *Charlemagne Péralte Le Caco*. Port-au-Prince, Haiti: R. Gaillard.
Gonzalez, Johnhenry. 2019. *Maroon Nation: A History of Revolutionary Haiti*. New Haven, CT: Yale University Press.
Haiti Libre. 2018. "Summary, challenges and perspectives of the textile sector." https://www.haitilibre.com/en/news-26479-haiti-economy-summary-challenges-and-perspectives-of-the-textile-sector.html
IDB. 2012. "Fact Sheet: The IDB and Haiti's Caracol Industrial Park." https://www.iadb.org/en/news/background-papers/2012-07-06/caracol-industrial-park-key-facts percent2C10054.html.
Joos, Vincent A. 2021a. *Urban Dwellings, Haitian Citizenships: Housing, Memory, and Daily Life in Haiti*. New Brunswick, NJ: Rutgers University Press.

———. 2021b. "Developing Disasters: Industrialization, Austerity, and Violence in Haiti since 1915." In *The Struggle of Non-Sovereign Caribbean Territories*, ed. Adlai Murdoch. New Brunswick, NJ: Rutgers University Press.

Katz, Jonathan. 2013. *The Big Truck That Went By: How the World Came to Save Haiti and Left Behind a Disaster*. New York: Palgrave Macmillan.

Kolektif Peyizan Viktim Tè Chabè. 2017. "Haiti: Caracol Industrial Park." Accountability Counsel website, https://www.accountabilitycounsel.org/client-case/haiti-caracol-industrial-park/#timeline.

Lucien, Georges Eddy. 2018. *Le Nord-Est d'Haïti: La perle d'un monde fini; entre illusions et réalités (Open for Business)*. Paris: L'Harmattan.

Lundahl, Mats. 2013. *The Political Economy of Disaster: Destitution, Plunder and Earthquake in Haiti*. New York: Routledge.

Morison, Samuel E. 1940. "The Route of Columbus along the North Coast of Haiti, and the Site of Navidad." *Transactions of the American Philosophical Society* 31(4): 239–85, https://doi.org/10.2307/1005582.

Naimou, Angela. 2015. *Salvage Work: U.S. and Caribbean Literatures amid the Debris of Legal Personhood*. New York: Fordham University Press.

Péan, Leslie. 1987. "Trade in Manufactures: Haiti 1970-79." IESCARIBE Study for Interamerican Development Bank.

Pettigrew, Robert. 1958. *The Story of Fort Liberty and the Dauphin Plantation*. Richmond, VA: Cavalier Press.

Philogène, Jerry. 2015. "'Dead Citizen' and the Abject Nation: Social Death, Haiti, and the Strategic Power of the Image." *Journal of Haitian Studies* 21(1): 100–26.

Schuller, Mark. 2007. "Haiti's 200-Year Menage-a-Trois: Globalization, the State, and Civil Society." *Caribbean Studies* 35(1): 141–79.

———2009. "Gluing Globalization: NGOs as Intermediaries in Haiti." *PoLAR: Political and Legal Anthropology Review* 32: 84–104.

Shamsie, Yasmine. 2014. "La construction d'un parc industriel dans l'arriere-pays rural d'Haiti. Quelques observations sur le partenariat etat-societe et les capacites de l'etat." *Cahiers des Amériques latines* 75: 79–96.

———2019. "Reflections on Haitian Democracy: Zooming in on a Megaproject in the Hinterland." *Latin American Research Review*, 54(1): 35–49.

Sheller, Mimi. 2012. *Citizenship from Below: Erotic Agency and Caribbean Freedom*. Durham, NC: Duke University Press.

Sontag, Susan. 2012. "Earthquake Relief Where Haiti Wasn't Broken." *New York Times*, 6 July, https://www.nytimes.com/2012/07/06/world/americas/earthquake-relief-where-haiti-wasnt-broken.html.

Trouillot, Michel-Rolph. 1990. *Haiti, State against Nation: The Origins and Legacy of Duvalierism*. New York: Monthly Review Press.

Vansteenkiste, Jennifer. 2017. "Haiti's Peasantry as Poto Mitan: Refocusing the Foundations of Prosperity and Development." *Canadian Journal of Development Studies*. Volume 38, 2017 - Issue 4, 523-541.

CHAPTER 4

Post-Katrina Intrusions on African American Cultural Traditions in New Orleans

SHEARON ROBERTS

Introduction

Tremé is considered America's oldest Black neighborhood. Between 1775 and 1841, Black people who had earned their freedom from slavery, mixed with recent immigrants from Saint Domingue (Haiti), owned 80 percent of Tremé. They created businesses, started the first daily Black newspaper, *L'Union* (later the *Tribune*), and centered Congo Square at the heart of the neighborhood as the spiritual public space to celebrate and preserve their African heritage in spite of enslavement (Johnson 1991).

Three centuries later, Tremé is struggling to remain a predominantly Black space in a majority Black city. The Housing Authority of New Orleans noted that several sections of Tremé had shifted from majority Black to majority white (Rose 2020; LaBorde 2016). In addition to Tremé, traditionally Black neighborhoods that spread out from Uptown, such as Broadmoor and Central City, heading east past Tremé, then to the Seventh Ward, Gentilly, and on to the Ninth Ward, also experienced rapid gentrification. The Louisiana Fair Housing Action Center noted in 2020 that since Hurricane Katrina, New Orleans had a total of thirteen gentrifying neighborhoods with an additional fifty-one showing early signs of gentrification. Altogether, the city now ranks as the fifth most gentrified in America (Rose 2020).[1]

Gentrification is one of the more far-reaching postdisaster effects of Hurricane Katrina, a decade and a half later. When the waters receded in New Orleans, it stripped the ability of generations of Black New Orleanians to rebuild life, community, and to hold on to heritage. Along Claiborne Avenue, where second lines and jazz funerals take place, over 1,000

Black households have disappeared, and the stretch has gained 120 white households, 50 Latino households, and 5 Asian households, according to the latest census data for that neighborhood (Rose 2020).

More than fifteen years since Hurricane Katrina, New Orleans remains an important case study of how post-disaster recovery can be persistently unequal in the long term. Many post-disaster case studies often mark the ten-year anniversary of a natural disaster, noting infrastructure renovations and the return of economic activity and population density as overall indicators that a disaster-vulnerable space has "returned to normal."

This chapter dives deeper into postdisaster recovery, centering marginalized communities within disaster spaces and the ways in which their lives and communities remain forever changed by a disaster. In fact, while Hurricane Katrina was the perfect collision of mother nature (a hurricane) and a man-made crisis (failed levees, slow federal response), resulting in the flooding of a city, the uneven return of New Orleans is entirely a man-made crisis in which policies or the lack of system protections failed to allow a fair opportunity for marginalized peoples to regain what was lost from a natural disaster. The gentrification of Black communities in New Orleans is therefore the consequence of a lack of intervention to protect African American families from market forces, and of the policies of urban revitalization that drive such forces in postdisaster spaces.

A further form of marginalization is that the cultural capital of New Orleans is rooted in African American traditions that were first birthed in Black neighborhoods across the city and controlled within neighborhoods in order to pass this unique heritage down through several generations. This chapter describes first the ways in which gentrification of Black neighborhoods in New Orleans, after Hurricane Katrina, threatens the survival of cultural practices that are crucial to livelihoods and community cohesion in Black neighborhoods. These traditions were born out of resistance that first began in enslavement, and persisted through three hundred years of oppression, and that bring joy and upliftment to souls in addition to economic means and empowerment.

To their credit, New Orleans residents continue to act as gatekeepers of what is left of their communities and to serve as watchdogs of the erasure of their communities and the settlement into them by "transplants" (the name given to mostly white residents who have made New Orleans their home after Hurricane Katrina). While grassroots organizing is one way in which residents continue to push back against their displacement, digital spaces also allow residents to draw national attention to the ways in which the place that was the home of Louis Armstrong is under cultural assault, precipitated by the aftermath of a disaster.

Cultural Gentrification

As the demographic shifts into historically Black neighborhoods rapidly continue in the city, African Americans have decried the cooption of communal practices that were the exclusive and traditional domain of culture bearers. These physical displacements and cultural intrusions are evident in the ways in which Black residents continue to fight to preserve their sacred spaces and sacred traditions.

The movement of "transplants" into Black spaces in New Orleans takes on a slightly different nature than in other gentrified Black communities across the country. The appeal of Black culture in this city to outsiders places a premium on escape, relish, and entertainment, which makes living in Black neighborhoods in New Orleans quaint, faux-authentic, and hip. The participation of outsiders in the sacred practices of marginalized groups is an extension of the privilege that those who hold power are able to exert over disenfranchised groups (Thomas 2012).

Particularly for Black people, the consumption of their lived experiences is not new. The fetishizing and exoticizing of Black bodies and Black cultural traditions is rooted in Frantz Fanon's theorizing of the white gaze.

Recalling Afro-Caribbean philosopher Frantz Fanon's *Black Skin, White Masks* (Fanon 2008), scholar Dianca London (2017) contemplates the dangers of the "white gaze." "When race is signified via the white gaze," London writes in a scholarly essay, "narratives involving people of color are otherized. Their stories become tangential, contingent upon their proximity to or distance from whiteness. When the white gaze is privileged, all other identities are jeopardized, confining marginalized bodies to typecast tokenism or, even worse, erasure."

The city was predominantly Black before Hurricane Katrina, dropping to 59 percent from 67 percent prior to the storm. The white population in New Orleans has grown by over 10 percent since 2005, with 90 percent of white native residents returning to the city (Rose 2020). Therefore, the city grew in white residents who were not native to New Orleans and familiar with its unique Black culture. Nor did new residents fully understand the ways in which native white residents adhered to socially understood but unwritten rules of mutual respect while engaging in citywide events.

Estimates of returning white residents and new transplants to the city (those who moved to New Orleans after the storm) outpaced the rate of return of native African American residents threefold (Population Reference Bureau 2010). Younger transplants, in particular, also faced the city's rising housing costs and shortage of units and were lured to traditionally African American wards and neighborhoods that have lower costs of living. The result has been the rapid gentrification of historic African American neighborhoods, wards, and blocks, which were traditionally located along public transit lines, or within short walking or biking routes to the French Quarter or to downtown.

As transplant residents began to purchase homes or rent in Black neighborhoods, boutique businesses from coffee shops like Starbucks to sandwich café's and even a Whole Foods emerged for the first time in predominantly Black neighborhoods. White residents also lobbied for and supported the expansion of bike lanes, more pedestrian friendly sidewalks, greenways, and the extension of the streetcar line further past the French Quarter and into Mid-City. This changed the nature of Black communities both visually and communally and became a source of both tensions and, later on, cultural clashes between residents and transplants.

The visual change was particularly painful for residents because of the significance of Tremé and its beating heart, Congo Square. Enslaved Africans and free people of color founded Congo Square as a space to preserve African traditions and create community in the face of enslavement. Many of the cultural traditions of New Orleans: music, dance, art, Vodou, and Black masking were forged and preserved first at Congo Square. Efforts by the city council to revive Congo Square in 2021 generated widespread resistance online and through organized protests from Black residents across the city who argued that this sacred public space remains a target for urban revitalization, primarily because of the gentrification taking place around it. The desire by the city to repurpose space around Congo Square in 2021 triggered fears that the site is marked as a space for redevelopment primarily because of its proximity to and appeal for transplants, rather than to protect it as a sacred Black public space.

In addition to Congo Square and its use today as a site for community gathering, Black communities created Black Mardi Gras and public performance traditions that were defined by the geographical spaces where they forged community. Black masking traditions in particular in New Orleans, which are a part of major city events such as Mardi Gras, Super Sunday, and Jazz Festival, are to this day rooted in the earliest forms of resistance by people of African descent in this city.

Their practices are contextualized in the lived experiences of African Americans in New Orleans, and their performance today through festivals are tributes to their ancestors, rallying cries for continued forms of resistance to systemic oppression, and a source of joy and escape from the hardships of life. They are not performances for external entertainment, although they are featured parts of the carnival and festival public events that attract tourists and bring economic means into the city. Rather they are community cultural practices passed down from generation to generation, and their performance annually takes place in the spaces where Black residents have lived.

Indeed, African Americans in New Orleans do not see the performance of their cultural heritage as a spectator sport. For instance, Black masking traditions like Mardi Gras Indians pay tribute to marronage and to Native Americans who allowed African Americans to survive as runaways (Smith 1994; Wehmeyer 2010). After emancipation, Black women created the Baby Dolls as a form of empowerment to reclaim their dignity as sex workers in the French Quarter (Vaz 2013). Second-lining can be found in births and deaths, is a core form of celebrating life, and its music and dance are passed down from generation to generation (Turner 2016). While tourists and white native New Orleanians are spectators to these Black practices, the unspoken rule and understanding is the need for distance and respect.

As a result of the celebration and homage these customs display, spectators who are not part of these communities or clubs or tribes must remain on the outskirts of these processions and can only engage performers if invited in. For the most part, this is how tourists have engaged these cultural practices during Mardi Gras season and across the year. With new transplants who reside in the spaces where these customs are performed yearly, the shared ownership of a historic space results in a battle between a community that sees its streets as ancestral and transplants who also see those streets as boundaries for the property they now own. Through ownership of former Black spaces that are rooted in history and the economic power ownership provides, rights accrue to transplants that privilege one form of existence over another.

These physical intrusions on Black cultural practices in New Orleans have real consequences beyond mere annoyance, objectification, or disrespect (Barrios 2010). These postdisaster physical intrusions correspond to three consequences: economic loss through appropriation, increased forms of criminalization, and the rupturing of Black safe communal spaces.

First, these intrusions result in economic loss when Black practices are appropriated and exploited by transplants. Cultural traditions created by African Americans in the city are frequently used in backdrops by Hollywood South (Louisiana's film industry) and for other parts of the entertainment industry; however, the bearers of these cultural practices continue to deplore the lack of recognition or compensation for native Black New Orleanians.

Second, these intrusions enhance criminalization of Black practices and Black bodies. Transplants have been successful in activating and proposing new ordinances to enforce "noise pollution" from African American street traditions ranging from block parties, party buses, street performers, and second-lining. The city's police have been used to shut down such events and make arrests following complaints by transplants about what have been traditional community practices at different times of the year.

Third, these intrusions further rupture Black safe communal spaces, adding a second level of violence inflicted on Black communities in the city after Katrina and its mismanagement tore the soul of Black New Orleans and scattered it across the South. Indeed, native Black New Orleanians and their children who moved away from the city after Katrina use the following phrase or hashtag: Nola born, elsewhere raised. To be born Black in New Orleans is a distinctive cultural marker that displacement from Katrina could never erase. All native New Orleanians wish to travel home, physically or spiritually. The cultural practices born in the city are a line that connects displaced residents and even Katrina Babies (those born outside of the city to New Orleans families or New Orleans children displaced by the storm). While their physical spaces are disrupted, their distinct cultural heritage allows New Orleans to be transported as an omnipresent sense of identity and belonging.

Cultural Intrusions

Cultural Appropriation for Economic Gain

Pop star Miley Cyrus's hip-hop phase can be traced back to post-Katrina New Orleans. The country singer and actress made a dramatic image and musical style transition that started in 2013 and ended around 2017, followed by several apologies for comments Cyrus made in response to her being labeled a "culture vulture." However, in Cyrus's short hip-hop phase, she produced the album *Bangerz*, which went triple platinum and number one on the Billboard chart when it debuted in 2013.

So what did Cyrus's success have to do with the mainstreaming and appropriation of Black New Orleans culture? She first encountered bounce music while shooting a film in the city, which emerged as the hub of Hollywood South through a Louisiana effort to lure West Coast film and TV projects to the state with the goal of revitalizing the city and southeast, Louisiana (Morgan Parmett 2014). The key to selling Black New Orleans culture was partly Hollywood South's arrival in a postapocalpytic New Orleans that made for good television and films (Roberts 2017: 23). In other words, New Orleans's physical disaster was an economic boom for Hollywood production and for storytelling. The movement of creatives into New Orleans brought a first group of transplants to the city who stayed and became part of the city's new residents.

While shooting the comedy film *So Undercover* in 2012, Cyrus spent time with other transplants, and while experiencing the city's culture, learned how to twerk. On her Facebook account she posted a short viral video of her twerking to bounce music. She then nationally debuted twerking as part of her new performing hip-hop persona at the 2013 MTV Video Music Awards, mainstreaming it and popularizing it among white pop culture consumers. Entertainment media at the time described Cyrus as having "invented" twerking ("Miley Cyrus" 2015). The dance became so popular after Cyrus's performance on national TV that both the Merriam-Webster and Oxford dictionaries added it as a new word in 2013, the same year as her performance.

Prior to Cyrus's demonstration of twerking, this form of dancing had been derided as part of Black culture that society deemed hypersexualized, provocative, and dirty (Baskerville 2014; Halliday 2020). In New Orleans, in particular, where Cyrus first learned her moves, twerking had its roots among low-income residents in the city's housing projects and was a key feature of bounce music, which was pioneered by rappers like Magnolia Shorty and Big Freedia. Hurricane Katrina destroyed public housing projects in the city and scattered those residents into other neighborhoods or cities. This cultural form that was often described as being "ghetto" was a feature of block parties, street parties, and spontaneous dance-offs by DJs in the projects. Big Freedia became a postdisaster icon for former residents of public housing because her music restored memory of the life and community that was lost when Katrina destroyed many of the city's projects, which were later demolished by city decree.

While Miley Cyrus sold one million copies of her *Bangerz* album in 2013, New Orleans native Big Freedia and other bounce-music artists continue to sue and speak out against the use of the artform they innovated and popularized without credit and compensation by both well-known artists and other creatives who have become transplants in the city, and who routinely mine New Orleans culture for ways to freshen up popular culture. In response to Cyrus' performance of twerking and the interest generated in bounce, Freedia, who is called "The Queen of Bounce," said in an interview in 2013, "It's become offensive to a lot of people who've been twerking and shaking their assess for years, especially in black culture" (Superselected 2020). In her 2015 biography, Freedia wrote of Cyrus: "I want our culture to be credited" (Big Freedia & Balin, 2015, p. 237).

Joining more popular names like Big Freedia, local groups also spoke out at the time about Cyrus's appropriation of Black culture, specifically Black New Orleans culture. In 2013, the Millisia White New Orleans Baby Doll group began an effort to educate others on the origins of twerking culture, particularly as it originated in the city in the community and spaces where block parties were held ("News with a Twist" 2013).

Since Cyrus's appropriation of twerking culture in support of her successful musical transition into hip-hop, many other artists, both Black and white, have moved to New Orleans to co-opt parts of Black culture into mainstream art forms. While New Orleans's artists have recognized how their culture has become more mainstream, they critique the lack of credit and financial remuneration when their art and culture is co-opted.

Policing Gentrified Neighborhoods

Prior to Hurricane Katrina, New Orleans was the most incarcerated city in the US (Vargas 2020). In the immediate aftermath of the disaster, inmates at the city jail were left without basic food, water and shelter. Also dubbed the murder capital of the world, New Orleans pursued aggressive policing by its police department, which heightened tensions between law enforcement and Black communities. As the difficult days after the storm rolled on, hysteria over unfounded claims of mass looting ended in fatal police shootings of Black men, which only years later were determined to have been the source of a large-scale cover-up (Miller, Roberts, and LaPoe 2014).

In one of the more notable police shootings after Hurricane Katrina, New Orleans Police Department (NOPD) officers killed two unarmed men, one who was seventeen years old, James Brissette, and another, aged forty, Ronald Madison, who was determined to be mentally disabled. Four other unarmed Black men were also shot. The shootings took place six days after the storm on the Danzinger Bridge. It took five years for a federal jury to convict five NOPD officers. The cover-up led the Department of Justice to launch an investigation into the NOPD's practices, placing the department under consent decree monitoring to implement many reforms after the disaster.

Criminal justice reform in New Orleans is one of the main reasons that the state of Louisiana is the only one in the South with a Democratic governor, John Bel Edwards, whose victory was primarily determined by the city's residents. Edwards became a national model, cited even by President Donald Trump, for his comprehensive criminal justice reform plan. The model adopted longtime work by local activists to release first-time, nonviolent, and nonsex offenders, to reduce prison terms for petty offenders, particularly for marijuana charges, and to invest in programs that reduce recidivism and assist the formerly incarcerated in reentering society. The plan also aims to create alternatives to incarceration for petty offenses. The plan resulted in the largest release in the state's history of inmates on "good standing" while serving their sentence. It also took the state off the top of the list of most incarcerated states in the US and is projected to drop the prison population by 12 percent over the next decade (Office of the Governor 2020).

The first key to effective reentry is the community that many of the formerly incarcerated are returning to, and who supports them in ways that allow for successful return to society and the prevention of recidivism. With the arrival of new white residents and businesses into Black neighborhoods, longtime residents have spoken out about the increased surveillance by law enforcement in those communities, not for the overall safety of the neighborhood but primarily because of an increase in calls from white residents (Sinders 2021; Blumberg 2020). These calls range from reports of carjacking to alerts, reports of break-ins, or expressions by white residents of their need to walk, jog, or bike safely in neighborhoods that were, or still are, predominantly Black but still hold many abandoned homes.

The increased hypervigilance of law enforcement in gentrified neighborhoods often results in false arrests, profiling of Black residents, and general distrust between communities and police. The community that would have worked to reintegrate formerly incarcerated persons in the past is slowly becoming a shell of its former self, without the resources and support the state needs for sustained community-wide reentry efforts. As former inmates return to live with relatives or the elderly as a result of this state-wide effort, gentrified Black neighborhoods become riskier because white "transplant" residents activate law enforcement within these formerly predominantly Black neighborhoods, heightening the surveillance of the formerly incarcerated and resulting in probation violations for minor infractions. Ultimately the use of law enforcement to patrol gentrified Black neighborhoods, at the requests of newer white residents, weakens the ways in which the community worked in the past to support successful re-entry into society for the formerly incarcerated.

Physical and Spiritual Displacement

In 2017, actress Carrie Fisher died. Members of the Krewe of Chewbacchus announced they would hold a second-line to celebrate Fisher's life. It set off an outcry on Facebook among Mardi Gras krewes about the sacredness of second-lines. One Facebook user, Martha Alguera, posted: "Really Carrie Fisher needs a second-line?" (Brasted 2017) The question set off a series of public outcries that prompted the krewe to remove the word second-line from the event. The krewe's cofounder Ryan Ballard told the *Times-Picayune* that "this debate was waiting to happen. It's all about all the changes in New Orleans that have taken place over the last few years. Some good, some bad. It's the new New Orleans, post-Katrina world where the city is evolving" (Brasted 2017)

The public outcry over the Carrie Fisher second-line wasn't the first. Previously a second-line planned for David Bowie created a public outcry among the Black community. Second-lines, which are street musical processions, originated in West Africa and were retained by enslaved Africans in New Orleans (Berry 1988). Jazz funerals are a component of second-lines aimed at celebrating the lives of loved ones who are no longer with the community (Turner 2016). They are practices specifically tied to the desire by people of African descent to hold onto their heritage and to celebrate life. Tulane University researcher Matt Sakakeeny noted in the *Times-Picayune* article that "white people like me do a lot of hand-wringing over these traditions. . . . I'm a guest when I join these traditions nurtured by black New Orleanians" (Brasted 2017).

The public outcry over second-lines for white celebrities is more than just an annoyance about a "new New Orleans." Indeed, in the pre-Katrina context, white performers were members of Black Mardi Gras krewes, Black jazz bands, Baby Dolls, Skulls and Bones, and many other practices, with the exception of Mardi Gras Indians. In fact the presence of white members in the Zulu Social Aid and Pleasure Club became the subject of debate among the Black community as the krewe's members often paint their faces black, meaning that white members inadvertently participated with "blackface" during Mardi Gras.

The displacement of native Black New Orleanians after Hurricane Katrina is an experience that is mourned. As mentioned already, children who were forced to relocate and grow up in other cities often describe themselves as "Nola-born, elsewhere raised." These "Katrina babies," as they call themselves, saw their childhood interrupted by postdisaster relocation, alienation from community and culture, and a desire for belonging.[2]

Lower-income New Orleans families, particularly those displaced from public housing, experienced discrimination in the cities they relocated to, heightening the desire to return to a place of community they are being priced out of (Chamlee-Wright and Storr 2009). Yet these cultural practices are kept alive across the city's diaspora of Black residents. That these practices are becoming whitewashed since Katrina intensifies the stripping away of central markers of Black New Orleans cultural life that many of those who wish to return home, but cannot afford to do so, see as the eroding of a place they continue to call home.

Resistance to Intrusions on Cultural Practices

New Orleans residents have always pushed back and acted as gatekeepers to their communities as they worked to rebuild after Katrina. As gentrifi-

Figure 4.1. Flyer by Greater New Orleans Housing Alliance's march of 2 November 2019. Posted on Facebook on 23 October 2019.

cation has accelerated, they have taken to protests offline and online to call attention to the ways in which their communities are eroding.

Veteran New Orleans musician and native Kermit Ruffins convened a meeting of musicians and friends at his Tremé lounge within the first few years after Katrina to respond to what African American newspapers described as an "attack on live music [that] has been achingly long, pervasive and ongoing" (Wyckoff 2014).

The meeting led to the creation in 2014 of the Music & Culture Coalition of New Orleans, a mix of musicians and their allies that began to formally advocate on behalf of the city's culture bearers as newer residents increasingly called on the city council to enact some of the most stringent noise ordinances the city has put in place in its post-Katrina residential codes.

The coalition joined forces with other grassroots organizations with goals running from housing equity to the removal of Confederate monuments to linking the enforcement of cultural practices through city codes with other forms of systemic displacement of the city's Black residents.

The coalition aimed, as well, to acknowledge all of the impacts of unaffordable housing, urban renewal, short term rentals like Airbnb, and gentrification.

On 2 November 2019, a collective of several New Orleans grassroots organizations scheduled the #PutHousingFirstMarch, highlighting that housing was an issue of social justice in post-Katrina New Orleans and impacted Black communities and their way of life. As the slogan for its march, the Greater New Orleans Housing Alliance carried the tag line: "Will New Orleans still be cool after we displace everyone that makes it cool?"[3]

What precipitated the November march was a string of viral events during festival season in 2019—spanning dozens of live musical events from Mardi Gras through the Jazz Festival and the French Quarter Festival—in which white residents, transplants, and even tourists had called the police on street musicians, brass bands, artists, and Black residents. Echoing similar national social media documenting the policing of Black bodies, the New Orleans context specifically had involved the public expression of Black communal cultural practices in public spaces. As is the case nationally, when white residents call the cops on Black neighbors, it often leads to the use of excessive force by law enforcement, and can potentially be deadly.

In New Orleans, these calls heightened tensions between local residents and transplants. As gentrification has accelerated after the ten-year anniversary of Hurricane Katrina, Black residents have taken to Black-owned media and social media spaces to call out the effects of policing cultural practices.

During summer festival season in 2019, Twitter user @KyleDeCoste504 caught the attention of The Roots band frontman and drummer Ahmir Khalib Thompson, better known as QuestLove. The Roots is the house band for NBC's Late Night with Jimmy Fallon.

Invoking the #BlackLivesMatter hashtag, DeCoste deplored the arrest of brass musician Eugene Grant due to a call "from a colonizing business owner." DeCoste wrote, "He was just making a couple honest bucks playing music on Frenchmen Street and they tackled him to the ground and locked him up."[4]

The owners of Frenchman Art & Books had called the police to complain about "noise." When the police arrived, a confrontation ensued between the officers and Grant. The police stated that Grant struck an officer in his chest with his trumpet. Grant's attorney and mother argued that the twenty-seven-year-old is on the autism spectrum, and that the officers attempting to arrest and taser him confused and frightened him. Grant was thrown to the ground by officers, pinned there, and arrested. The arrest was recorded by bystanders and shared on social media. Dozens of resi-

Figure 4.2. Screengrab of viral social media video of brass musician Eugene Grant's arrest on Frenchman Street posted on Facebook by the Music & Culture Coalition of New Orleans and included in an editorial published on 18 July 2019.

dents flooded to the bookstore's Yelp account to post negative reviews for the business's actions.

One negative Yelp review stated: "They may be angry at us for playing our music too loud, but we are even more angry at them for trying to disrupt our tradition" ("Don't Mute" 2019). A Twitter user named @YesICandice posted on 9 July 2019 in response to the viral video: "If you're in New Orleans, please avoid Frenchmen Art & Books. They are new owners who called the police on a brass band playing outside which turned into 10–15 officers showing up and one musician being detained. MAKE NEW ORLEANS BLACK AGAIN."[5]

As the video gained national attention, QuestLove reposted it to draw attention to the calling of law enforcement on New Orleans street musicians and artists. He wrote to his millions of followers: "Reason 399 why gentrification sucks: live music is the bloodflow of Nawlins culture ESPECIALLY ON FRENCHMEN ST. This is like me calling the cops on South St cause of the cheesesteak aroma in the air. Y'all put lives in danger doing this passive aggressive ish. TALK TO FOLKS!"[6]

What QuestLove was pointing to was that when communities erode due to gentrification, widely acceptable forms of public performance and cultural practices are interpreted as law-breaking.

Grant's arrest sparked a series of community forms of surveillance of so-called "transplants," "gentrifiers," and "colonizers" who had been weaponizing noise ordinances as ways to police cultural traditions in the city.

In 2018, New Orleans City Council member Cyndi Nguyen introduced a proposal to regulate party buses, a well-known public spectacle of converted school buses and limousine buses popular with younger Black teens that provide a moving party experience across the city, with strobe lights and bounce music blasting from its speakers. While Nguyen stated in introducing the proposal that party buses are protected under the city's charter if they have party carrier permits, she told *Gambit* magazine that her office had been receiving "numerous calls about buses rolling through neighborhoods late at night with loud music" (Woodward 2018).

The ordinance would restrict party buses to major thoroughfares only and not residential streets, where they typically would have circulated in Black wards, now experiencing gentrification. Similar proposals were brought to the city council to regulate block parties and second-lines, placing higher thresholds for receiving permits, and regulating the time, format, and nature of these community events. These series of ordinances, city council members argued in public meetings, were a result of complaints and pressure leveled at the city to regulate these primarily Black cultural practices.

The Music & Culture Coalition also cited a series of events since Katrina that led to the public outburst in 2019. Referring to the decade since the storm, the coalition pointed to the "harassment of Mardi Gras/Black Masking Indians," specifically on St. Joseph's Night, the "arrest of several musicians in the Tremé in 2007 during a traditional second line," "the shutting down of To Be Continued Brass Band" in the French Quarter and downtown, and the "Hundreds Brass Band outside of Jazz Fest," in which the musicians were forced to stop performing "while an officer looked up what ordinance they were violating, and were allowed to continue, when there, in fact, wasn't one" (Ellstad 2019).

Later that summer, in August 2019, the NOPD arrested Kay Joe, a local rapper who goes by the name "Unscripted," as he performed on Frenchman Street. In addition to arresting Joe, police confiscated his equipment, his primary means of earning money, until his court case could be handled. Joe posted in an Instagram Live video that "I was locked up, handcuffed and everything. They towed my ride for street performing, something I've been doing for three and a half years, and all of a sudden it's illegal. I guess I'm being made the example."[7]

The rapper also said he fully knew the social contract with the neighborhood. He would only perform after the brass bands had completed, out of respect for them. He would keep his sound levels under eighty decibels, and not block door entrances. He had been fully educated about the changing levels of acceptance for street performances in and around the city. He stated in an interview with *Offbeat* magazine: "The biggest issue surrounding my arrest is there should have been a decibel reading to determine if I was in violation. NOPD can't determine that, only the Health Department, who is trained and equipped with a decibel reader, can" (Frank 2019).

Decibel readers had become a new tool of measuring community levels of tolerance for Black culture, and as the *Offbeat* article noted, "While Joe's late night performances may have been tolerated, and even celebrated in the past, recent changes to the local community have affected street performance culture" (Frank 2019).

Using Social Media to Resist

In 2019, social media lit up with New Orleans residents posting images of primarily white residents or their homes in predominantly Black neighborhoods or wards that are experiencing gentrification. They identified the ways in which cultural practices that were widely communal and shared had become criminalized against the original residents. Transplants weaponized several laws against Black residents, ranging from noise pollution to loitering, disturbing the peace, violations of newly enacted ordinances, public nuisance, reckless driving, defacing public property, trespassing, and suspicious activity—all as reasons to call law enforcement on Black cultural practices.

In response, Black folks used their cameras and social media to record police arrests, removal of street artists and musicians, shutdowns of block parties, raids, police harassment, and the enforcement of party buses during Mardi Gras and other festivals.

One Twitter user posted in 2019, "If you are a transplant living in New Orleans [and] feel the need to issue a noise complaint against musicians, you have moved to the wrong place and should leave ASAP."[8]

Others have asked transplants to respect the sacredness of second-lines. Twitter user @ShotByLu posted in 2019: "Dear transplants, visitors, and whom it concerns: Do NOT walk in the Second Line procession with your dog, keep that on the other side of the ropes. Thanks, Mgmt."[9]

Journalist and author Megan Braden-Perry,[10] a Seventh Ward native, has used her social media presence to document the impacts of gentrification on the city's culture. In particular, she has focused on the ways in which the large-scale purchasing of homes and lots in Black neighborhoods has created short-term rentals that attract tourists or transplants, housing them in Black communities, selling an "authentic" New Orleans experience.

Braden-Perry wrote in 2013 about the contrasts between what native New Orleanians have desired since Katrina and what the commercialized image of post-Katrina New Orleans has sold to transplants who now gentrify Black spaces.

> I feel like these newcomers and TV producers looked at our Facebook posts post-Katrina and said, "Yes, this is what New Orleanians love! Gumbo, second lines, red beans, this Schwegmann's place and these Hubig's pies!" That's what New Orleanians grieving for the city wanted. . . . Why are these people grieving for what they never knew? Who gave them the right to come to the pulpit and give our eulogy?

As Twitter user named Seventh Ward Sunflower noted in response to a question about why New Orleans culture is constantly at risk: "Because they [transplants] moving not realizing the culture isn't just when they decided to visit for x event but all the damn time."

The resistance to transformations in Black neighborhoods is more than just nostalgia. There have been real implications for how Black residents have been impacted through the co-optation and commercialization of the cultural spaces they created. In 2019 in particular, after a boom in film and television featuring New Orleans as a backdrop, residents pointed to the shift in who benefits from this rejuvenation of the city. Twitter user Jonathan Isaac Jackson (@jonisaacjackson) posted that "New Orleans independent cinema is now about transplants who are enjoying the culture at the expense of low paid, black citizens."[11]

While the gentrification of Black spaces in New Orleans is another form of systemic oppression, this is not to say that Black New Orleanians have taken intrusions without a fight. The social media discourse in itself is one space, but it also works in conjunction with offline forms of resistance.

These include protest second-lines and marches, graffiti and visual artists whose physical performance of resistance visually marks every neighborhood with the imprint of Black culture (as shown in Kermit Ruffin's Mother-in-Law Lounge in the Tremé neighborhood), and Brandom "B-mike" Odum's artworks of Black New Orleans culture that are placed around gentrifying neighborhoods. Someone scribbled "Yuppy = Bad" in blue graffiti on the side of the St. Roch Market in 2015, in what was historically a Black neighborhood in New Orleans (Bullington 2015).

New Orleans grassroots groups like Take 'Em Down Nola team up with artists and culture bearers to push back against the practices that perpetuate uneven recovery across the city, convening marches and protests to bring city action with regard to land use, education, access to jobs, health-care, and basic infrastructure, which still have not returned in many parts of Black streets and blocks.

While mainstream media in the city have largely framed post–Hurricane Katrina gentrification of Black neighborhoods as a debate between "progress versus preservation," native Black residents have used social media as a space to articulate how gentrification hurts communities even further, weakening community dynamics and eroding the sanctity of cultural practices.

On one end, native African American residents continue to see outsiders, whom they call "transplants," as responsible for increasing their vulnerability to hostile law enforcement, who now police what were traditionally acceptable communal cultural practices. Enhanced policing of African Americans also impacted cultural traditions, including the removal of street performers and the policing of Black cultural practices as public nuisances and noise violations. Native Black residents have also called out the cultural appropriation and disrespect for traditions when new residents monetize their culture without credit or compensation. The cultural tensions brought on by gentrification provide a window into how postdisaster recovery impacts the most vulnerable groups. More importantly, cultural intrusions impact the livelihood of Black residents whose informal and formal traditions are an economic means for these communities in a city that sells its culture, primarily Black culture, as its primary revenue draw for tourism.

Shearon Roberts is an assistant professor of mass communication and a faculty member in African American and diaspora studies at Xavier University in New Orleans. She has published on the role of the media in post-disaster communities, on Haitian media during and after the 2010 Haiti earthquake, and on new media use in Cuba. She studies the impact of digital media across the Caribbean and representations of race and gender in the media. She is coauthor of *Oil and Water: Media Lessons from Hurricane Katrina and the Deepwater Horizon Disaster* and coeditor of *HBO's Treme and Post-Katrina Catharsis: The Mediated Rebirth of New Orleans*. She has worked as a reporter in Latin America and the Caribbean, and holds a PhD in Latin American Studies from Tulane University's Stone Center for Latin American Studies.

Notes

1. On the broader context of post-Katrina New Orleans, see Johnson (2011) and Fox Gotham and Greenberg (2014).
2. As seen in the 2018 film by Edward Buckles, *Katrina Babies*.
3. Greater New Orleans Housing Alliance, Facebook post, 23 October 2019, https://www.facebook.com/events/511697759640332/?post_id=548875639255877&view=permalink.
4. Kyle DeCoste (@KyleDeCoste504), Twitter post, 9 July 2019, https://twitter.com/KyleDeCoste504/status/1148665244748845056?s=20.
5. Candice, right? (@YesICandice), Twitter post, 9 July 2019, https://twitter.com/YesICandice/status/1148748708940587008?s=20.
6. B.R.O.theR. ?uestion (@questlove), Twitter post, 10 July 2019, https://twitter.com/questlove/status/1148916694812901376?s=20.
7. Kay Joe (Unscripted), Instagram post, 16 August 2019, https://www.instagram.com/p/B1OXRFUAtoa/.
8. GJP (@jupiter_bunny), Twitter post, 12 September 2019, https://twitter.com/jupiter_bunny/status/1172218192007258112?s=20.
9. Pels in Six (@ShotByLu), Twitter post, 10 March 12019, https://twitter.com/ShotByLu/status/1104818686689492996?s=20.
10. Megan Braden-Perry (@megandoesnola) can be followed at https://twitter.com/megandoesnola?lang=en.
11. Jonathan Isaac Jackson (@jonisaacjackson), Twitter post, 2 October 2019, https://twitter.com/jonisaacjackson/status/1179526352334213122?s=20.

References

Barrios, Roberto E. 2010. "You Found Us Doing This, This Is Our Way: Criminalizing Second Lines, Super Sunday, and Habitus in Post-Katrina New Orleans." *Identities: Global Studies in Culture and Power* 17(6): 586–612.

Baskerville, Niamba. 2014. "Twerk It: Deconstructing Racial and Gendered Implications of Black Women's Bodies through Representations of Twerking," BA Thesis, Swarthmore College Department of Sociology & Anthropology, http://hdl.handle.net/10066/14354.

Berry, Jason. 1988. "African Cultural Memory in New Orleans Music." *Black Music Research Journal* 8(1): 3–12.

Big Freedia, and Nicole Ballin. 2015. *God Save the Queen Diva!* New York: Gallery Books/Simon & Schuster.

"Big Freedia Talks Miley Cyrus, Cultural Appropriation, Coming Out and More in New Memoir." 2015. Superselected website. Accessed 20 October 2020, https://www.superselected.com/big-freedia-talks-miley-cyrus-cultural-appropriation-coming-out-and-more-in-new-memoir/.

Blumberg, Lucy. 2020. "An Open Letter on Surveillance in New Orleans." *The Lens Nola*. 1 May, https://thelensnola.org/2020/05/01/an-open-letter-on-surveillance-in-new-orleans/.

Braden-Perry, Megan. 2013. "It Wasn't a Blank Slate." *Gambit*. 31 December, https://www.nola.com/gambit/news/article_fe65ad24-e70f-5d79-98b6-defd801ab154|.html.

Brasted, Chelsea. 2017. "Carrie Fisher Parade Sparks Public Conversation about Second-Lines, New Orleans Culture." *Nola.com/The Times-Picayune*. 5 January, https://www.nola.com/entertainment_life/music/article_692c8df8-334c-54ca-a37b-096563a64280.html.

Bullington, Johnathan. 2015. "Vandals Hit St. Roch Market," *Nola.com/The Times-Picayune*. 1 May, https://www.nola.com/news/crime_police/article_8246265a-92a5-5473-9ba9-6d5a8ef3aae7.html.

Chamlee-Wright, Emily, and Virgil Henry Storr. 2009. "'There's No Place Like New Orleans': Sense of Place and Community Recovery in the Ninth Ward after Hurricane Katrina." *Journal of Urban Affairs* 31(5): 615–34.

"'Don't Mute New Orleans!' Colonizers Call the Cops on Black Man for Playing the Trumpet." 2019. *Newsone* website. https://newsone.com/3881967/new-orleans-gentrification-black-man-trumpet/.

Ellstad, Ethan. 2019. "The Unacceptable Arrest of Musician Eugene Grant Should Be the Catalyst for Chang." *The Lens Nola*. https://thelensnola.org/2019/07/18/the-unacceptable-arrest-of-musician-eugene-grant-should-be-the-catalyst-for-change/.

Fanon, Frantz. 2008 [1970]. *Black Skin, White Masks*. London: Grove press.

Fox Gotham, Kevin, and Miriam Greenberg. 2014. *Crisis Cities: Disaster and Redevelopment in New York and New Orleans*. Oxford: Oxford University Press.

Frank, Michael. 2019. "Freestyle Rapper Unscripted Arrested for Performing on Frenchmen Street." *Offbeat*. https://www.offbeat.com/news/freestyle-rapper-unscripted-arrested-for-performing-on-frenchmen-street/.

Halliday, Aria S. 2020. "Twerk Sumn!: Theorizing Black Girl Epistemology in the Body." *Cultural Studies* 34(6): 874–91.

Johnson, Cedric., ed. 2011. *The Neoliberal Deluge: Hurricane Katrina, Late Capitalism, and the Remaking of New Orleans*. Minneapolis: University of Minnesota Press.

Johnson, Jerah. 1991. "New Orleans's Congo Square: An Urban Setting for Early Afro-American Culture Formation." *Louisiana History: The Journal of the Louisiana Historical Association* 32(2): 117–57.

LaBorde, Lauren. 2016. "New Orleans Gentrification Report: Many Formerly Black Neighborhoods Are Now Majority White." *Curbed* website. https://nola.curbed.com/2016/9/6/12821038/new-orleans-gentrification-report.

London, Dianca. 2017. "'Get Out' and the Revolutionary Act of Subverting the White Gaze." *Medium* website. 9 March, https://medium.com/the-establishment/get-out-and-the-revolutionary-act-of-subverting-the-white-gaze-c769cb620496#.nz7a4abb6.

"Miley Cyrus Didn't Invent 'Twerking'—It Dates Back to 1820." 2015. *Independent* website. 25 June, https://www.independent.ie/entertainment/books/book-news/miley-cyrus-didnt-invent-twerking-it-dates-back-to-1820-31328818.html.

Miller, Andrea, Shearon Roberts, and Victoria LaPoe. 2014. *Oil and Water: Media Lessons from Hurricane Katrina and the Deepwater Horizon Disaster*. Jackson: University Press of Mississippi.

Morgan Parmett, Helen. 2014. "Media as a Spatial Practice: Treme and the Production of the Media Neighbourhood." *Continuum* 28(3): 286–99.

"News with a Twist: 'Twerking,' 'Miley Cyrus' & 'Baby Doll Ladies.'" 2013. New Orleans Baby Doll Ladies YouTube channel. https://www.youtube.com/watch?v=obMxTvTZCis.

Office of the Governor. 2020. "Criminal Justice Reform." Accessed 20 October, https://gov.louisiana.gov/index.cfm/page/58.

Roberts, Shearon. 2017. "Selling Tremé through the Home Box Office." In *HBO's Treme and Post-Katrina Catharsis: The Mediated Rebirth of New Orleans*, ed. Dominique Gendrin, Catherine Dessignes, and Shearon Roberts, 23–40. Lanham, MD: Lexington Books.

Rose, Kate. 2020. "Gentrification a Growing Threat for Many New Orleans Residents." *Louisiana Fair Housing Action Center.* 24 July, https://lafairhousing.org/blog/gentrification-a-growing-threat-for-many-new-orleans-residents.

Sinders, Caroline. 2021. "How Musicians and Sex Workers Beat Facial Recognition in New Orleans." *Vice* website. 26 March, https://www.vice.com/en/article/xgznka/meet-the-musicians-and-strippers-who-beat-facial-recognition-in-new-orleans.

Smith, Michael P. 1994. "Behind the Lines: The Black Mardi Gras Indians and the New Orleans Second Line." *Black Music Research Journal* 14(1): 43–73.

Thomas, Lynnell L. 2012. "'People Want to See What Happened' Treme, Televisual Tourism, and the Racial Remapping of Post-Katrina New Orleans." *Television & New Media* 13(3): 213–24.

Turner, Richard Brent. 2016. *Jazz Religion, the Second Line, and Black New Orleans, New Edition: After Hurricane Katrina*. Bloomington: Indiana University Press.

Vargas, Ramon Antonio. 2020. "New Orleans Was Fourth-Deadliest U.S. City in 2019." *Nola.com/The Times Picayune*. 29 September, https://www.nola.com/news/crime_police/article_255bf308-0276-11eb-a38f-4f890c23241b.html.

Vaz, Kim Marie. 2013. *The "Baby Dolls": Breaking the Race and Gender Barriers of the New Orleans Mardi Gras Tradition*. Baton Rouge, LA: LSU Press.

Wehmeyer, Stephen C. 2010. "Feathered Footsteps: Mythologizing and Ritualizing Black Indian Processions in New Orleans." *Social Identities* 16(4): 427–45.

"Who Returned to New Orleans after Katrina?" 2010. Population Reference Bureau. Accessed 10 October 2020, https://www.prb.org/resources/who-returned-to-new-orleans-after-hurricane-katrina/.

Woodward, Alex. 2018. "New Orleans Party Buses Would Be Banned from Residential Areas under City Council Proposal." *Gambit*. 6 September, https://www.nola.com/gambit/news/article_fb38cfff-d774-53c1-a085-e7dc9d5c7c2c.html.

Wyckoff, Geraldine. 2014. "Artists Stand Up to Stick Up for Music." *The Louisiana Weekly*. 6 October, http://www.louisianaweekly.com/artists-stand-up-to-stick-up-for-music/.

CHAPTER 5

Cat Bonds and Necrocapitalism in Haiti and Puerto Rico

JANA EVANS BRAZIEL

Disasters have historically led to disaster profiteering, what Naomi Klein defined as "disaster capitalism," the buying and selling, trading and speculating—in short, profiting—from disasters, natural and unnatural. It happened after the Indian Ocean earthquake and tsunami in 2004, the Indonesia tsunami in 2005, Hurricane Katrina in 2005, monumentally and wastefully after the 2010 earthquake in Haiti, after the Tōhoku earthquake and tsunami of 2011, now known as 311 in Japan, and so on. Unsurprisingly, disasters and disaster capitalism resurfaced in the Caribbean archipelago after Hurricanes Irma and Maria in 2017, particularly in Puerto Rico, an island already wracked and ravaged by colonial disenfranchisement, debt restructuring, poverty, austerity, electrical grid failure, food importation dependency, and rolling power blackouts. As Yarimar Bonilla writes in her *Washington Post* op-ed sardonically entitled "Why Would Anyone in Puerto Rico Want a Hurricane? Because Someone Will Get Rich," natural disasters equal devastating losses for many, yet interest income for the financial few with capital to invest. She explains the situation in the opening paragraph of the editorial:

> Among those I interviewed this summer about Puerto Rico's economic crisis was a local wealth manager who was extremely upbeat about the economic climate. Anticipating government default, she had redirected her clients' assets toward U.S. stocks. Investments in the wake of President Trump's election had been doing very well, she said, adding, "The only thing we need now is a hurricane." She was referring to how such natural disasters bring in federal money for rebuilding and often become a boon to the construction industry. As I left her office, she encouraged me to buy stock in Home Depot.

What makes natural disasters profitable, however, is not just federal money driving supply and demand in consumer goods (water, food, lumber, nails, piping) from Lowes, Home Depot, Walmart, and other retailers, as Bonilla correctly if only partially notes; it is also (and more profitably) the speculative buying and selling and futures projections in catastrophe bonds.

In this chapter, I examine the collision of natural disasters and unnatural "structural adjustments" in the Greater Caribbean by interrogating neoliberal approaches to so-called "disposable" economies, for-profit debt refinancing, externally imposed austerity measures, and postdisaster rebuilding (or not) in the wake of Caribbean natural disasters. Taking the 2010 earthquake in Haiti, onomatopoeically referred to in Kreyòl as "Goudougoudou," and the 2017 fallout from Hurricane Maria in Puerto Rico as the two primary case studies, but also pointing to salient postdisaster parallels in New Orleans following Hurricane Katrina, I dismantle the inhumane policies and dehumanizing impacts of contemporary necrocapitalism, or the debased international trading in death and in disaster stocks, amounting to the for-profit investment in death-capital. Building on critical insights from Naomi Klein's *The Shock Doctrine: The Rise of Disaster Capitalism* (2008), *This Changes Everything: Capitalism vs. the Climate* (2014), and her most recent and germane (if brief) intervention in *The Battle for Paradise* (2018)—but also extending the analysis to meditations on speculative investments and even futures trading in profit-driven "disaster stocks," or catastrophe bonds—I argue that the Caribbean, long the resort for the rich and famous, then the site of offshore banking for corporate wealth, has now entered a perilous period of absolute necrocapital destruction before (and perhaps for) profit. In the chapter, I focus on Haiti and Puerto Rico, two small island states or territories in the Caribbean, both devastated in the wake of the 2010 earthquake and the 2017 hurricane by the further machinations of disaster capitalism

Opening Questions

Writing on the postearthquake reconstruction economies in Haiti after 2010, many cultural critics extended and expanded upon Klein's notion of "disaster capitalism" as first outlined in *The Shock Doctrine* (2007), including Mats Lundhal's *The Political Economy of Disaster: Destitution, Plunder and Earthquake in Haiti* (2013), John C. Mutter's *The Disaster Profiteers: How Natural Disaster Make the Rich Richer and the Poor even Poorer* (2015), Anthony Lowenstein's *Disaster Capitalism: Making a Killing out of Catastrophe* (2017), Kasia Mika's *Disasters, Vulnerability, and Narratives: Writing Haiti's Futures* (2018), Juliana Svistova and Loretta Pyles's *Production of Disaster and Recovery in Post-Earthquake Haiti: Disaster Industrial Complex*

(2018), Mark Schuller's *Killing with Kindness: Haiti, International Aid, and NGOs* (2012), and Schuller and Pablo Morales's edited volume, *Tectonic Shifts: Haiti since the Earthquake* (2012). Naomi Klein's *The Battle for Paradise: Puerto Rico Takes on the Disaster Capitalists* (2018) continues her analyses of disaster capitalism in austerity-strapped postdisaster Puerto Rico; and scholars Yarimar Bonilla and Marisol LeBrón extend these intellectual and political critiques to post-Maria Puerto Rico in their edited collection, *Aftershocks of Disaster: Puerto Rico Before and After the Storm* (2019), as do Sara Molinari and the other contributors to the volume.

I join that ongoing critical conversation, but in doing so, I foreground the proliferation in trade of catastrophe bonds, or "cat bonds" as they are also called. My comparative interdisciplinary framework foregrounds rhetorical and political theoretical meanings, as well as the material impacts and, of course, financial rationale, of cat bonds. I analyze the consequences of catastrophes and of cat bond yield socially, culturally, historically, and demographically, not merely the economic justification (distribution and financialization of loss) for issuing the bonds. My own theorizations of disaster capitalism are informed by the neoliberal "politics of disposability," what Henry A. Giroux defines as the "expendable" people and places within capitalism,[1] and by the term necrocapitalism, or buying and selling, trading and investing, profiting and speculating in the political economies of death and disaster. I begin by posing a series of questions about cat bonds, before analyzing the global market in cat bonds as necrocapitalism, and then analyzing online financial journalism or cat bond blogs as necromedia.

I thus open with a series of interrelated questions. First, what are cat bonds? And how are catastrophe bonds both, and perhaps ironically, the literal and yet also abstract manifestations of disaster capitalism in the twenty-first century? How are catastrophe bonds—ostensibly introduced and initially issued to offset the risks of damages from natural disasters and to mitigate the deleterious impacts of climate change—actually trading and profiting in the financialization of disaster, while racking up returns that are invested in (not divested from) the destructive, even at times fatal, impacts of greenhouse gases, global warming, rising sea levels, and the increased frequency, intensity, and severity of tropical storms and hurricanes? In brief, to answer the first question, cat bonds are collateralized risk and the economic transformation (through financialization) of liability into asset, a bond that investors purchase, whose maturation date they await (typically but not necessarily three years), and which they then cash in with a coupon in exchange for principal plus interest income. This happens unless, of course, the bonds are catastrophically catalyzed, activated, or disbursed—paid out as insurance and reinsurance payments for damages wrought by natural disaster. Then the investor forfeits a portion of interest income, accordingly, and in proportion to her share (or percentage) of investment in or against liability or loss. Not surprisingly, the rates of return remain consistently high—even in disastrous seasons—and sales of cat bonds also remain vigorous. Individual liability is minimized (spread microscopically across myriad bond holders), and the outstanding market for cat bonds persists as a booming industry in global financial markets. Even during the 2017 hurricane season, which resulted in reduced profits, configured as industry "loss," cat bonds remained profitable, the industry strong, the returns high.

How high? We'll take a look momentarily, but first some requisite history.

Catastrophe Bonds: A Brief History

Following $27 billion in damages and $15.5 billion in insurance payouts, as a result of Hurricane Andrew in 1992, cat bonds were first issued on the international global market in 1997. Keep in mind that we are, by 1997, eight years after the fall of the Berlin Wall in 1989 and six years removed from the 1991 collapse of the Soviet Union and the ostensible "triumph" of capital, the death of communism, and the "end of history"; we are firmly in the period of neoliberal economics and global capitalism. One decade later, in 2007, the Caribbean Catastrophe Risk Insurance Facility (CCRIF), a multicountry regional insurance pool, was created.[2] Barely one year later, of course, the world witnessed the economic collapse of Lehman Brothers. This triggered the onset of a global recession, also a consequence of collateralized, financialized risk, this time through the packaging, buying, and selling of subprime mortgages as assets, which, not surprisingly, led to the subsequent expansion of the cat bond market as funds sought to diversity investments, particularly those not directly linked to a volatile stock market. In 2010, the CCRIF paid $8 million ($7,753,579 to be precise) to Haiti following the 12 January earthquake in the country. In 2014, as tropical storms and hurricanes increased in frequency, intensity, and severity, as well as in total damages wrought, the World Bank launched the idea of a Caribbean regional catastrophe bond: the CCRIF became the CCRIF SPC, or the Caribbean Catastrophe Risk Insurance Facility Segregated Portfolio Company. In other words, it went from being a regional insurance pool to a regional catastrophe bond issuer. Caribbean countries purchase insurance; insurers purchase reinsurance; and reinsurers purchase insurance-linked securities (ILS), using a special-purpose vehicle, nebulous to say the least, through which collateralized risk (against poten-

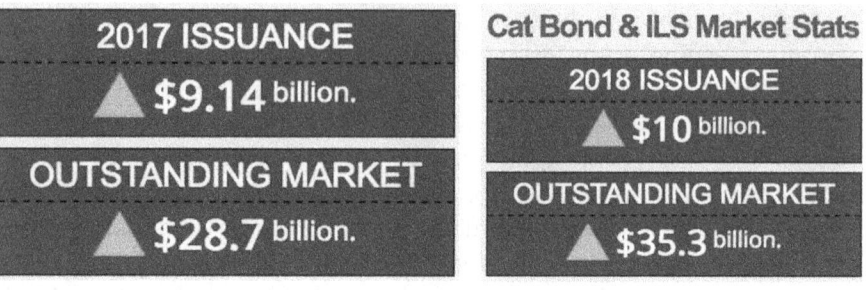

Figure 5.1. 2017 and 2018 issuance for cat bonds. Source: artemis.bm.

tial catastrophic loss) is repackaged as an asset and issued as cat bonds, which investors buy.[3] This recent history, of course, precedes 2017; and 2017, suffice it to say, was a devastating year in natural disasters for the Caribbean, bringing Hurricanes Harvey, Irma, and Maria.

"At $353 billion, 2017 was the costliest year for insurers for weather disasters. Under those circumstances," the authors of "How Record Catastrophe Bond Issuances Are Changing the Alternative Investment Landscape" write, financial investors "might [have] expect[ed] that the market for cat bonds would [have] suffer[ed]." Indeed, after the devastations of the 2017 hurricane season, "there was uncertainty about the response of the capital markets"; however, as the authors continue, "[o]ne asset class that could have been hit hardest by these events—catastrophe bonds—showed no signs of losing its appeal. In fact, in 2017 a record number of catastrophe bonds were issued—more than $10 billion worth. In 2018, this momentum . . . continued." And in February of 2018, the World Bank sponsored and issued a "record-breaking $1.4 billion" multilateral earthquake catastrophe bond." To be exact, it was $1.36 billion, but financial investors have a proclivity toward excess and exaggeration ("How Record Catastrophe Bond Issuances"). I quote at length to underscore the ways in which profiting in loss and hedging bets against devastating losses are too often rhetorical gestures that ardently defy rational common sense. To reiterate and underscore the basic financial realities of cat bonds, reinsurance, and insurance-linked securities: the annual market (or sales in cat bonds) have historically (and exponentially) exceeded disaster-related losses; and based on ongoing and unabated projected growth in the industry, future sales will also outpace future, disaster-related losses, however substantial. Also, cat bonds are the final layer of collateralized risk sold as asset and rarely liquidated against loss, though always theoretically possible.

Now, let's return to the global market and its consistently high rates of return on investment. And let's begin, not arbitrarily but deliberately, with

Figure 5.2. 2019, 2020, and 2021 issuance for cat bonds. Source: artemis.bm.

2017. The 2017 issuance for cat bonds totaled $12.56 billion, and the total outstanding market for 2017 was $31.06 billion. In 2018, the total issuance for the fiscal year totaled $11 billion, and the outstanding market was $36 billion.

Despite a decrease in issuance of cat bonds in 2019, the total issuance for 2019 was still $7.7 billion, and the outstanding market was $40.1 billion. By Q1 (first quarter) 2020, the cat bond and ILS market issuances already totaled $3 billion, reaching $15.4 billion by Q4 (fourth quarter), and the outstanding market was $41.4 billion and $45.29 billion, respectively, for Q1 and Q4 of 2020. For 2021 (as of April 2021), the issuance for Q1 totaled $4.6 billion and the outstanding market $48.13 billion.

One incontrovertible fact is clearly isolable: the global markets in insurance, reinsurance, insurance-linked securities and cat bonds shift the economic and political debates—both within the industry itself and within the corporate-backed US Congress—away from concerns about climate change mitigation and natural disaster reduction and decisively toward investiture in risk, resilience, preparedness, and rapid response. As Sarah Molinari asks in a paper presented at the Puerto Rican Studies Association at the University of Texas–Austin in fall 2019: ¿Tu estás preparado (Are you prepared)?

Who profits from this shift?

And who loses?

According to the Artemis Q4 2019 Catastrophe Bonds & ILS Market Report, the "catastrophe bond and ILS issuance in the fourth-quarter of 2019 [was] the highest ever recorded in the period," at what they define as "an

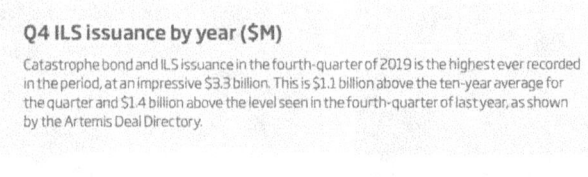

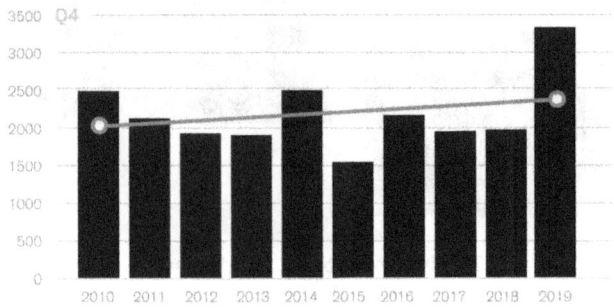

Figure 5.3. Fourth quarter cat bond issuances by year (2010–19). Source: artemis.bm.

impressive $3.3 billion," which was "$1.1 billion above the ten-year average and $1.4 billion above the level seen in the fourth-quarter of last year, as shown by the Artemis Deal Directory."

Of this Q4 issuance, the overwhelming majority of cat bond sales were in the area of "international multi-peril," which "accounted for the largest slice of Q4 issuance, at $1.33 billion, or 40 percent of total issuance," and the authors further note that "Q4 issuance took the total outstanding market size to a new end-of-year high, of $41 billion." Significantly, if also curiously, the Artemis Deal Directory of Q4 2019 includes "seven private deals featured in Q4, bringing a combined $157 million of U.S. and unknown property catastrophe risks" (Artemis Q4 2019).

Let's think about this fact for a moment: seven private deals, $157 million in trade, and "unknown property catastrophe risks." In other words, where other Q4 deals have identified and identifiable sponsors—Everest Re, XL Bermuda Ltd., California Earthquake Authority, Genworth Mortgage Insurance, Covéa Group, USAA, Arch Capital Group Ltd., even the Republic of the Philippines—seven of the Q4 trade deals totaling $157 million have "unknown" listed as the sponsor. It certainly begs the questions: Who are the buyers here, and who the sellers, and who the sponsors? And what risk is being collateralized as asset and bought and sold as insurance-linked securities (ILS) and cat bonds? On whose behalf? To whose gain? And to whose loss? Whose devastation is at risk? And who will profit from this devastation?

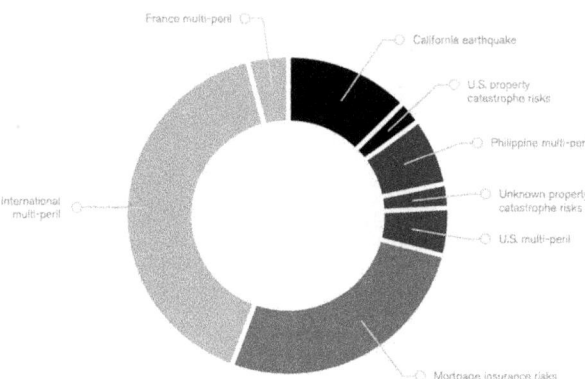

Q4 2019 ILS issuance by peril
The rebound of cat risk in the quarter was helped by an $850 million deal from Everest Re, providing protection against multiple international perils, including U.S. and Canada named storm and quake risks, among others. XL Bermuda's $475 million deal also covered multiple international perils, such as Australia, Canada and U.S. quake, European windstorm and Australian tropical cyclone risk, alongside additional named storm and severe thunderstorm risks.

Figure 5.4. Cat bonds by geographical regional for Q4 2019. Source: artemis.bm.

So, what are the symbolic values and, more importantly, the human and ecological liabilities that are registered in the capital gains and losses of this global market? In this international buying and selling of cat bonds? What are the philosophical valences of cat bond returns or even diminished returns? Its financialization of risk and its reverse liquidity of capital during catastrophic events or disasters? What is truly (or also) being bought and sold? In addition to bonds as collateralized risk, the lives and landscapes of those impacted by natural disasters, their losses, their devastations, are also being trafficked on the international financial market. We must not lose sight of this fact. To underscore this point, I pose a hypothetical scene of disaster and a series of interrelated hypothetical questions: *If* I am buying collateralized risk against loss (as cat bond and as asset), *if* I profit from unliquidated cat bonds through bond yields at the end of the three-year period, *even if* your home is destroyed, *even if* your home owner's insurance policy only reimburses your loss at a fraction of the actual damages, and *even if* you or your family experience death and dismemberment, then am I complicit (to some degree) in a necrocapitalist system that traffics in loss, even loss of life, as bond holder and yield receiver? What stake, ultimately, do I have in your loss (of property, of money, of limb, of life)? And by what right do I buy into that collateralized

ISSUER / TRANCHE	SPONSOR	PERILS	SIZE ($M)	DATE
Artex SAC Limited - Series IX Notes	Unknown	Unknown property cat risks	50.255	Dec
Seaside Re (Series 2020-2)	Unknown	U.S. property cat risks	20	Dec
Seaside Re (Series 2020-1)	Unknown	U.S. property cat risks	7	Dec
Seaside Re (Series 2020-51)	Unknown	U.S. property cat risks	50	Dec
LI Re (Series 2019-1)	Unknown	California earthquake	10	Dec
Kilimanjaro III Re Ltd. (Series 2019-1/2019-2)	Everest Re	International multi-peril	850	Dec
Galileo Re Ltd. (Series 2019-1)	XL Bermuda Ltd.	International multi-peril	475	Dec
Ursa Re Ltd. (Series 2019-1)	California Earthquake Authority	California earthquake	400	Nov
Triangle Re 2019-1 Ltd.	Genworth Mortgage Insurance	Mortgage insurance risks	302.791	Nov
IBRD CAR 123 / 124	Republic of the Philippines	Philippine multi-peril	225	Nov
Residential Reinsurance 2019 Limited (Series 2019-2)	USAA	U.S. multi-peril	160	Nov
Hexagon II Reinsurance DAC (Series 2019-1)	Covéa Group	France multi-peril	132.93	Nov
Eclipse Re Ltd. (Series 2019-07A)	Unknown	Unknown property cat risks	20	Oct
Bellemeade Re 2019-4 Ltd.	Arch Capital Group Ltd.	Mortgage insurance risks	577.28	Oct
ILN SAC Ltd. Series 2019-1	Unknown	Unknown property cat risks	10	Oct

Figure 5.5. Cat bonds by sponsor (including unknown) for Q4 2019. Source: artemis.bm.

risk (virtual) as cat bond—which is your loss—and profit rather than pay or participate in the paying back your real losses?

This global market traffics in disaster, destruction, devastation, and even death. This global market manifests the nefarious machinations of necrocapitalism, or death-capital. We are far removed from 1947, the ravages of World War II, the abyss of six million deaths during the Shoah as the wages and returns of the Nazi war-and-death machine of the Third Reich and its final solution, *die Endlösung*; and yet we are still perilously close—historically, economically, geopolitically—to what Georges Bataille diagnosed in 1947 as *la part maudite*, the "accursed share," and its logical ends, the waste economies and destructive economics of the Marshall Plan—perhaps one genealogical node of development for globalization and global capitalism in the mid-twentieth century, one node that gave rise to the Cold War and its ideological divides of politics, economics, and geography.

This international trade, this global financial market, clearly manifests the inhumane policies and dehumanizing impacts of contemporary necrocapitalism, or the debased international trading in death and disaster stocks and catastrophe bonds, the for-profit investment in death-capital.

The Caribbean, long the resort for the rich and famous, then site of offshore banking for corporate wealth, has now entered a perilous period of absolute necrocapital destruction before (and perhaps for) profit. I thus frame my argument through the concept of necrocapitalism, which builds on several interrelated concepts: biopolitics, necropolitics,[4] and necromedia.[5] And I offer intellectual and political deconstructions of this death-for-profit phase of capital.

Necrocapitalism and Neoliberal Disposability

We are inexorably, or so it seems, in the quicksand terrain of *Necro-Capital, Inc.*—the dazzling rich, the disposable poor. While some have defined technology as the "master of war" and the distributor of death,[6] I argue that it is the nefarious mechanisms (production, circulation, investiture, divestiture, privatization, consumption, and disposal) of for-profit destruction, disaster, and disposability that defines the "death phase" of neoliberal, late expenditure capitalism—or what I am designating as necrocapitalism. In other words, cat bonds, as necrocapital, manifest transactional investing in and profiting from disaster as risk and as reality, and in death as risk and as reality. Necrocapital deals in death. It deals out death. Its death blows strike at point *a* and blowback to point *b*, and on and on.[7] It miasmically spreads. And like other neoliberal malaprops and geoeconomic misnomers—such as, strikingly, "cat bonds" (instead of catastrophe bonds)[8] and *Citizens United* (with its legal transformation of corporations into juridically protected persons in the United States)—these are the machinations of death-for-profit incorporated: Necro-Capital, Inc. These are the biopolitics of disaster, the necropolitics of savage capitalism—necrocapitalism.

Haiti offers, tragically, a compelling case study in the nefarious machinations of necrocapitalism and its devouring of so-called disposable people.[9] The devastating 2010 earthquake in the country killed between 240,000 and 316,000 people, most of whom were buried in mass graves or simply dumped at Titanyen, a historical dump site where the Duvaliers also notoriously left bodies exposed in the baking, oppressive Caribbean sun to rot. Alex Dupuy indicts the contemporary, collapsed state of Haiti: in his estimation, the World Bank and other international financial institutions (IFIs) have both "abet[ed] dictatorship and undermin[ed] democracy" (*Haiti*, chapters 5 and 6). Or as Robert Fatton similarly laments: Haiti remains "trapped" in the "outer periphery" (*Haiti: Trapped in the Outer Periphery*). With Giroux, we also insist that necrocapitalism makes manifest and real the politics of disposability, which renders human beings expendable or disposable within its systemic ravages. Cat bonds, like structural adjustment programs, only "return to sender" as "return on investment" (ROI), rarely if ever delivering as promised (promissory) to the concessionary signatory (or constrained state government). In addition to the staggering death toll, there are the injured survivors. The earthquake left many more maimed, mutilated, and severely injured (crushed limbs and amputations were common), not to mention traumatized, and ultimately, it resulted in approximately 1.5 million internally displaced persons living in makeshift tent camps for almost two years. Lamentably the same could be argued about Puerto Rico. Within the mechanisms of disaster capitalism, or necrocapitalism, and even as ostensible citizens (an empty cipher to be sure), Puerto Ricans have been repeatedly rendered expendable to capital: in the face of death and destruction, the residents of the island are thrown paper towels in a Trumpian move that defies the devastations of Hurricane Maria.

Necromedia

Necrocapitalism, as I conceptualize, codify, and apply the term, resonates with recent meditations on necromedia, first by Marcel O'Gorman (though surprisingly insufficiently) and later by Jason Cortés, whose work explores "indebted subjectivity" and "necromedia"—as the "prevailing mode of representing social death"—in the "Puerto Rican Debt State." As Cortés explains, "[w]ithin this necropolitical logic, disposable populations, defined as an excessive burden on the state, are left to die" (2018b: 1). Critiquing the 2015 declaration by then Governor Alejandro Padilla of the Puerto Rican debt—$72 billion—as "unpayable," and analyzing the financial and political fallouts of the June 2016 ratification and installation of the Puerto Rico Oversight, Management, and Economic Stability Act (PROMESA) as "laughable," Cortés notes, ironically, that the "austerity measures do not put labour back to work, but capital, hence generating new forms of debt and producing necrocitizens (indebted subjectivities) cast as disposable excess" (6). Debt, as Cortés explains, "is a disciplinary apparatus ... deployed to control public policy, citizens, and fragile sovereignties" (5). Cortés thus describes "the imposition" of "US citizenship in Puerto Rico" as "a citizenship associated with death," "devoid of political agency," and without "emancipatory effect" (10n3). Puerto Ricans, for Cortés, are necrocitizens, in which citizenship becomes emptied of life and livelihood, affiliated only with debt and death. In describing Puerto Ricans as necrocitizens within the US, Cortés is drawing upon Russ Castronovo's work *Necro Citizenship* (2001). Cortés's theorizations of indebted subjectivities are influenced by Lazzarato's *The Making of the Indebted Man: An Essay on the Neoliberal Condition* (2012). As in Puerto Rico, so in Haiti, which has remained indebted to colonial powers, now Global North states, since its inception as a state. Forced to pay war indemnities to France in 1825 for its revolution, its independence, and for acknowledgement of its sovereignty, Haiti has since the mid-nineteenth century, following decades of economic isolation and trade embargos by the US, UK, and France as payback for its successful revolt, been immiserated in debt and poverty. These cycles of colonialist intervention and forced debt repayment also served as the justification (or at least one justification) for the US Occupation from 1915 until 1934, as well as later in the twentieth century with the 1995 Governors Accord and in the Economic Emergency Recovery Program (EERP), forced onto Haiti and the Jean-Bertrand Aristide administration.

Necromedia is not only the collision of technology and death, but also the death blow, or the coup de grâce, manifest in what Jean Baudrillard isolates as *symbolic exchange and death*, the gift which can never be paid back. In this sense, all debt is unpayable, all media necromedia. And the investment blogs and online financial articles on cat bonds are exemplary of necromedia and necrocapitalism, the buying and selling, trading and investing, profiting and speculating in death: death-capital. Administrative accounting that does not and cannot account for death is willful forgetting, a will to ignorance à la Charles Mills's *The Racial Contract*, an inadmissibility of death counts, body counts, precisely because there can be no accounting of disposable bodies consumed by disposable economies. These are the biopolitics of disaster, the necropolitics of savage capitalism—necrocapitalism. Online financial articles on catastrophe bonds, which have boomed since their introduction onto financial markets in 1997, are exemplary of necromedia and necrocapitalism

Cat Bond Blogs: Capitalism with Its Clothes Off

Postdisaster profiteering reveals a shameless, naked, capitalism-with-its-clothes-off trend toward greed at all costs, profit in all circumstances. In an April 2010 article entitled "Profiting from Disasters," wealth advisor James Altucher asks his readers, tongue in cheek, in the *Wall Street Journal*, "Afraid of a hurricane? Pandemic? Global Warming?" before reassuring nervous investors, "Consider these stocks." Writing for *Forbes* in April 2011, Daniel Diermeier blatantly echoed the point: "Every Disaster is an Opportunity You Must Seize." In August 2011, writing for *The Street*, an investment blog affiliated with crass capitalist Jim Cramer, the investment journalist Joe Mont explained that "tragedy and disaster hurt many, but can benefit a few in the right industries or investments." Mont goes on to demonstrate "how they" (multinational corporations), "and you" (the investor), can "make money on disasters." Sean Williams sheepishly adds, in an afterthought of moral equivocation in his May 2012 online investment article "5 Stocks to Prepare Your Portfolio for Natural Disasters": "I'm not wishing for a natural disaster, I'm merely pointing out stocks that could provide a hedge against Mother Nature's wrath." Simone Foxman, in QZ in September 2013, went further in her claims for cat bonds, writing, "Betting on natural disasters has been one of the best investments since the financial crisis." She explains:

> Catastrophe bonds—essentially a gamble on the likelihood of natural disasters—have been the fifth best-performing asset class since the financial crisis, according to research conducted by Deutsche Bank.... If you had invested your money at the fall of Lehman Brothers in September 2008, only silver, gold, and high-yield debt from the US and the European Union would have made you more money.

For inexperienced readers and investors, Foxman provides a brief summary of how cat bonds yield profit.

> As we've written before, catastrophe bonds—cutely called "cat bonds"—are a relatively new breed of investment. They are issued by companies, public organizations, or insurers that are vulnerable to unpredictable, weather-related disasters. As with any other bond, the issuer usually pays back a cat bond's value after a certain period, with interest. But with cat bonds, if some kind of natural disaster lands the issuer with unexpected costs—an unusually high number of insurance claims, for instance—then it doesn't have to pay back the full amount on the bond or all the interest.

Michelle Toovey also reassures her readers in Investopedia in February 2016 that although "impacts can be severe when storms bear down on areas with dense populations" and "can cause millions of dollars worth of damage to individuals and companies, there are some businesses that walk away with positive impacts."

Joshua Rogers, writing about "Catastrophe Investing" for *Forbes* in October 2016, wryly notes, "Investors seeking better returns without loading up on unwanted risk are turning towards something unexpected: catastrophe." Rogers also reassures risk-averse investors that disasters aren't financially risky: "What if you're risk-averse? Some of the wealthier, more conservative investors I know have been putting money into catastrophe bonds. These so-called 'cat bonds' are essentially slices of reinsurance. And some wealthy investors have found that cat bonds can provide a decent yield during a low-yield era" ("Catastrophe Investing"). As Rogers continues, "The market for cat bonds has grown in recent years, with almost $25 billion such bonds issued to date, covering losses from hurricanes, earthquakes and other horrendous events" ("Catastrophe Investing"). Rogers then assuages the worried minds of more morally driven investors, promising that "owning cat bonds doesn't mean you'll be cheering if disaster strikes" because "the bonds pay higher yields if little or nothing goes wrong in a calendar year," adding that if "hurricanes hit, returns can be very, very good" ("Catastrophe Investing"). If catastrophe (cat) bonds and disaster stocks were already big business during the previous presidential administration, and undeniably they were, then such buying and trading in catastrophes further escalated and accelerated after November 2016.

Unapologetically, John Persinos ominously intones "Disaster Looms" before almost gleefully adding in his subtitle, "3 Stocks That Rise on Global Upheaval." In his article for *The Street* in December 2016, after the election and before the inauguration, Persinos offered this agnostic advice: "Whatever your political persuasion, you have to admit at least one thing: The unexpected election of a former reality television star with no government experience to the most powerful job on the planet was a 'black swan' event" ("Disaster Looms"). And he alerted his readers to "[b]race yourself for more shocks in 2017." Disavowing any true political, ideological, or intellectual commitments—beyond global capitalism, that is—Persinos urged readers and investors to "take the world as it is, not as you want it to be," and he advised that "the best way to make new money in the new year is to . . . tap into trends that will inexorably march forward, regardless of temporary economic cycles" ("Disaster Looms"). In other words, the question was how best to "profit from grim global realities," such as "severe weather incidents, terrorist attacks, armed strife, famine, environmental destruction, social unrest" ("Disaster Looms"). For Persinos—in words that parody or mock the passionately held convictions of anticapitalist environmental activists, notably Naomi Klein herself—"'disaster capitalism' is one of your best investment bets today."

Even in the aftermath of Hurricane Harvey on 5 September 2017, Christopher Versace, founder of the Cocktail Investing Podcast, and noting the catastrophic damages and losses left in the storm's wake in the city of Houston, nevertheless wrote: "As uncomfortable as it might be, we must view this storm as investors." Like Persinos, Versace is unapologetically cutthroat. "One of the wisest words I've heard in the investing world is to be 'cold-blooded' when it comes to one's investments—don't fall in love with your holdings, and in times of uncertainty or tragedy remain focused." Versace added that "the rebuilding effort to come over the ensuing months will be massive." Also writing after Harvey but before Hurricanes Irma and Maria, Matt Thalman, in an online article, admits that "investing with the mindset of making money before or after a natural disaster" is "a touchy subject"; however, if investors can make peace with "investing in this 'morally gray' area," there is, he assures, profit to earn. While noting global warming, rising sea levels, and the increasing intensity and severity of storms (though he does not catalogue their probabilities), Thalman isolates hurricanes, specifically, as "predictable" disasters that (fortuitously?) yield profit before *and* after the storm.

Even as recently as late May 2018, and despite the atrocities wrought by the 2017 hurricane season in the Caribbean and in North America, April Joyner (for Reuters Business News) acknowledged the devastation but also championed the profits: "Several Atlantic Ocean hurricanes in 2017 wrought heavy damage in the Caribbean and U.S. mainland, but for U.S. stocks in several industries, including hotels and transportation, they were a tailwind" ("Factbox"). Even as she tallies the 2017 devastations, Joyner does so in losses and damages, not lives and deaths. "In 2017," she writes, "the hurricane season, which typically runs from June to November, caused more than $250 billion worth of damage in the United States" ("Factbox"). Joyner's only nod to the human impacts of the hurricanes is calculated in customers and in profits. She observes that "car rental, hotel and home improvement companies benefited from an influx of customers seeking emergency resources in the wake of the storms," and that "[f]reight companies commanded higher prices as capacity tightened due to increased demand for supplies in areas struck by the hurricanes" ("Factbox").

Investopedia defines catastrophe bonds as "high-yield debt instruments" linked to insurance and "meant to raise money in case of a catastrophe such as a hurricane or earthquake." Moreover, cat bonds have "a special condition that states if the issuer, such as the insurance or reinsurance company, suffers a loss from a particular predefined catastrophe, then its obligation to pay interest and/or repay the principal is either deferred or completely forgiven" (Murphy 2020). Reinsurance is a related financial term. According to Investopedia, reinsurance, "also known as insurance for insurers or stop-loss insurance, is the practice of insurers transferring portions of risk portfolios to other parties by some form of agreement to reduce the likelihood of paying a large obligation resulting from an insurance claim" (Banton 2022). In other words, and more to the point: catastrophe bonds and reinsurance are financial repackaging and investing in risk, loss, damages, and debt. So, we are back, once again, and this time even more precariously and immorally, to the convoluted and corrupt accounting calisthenics and financial games of subprime mortgages and collateralized, refinanced debt. Rewind to 2008.

While hurricanes can be devastating, for many cat bond investors they are also sources of profit. For financial analysts, general obligation bonds necessitate all measures, including the possibility of increasing taxes (if necessary) to ensure that bondholders are paid. So much for no state intervention in the economy. Michael Shum, writing in fall 2017 in the midst of the hurricane season for *Investment Frontier*, also connects catastrophe bonds to insurers, reinsurers, and insurance-linked securities: "While broader markets have not been impacted in the aftermath of these disasters, insurance companies have the most direct exposure to catastrophic events. To defray the risks, most insurance companies will work with even larger re-insurers. But another method of hedging out their risk has been to package these policies and sell them as insurance-linked securities (ILS)" ("Investing in Natural Disasters").[10] Clearly, Shum's and investors' calculations of "most direct exposure" differ radically from my own and likely from those of people residing in Puerto Rico and in Haiti. More obvious still, there seem to be endless, even infinite, financial and investment possibilities when profiting from loss. Even from death. Necrocapitalism will save the economy! At least the economy will survive.

Conclusion

Disaster capitalism has indeed entered a lethal phase—that of necrocapitalism. To conceptualize how we have moved from necropolitics to the echoing death chamber of necrocapitalism, I formulate urgent questions that demand answers: Have we now entered the stage of capitalism that may be aptly defined as necrocapitalism and that hyperproduces unneeded commodities, absurd consumer and fashion fetishisms, infinitely disposable products, and also, unforgivably, disposable people, disposable lives? Have economic frames become indistinguishable from political ones, and the economy indistinct from the necropolitics of perpetual war?[11] What happens, moreover, when biopolitical governmentality becomes necropolitical rule by constant warfare not only against terrorist organizations, rogue states,[12] citizens, and publics, but against life itself and especially in 'inconvenient' continents (Ferguson, *Global Shadows*) and disposable "shithole" countries, where lives are rarely documented by censuses and deaths are too infrequently tallied? What happens, in short, when biopower nefariously becomes exercised as necropower? Is neoliberal, late-expenditure capitalism, then, predicated upon necrocapital, the profit from death and destruction? Is not disaster capitalism, then, by default, by definition, and by extension actually necrocapitalism?

Other questions also demand to be asked: What does it mean, for example, to "capitalize" death? What does it mean when profits are intensively and inextricably entangled not only with destruction and disposability, but also with death? Why are there speculative markets that wager losses and gains in death and destruction? And are there futures in death profits? War and its surplus capital offer only one model. But what of deaths wrought through natural disasters, and the capital gained from postdisaster reconstruction? What of mortal, manmade disasters caused by a strategic decades-long dismantling of the state, the public, and welfare across the globe? What of the rapid descent to the bottom of increasingly low-wage and ever-outsourced labor pools internationally, which has left abandoned warehouses, defunct mills, and empty factories standing—or dilapidated and collapsing—like the skeletal remains of industrial capitalism on almost every continent? And what happens to those laid-off laborers? Where are toxic chemicals dumped and why? In a now infamous (yet still no less shocking) memorandum, Lawrence Summers coldly advocated for toxic dumping in poor countries, rationalizing that the lives of people living there were both shorter in duration and less valuable in monetary calculations. What, finally, of the looming point of no return for the earth's ecology? Parr has aptly diagnosed this as *The Wrath of Capital* (2012), and Klein correctly, if also scarily, notes in her title that *This Changes Everything*. Corporate "solutions" to ecological degradation, of course, equal "hijacking sustainability" (as Parr demonstrates in his 2009 book by that name). And what of cost/benefit analyses that determine CEO decisions to divest in some regions, countries, or even large swaths of entire continents rendering those areas and the people living in them as expendable and disposable?

Jana Evans Braziel is Western College Endowed Professor in the department of global and intercultural studies. Dr. Braziel (PhD, University of Massachusetts-Amherst) held the Five College Postdoctoral Fellowship in the Center for Crossroads in the Study of the Americas (CISA) while serving as visiting assistant professor of Black studies and English at Amherst College. Before joining the faculty at Miami University, she was Professor of Africana Studies at the University of Cincinnati. Braziel is author of five monographs, including *"Riding with Death": Vodou Art and Urban Ecology in the Streets of Port-au-Prince* (2017) and *Duvalier's Ghosts: Race, Diaspora, and U.S. Imperialism in Haitian Literatures* (2010).

Notes

1. To understand this obdurate and obfuscatory accounting—or what Henry Giroux perhaps more accurately calls the "violence of organized forgetting"—we need to return to the machinations and ruinations wrought by neoliberal disposability. The "politics of disposability" was first conceptualized as the plight of precarious labor in the postmodern, late capitalist, informatized economies by Michael Hardt and Antonio Negri in *Empire* (2001), manifested in the 'ungrievable' losses of the global terror war as documented by Judith Butler in *Precarious Life* (2004), more fully elaborated in Zygmunt Bauman's *Wasted Lives* (2004), and further developed in Henry A. Giroux's *Stormy Weather: Katrina and the Politics of Disposability* (2006). It was also centrally important in the collaborative and extended multipart "Disposable Life" project of Brad Evans. And it was notable in *Disposable Futures* (2015), coauthored with Giroux, and particularly in chapters two and three, "The Politics of Disposability" and "The Destruction of Humanity." These intellectual threads and key ideas—disposability, disposable economies, disposable people, and necrocapitalism—also genealogically emerged from the many provocative and productive philosophical writings around biopower, biopolitics, bare life, and necropolitics by Michel Foucault, Giorgio Agamben, and Achille Mbembe, among others.
2. As its own nature and history is delineated on the Caribbean Catastrophe Risk Insurance Facility (CCRIF) website:

    > In 2007, the Caribbean Catastrophe Risk Insurance Facility was formed as the first multi-country risk pool in the world, and was the first insurance instrument to successfully develop parametric policies backed by both traditional and capital markets. It was designed as a regional catastrophe fund for Caribbean governments to limit the financial impact of devastating hurricanes and earthquakes by quickly providing financial liquidity when a policy is triggered. . . . In 2014, the facility was restructured into a segregated portfolio company (SPC) to facilitate expansion into new products and geographic areas and is now named CCRIF SPC. The new structure, in which products are offered through a number of segregated portfolios, allows for total segregation of risk.

3. As explained by Rosalyn Retkwa for *Institutional Investor* in a 2012 online article: "Cat bonds add another layer of capital, which is the last to be tapped should claims from an event exhaust all the usual lines of insurance and reinsurance. The money raised by a cat bond issue is held in a trust—typically for a three-year term, though some bonds mature in as little as a year. Usually, the bonds pay interest and expire without being triggered. 'Cat bonds kick in at the top of the food chain' ... noting that the 'risk of attachment'—that is, the risk the principal raised through a bond issue will actually be used to pay claims and that investors will lose some or all of their money—is 'very, very remote.'"
4. See Mbembe (2003) and his recent book *Necropolitics*. See also Fischer's "Haiti: Fantasies of Bare Life," in *Small Axe*.
5. On necromedia, see O'Gorman (2015) and Cortés (2018a), whose theorizations of "indebted subjectivities" are informed by Lazzarato's *The Making of the Indebted Man* (2012).

6. In *From Communism to Capitalism: Theory of a Catastrophe*, Michael Henry argues that technology will overtake and eventually dominate capitalism; and when this technological triumph transpires, we will pass from the "capitalist world to the world of technology," in which the "power for destruction and death" will "dramatically increase" (2014: 113).
7. See Johnson's provocative and pointed *Blowback* (2004).
8. I more fully address cat bonds as exemplary of disaster capitalism in a book manuscript in progress tentatively entitled *Global Studies: Lessons from Haiti and Puerto Rico*.
9. On biopower, biopolitics, bare life, and necropolitics, see Foucault, Agamben, Mbembe, and Fischer.
10. As Shum further explains: "Many kinds of financial products, particularly mortgages and credit, can be securitized and sold off to other investors. Insurance-Linked securities serve a similar purpose in that insurers are able to aggregate policies to reduce overall risk, then sell them to other investors. Catastrophe (CAT) bonds, which aggregate policies on natural disasters, are a form of insurance-linked securities. They cover all kinds of natural disasters including earthquakes, storms, volcanoes and meteorites." And while cat bonds may prove less profitable "[i]f natural disasters are to become more frequent due to either climate change or fracking (in the case of earthquakes), insurance-linked securities are more steadfast and sure returns on investment."
11. See Vidal's *Perpetual War for Perpetual Peace* (2002). Vidal adopts his title from Harry Elmer Barnes's *Perpetual War for Perpetual Peace*, which was written in alarm at the expansionary foreign policies of Franklin D. Roosevelt and, after 1947, of Harry Truman.
12. See Derrida's "The Last of the Rogue States" (2004).

References

Agamben, Giorgio. 1998. *Homo Sacer: Sovereign Power and Bare Life*, trans. Daniel Heller-Roazen. Stanford, CA: Stanford University Press.

———. 2005. *State of Exception*, trans. Kevin Attell. Chicago: University of Chicago Press.

Artemis ILS Market Reports: https://www.artemis.bm/artemis-ils-market-reports/

Baggesgaard, Mads Anders. 2015. "The Migrating Earth: Cinematic Images of Haiti after the 2010 Earthquake." In *The Culture of Migration: Politics, Aesthetics and Histories*, ed. Sten Pultz Mosland, Anne Ring Petersen, and Moritz Schramm, 309–26. London and New York: I. B. Tauris.

Bales, Kevin. 1999. *Disposable People: New Slavery in the Global Economy*. Berkeley: University of California Press.

Balogun, Fidelis Odun. 1995. *Adjusted Lives: Stories of Structural Adjustments*. Trenton, NJ: Africa World Press.

Banton, Caroline. 2022. "Reinsurance Definition, Types, and How It Works." Investopedia. 3 April, https://www.investopedia.com/terms/r/reinsurance.asp#ixzz5RBt322a0.

Barnes, Harry Elmer. 1947. *Perpetual War for Perpetual Peace*. Caldwell, ID: Caxton Printers.

Baudrillard, Jean. 2017. *Symbolic Exchange and Death*. London and New York: Sage Publishers.
Bauman, Zygmunt. 2003. *Wasted Lives*. London: Polity Press.
Bonilla, Yarimar. 2015. *Non-Sovereign Futures? French Caribbean Politics in the Wake of Disenchantment*. Chicago: University of Chicago Press.
———. "Why Would Anyone in Puerto Rico Want a Hurricane? Because Someone Will Get Rich.: *Washington Post* op-ed (22 September 2017): https://www.washingtonpost.com/outlook/how-puerto-rican-hurricanes-devastate-many-and-enrich-a-few/2017/09/22/78e7500c-9e66-11e7-9083-fbfddf6804c2_story.html
Butler, Judith. 2004. *Precarious Life*. New York: Verso.
The Caribbean Catastrophe Risk Insurance Facility (CCRIF), https://www.ccrif.org/
Castronovo, Russ. 2001. *Necro Citizenship: Death, Eroticism, and the Public Sphere in the Nineteenth-Century United States*. Durham, NC: Duke University Press.
Cortés, Jason. 2018a. "Necromedia, Haunting, and Public Mourning in The Puerto Rican Debt State: The Case of 'Los Muertos.'" *Journal of Latin American Cultural Studies* 27(3): 357–69, https://doi.org/10.1080/13569325.2018.1485562.
———. 2018b. "Puerto Rico: Hurricane Maria and the Promise of Disposability." *Capitalism Nature Socialism* 29(3): 1-8, https://www.tandfonline.com/doi/full/10.1080/10455752.2018.1505233.
Derrida, Jacques. 2004. "The Last of the Rogue States: The 'Democracy to Come,' Opening in Two Turns," trans. Pascale-Anne Brault and Michael Naas. *South Atlantic Quarterly* 103(2/3): 323–41.
Duffield, Mark. 2001. *Global Governance and the New Wars*. London and New York: Zed Books.
Dupuy, Alex. *Haiti: From Revolutionary Slaves to Powerless Citizens: Essays on the Politics and Economics of Underdevelopment, 1804-2013*. New York and London: Routledge, 2014.
Evans, Brad, and Henry A. Giroux. 2015. *Disposable Futures: The Seduction of Violence in the Age of Spectacle*. San Francisco: City Lights Books.
Fatton, Robert. *Haiti: Trapped in the Outer Periphery*. Boulder, Colo: Lynne Rienner, 2014.
Ferguson, James. 2006. "Globalizing Africa? Observations from an Inconvenient Continent." In *Global Shadows: Africa in the Neoliberal World Order*, 25–49. Durham, NC: Duke University Press.
Fischer, Sibylle. "Haiti: Fantasies of Bare Life," *Small Axe* 11(2), 1-15. https://www.muse.jhu.edu/article/220143.
Foucault, Michel. 1976. *La Volonté de savoir*. Paris: Éditions Gallimard.
———. 1978. *The History of Sexuality*, trans. Robert Hurley. New York: Pantheon Books.
———. 2004. *Naissance de la Biopolitique: Cours au Collège de France, 1978–1979*, ed. Michel Senellart. Paris: Éditions de Seuil/Gallimard.
———. 2008. *The Birth of Biopolitics: Lectures at the Collège de France, 1978–79*, ed. Michel Senellart, trans. Graham Burchell. London and New York: Palgrave Macmillan.
Giroux, Henry A. 2006. *Stormy Weather: Katrina and the Politics of Disposability*. Boulder, CO: Paradigm Books.
Glissant, Édouard. 1997. *Poetics of Relation*, trans. Betsy Wing. Ann Arbor: University of Michigan Press.
Henry, Michael. 2014. *From Communism to Capitalism: Theory of a Catastrophe*. London and New York: Bloomsbury.

"How Record Catastrophe Bond Issuances Are Changing The Alternative Investment Landscape," *The One Brief*, AON: https://theonebrief.com/how-record-catastrophe-bond-issuances-are-changing-the-alternative-investment-landscape/

Johnson, Chalmers. 2004. *Blowback: The Costs and Consequences of American Empire*. New York: Holt Books.

Joyner, April. "Factbox: Hurricane season U.S. stocks to watch." Reuters (27 May 2018): https://www.reuters.com/article/us-storm-atlantic-stocks-factbox/factbox-hurricane-season-u-s-stocks-to-watch-idUSKCN1IT00N

Katz, Jonathan. 2013. *The Big Truck That Went By: How the World Came to Save Haiti and Left Behind a Disaster*. London and New York: Palgrave Macmillan.

Kaussen, Valerie. 2011. "States of Exception—Haiti's IDP Camps." *Monthly Review*. 1 February, https://monthlyreview.org/2011/02/01/states-of-exception-haitis-idp-camps/.

Klein, Naomi. 2007a. *The Shock Doctrine: The Rise of Disaster Capitalism*. New York: Metropolitan Books.

———. 2007b. "Disaster Capitalism: The New Economy of Catastrophe." *Harper's Magazine* (October): 47–58.

———. 2014. *This Changes Everything: Capitalism vs. the Climate*: New York: Simon & Schuster.

———. 2017. "How Power Profits from Disaster." *The Guardian*. 6 July, https://www.theguardian.com/us-news/2017/jul/06/naomi-klein-how-power-profits-from-disaster.

———. 2018. *The Battle for Paradise: Puerto Rico Takes on the Disaster Capitalists*. Chicago: Haymarket Books.

Lazaarato, Maurizio. 2012. *The Making of the Indebted Man*. London: MIT Press, Semiotext(e).

Mbembe, Achille. 2003. "Necropolitics," trans. Libby Meintjes. *Public Culture* 15(1): 11–40.

Molinari, Sarah. ¿Tu estás preparado (Are you prepared)? Conference paper presented at *Symposium: Puerto Rican Studies at 50*, Puerto Rican Studies Association (PRSA), University of Texas–Austin, 2019: https://liberalarts.utexas.edu/latinostudies/events/symposium-puerto-rican-studies-at-50

Murphy, Chris B. 2020. "Catastrophe Bond." Investopedia. 29 May, https://www.investopedia.com/terms/c/catastrophebond.asp#ixzz5RBsMid68.

O'Gorman, Marcel. 2015. *Necromedia*. Minneapolis: University of Minnesota Press.

Paravisini-Gebert, Lizabeth. 2017. "The Caribbean's Agonizing Seashores: Tourism Resorts, Art, and the Future of the Region's Coastlines." In *Routledge Companion to the Environmental Humanities*, ed. Ursula K. Heise, Jon Christensen, and Michelle Niemann, 278–88. New York and London: Routledge.

Parr, Adrian. 2009. *Hijacking Sustainability*. Cambridge, MA: MIT Press.

———. 2012. *The Wrath of Capital: Neoliberalism and Climate Change Politics*. New York: Columbia University Press.

———. 2017. *Birth of a New Earth*. New York: Columbia University Press.

Retkwa, Rosalyn. 2012. "Catastrophe Bonds Could Break $5 Billion Mark This Year." *Institutional Investor*. 20 March, https://www.institutionalinvestor.com/article/b14zplzytvv640/catastrophe-bonds-could-break-$5-billion-mark-this-year.

Schuller, Mark. 2012. *Killing with Kindness: Haiti, International Aid, and NGOs*. New Brunswick, NJ: Rutgers University Press.

Schuller, Mark, and Pablo Morales, eds. 2012. *Tectonic Shifts: Haiti since the Earthquake*. Sterling, VA: Kumarian Press.

Shum, Michael. "Investing in Natural Disasters." *Investment Frontier* (18 September 2017): https://investmentfrontier.com/2017/09/18/investing-natural-disasters/
Seitenfus, Ricardo. 2015. *L'échec de l'aide international à Haïti: Dilemmes et égarements*, trans. Pascal Reuillard. Port-au-Prince: Éditions de l'Université d'État d'Haïti.
Sontag, Deborah. 2012. "Rebuilding in Haiti Lags After Billions in Post-Quake Aid." *New York Times*, 23 December.
Vidal, Gore. 2002. *Perpetual War for Perpetual Peace*. New York: Nation Books.
Wallerstein, Immanuel, Randall Collins, Michael Mann, Georgi Derluguian, and Craig Calhoun. 2013. *Does Capitalism Have a Future?* Oxford and London: Oxford University Press.

CHAPTER 6

Wake Work in Post-Maria Puerto Rico and Beyond

JOHN RIBÓ

In the summer of 2019, Puerto Ricans protested en masse, forcing then-governor Ricardo Roselló to resign. The massive mobilization and unprecedented ouster were the culmination of a series of events including the US government's imposition of the Puerto Rico Oversight, Management, and Economic Stability Act (PROMESA) in 2016, the mishandling of the aftermath of Hurricanes Irma and Maria in 2017, and a string of political scandals that reached their apex in 2019 when Puerto Rico's Centro de Periodismo Investigativo published 889 pages of group chat transcripts between Roselló, members of his administration, and private contractors. Colloquially called Telegramgate or RickyLeaks, the release of the transcripts, which included racist, misogynistic, and homophobic slurs and crude commentary mocking the dead of Hurricane Maria, sparked the social unrest that eventually unseated Roselló.

While each of these events leading up to and including Roselló's resignation merit analysis and would be appropriate subjects for an edited volume on disaster in the circum-Caribbean, this chapter focuses on the role of the dead in Puerto Rican cultural practices of protest. More specifically, through close readings of Pedro Pietri's poem "Puerto Rican Obituary" (1971), Hurray for the Riff Raff's song "Pa'lante" (2017), and video footage of Puerto Rican protesters occupying Grand Central Station in New York City to dance the electric slide during the 2019 protests, I analyze how Puerto Rican activists, writers, and artists invoke the dead to empower the living to resist injustices rooted in US colonial rule. I read these engagements with the dead as manifestations of what scholar and cultural critic Christina Sharpe calls wake work—a term that describes a range of strategies for defending the dead. Puerto Rican wake work has deep roots in performance. Like the Puerto Rican protesters dancing the electric slide, Pedro Pietri's classic poem "Puerto Rican Obituary" and Hurray for the Riff Raff's more recent song "Pa'lante" originated in public performance, and the live element of their poetry and music has made their art particularly useful for educating, organizing, and bringing together broad publics. Moreover, the intertextual relationship connecting "Puerto Rican Obituary" and "Pa'lante" also replicates the dynamic of wake work. Through intentional engagement with Pietri's poem, Hurray for the Riff Raff's Bronx-born Puerto Rican singer-songwriter Alynda Segarra invokes the struggles of previous generations as inspiration for continued resistance to injustice today. Finally, drawing on the scholarship of Yarimar Bonilla and Beatriz Llenín-Figueroa, I situate these examples of Puerto Rican wake work within the larger context of the circum-Caribbean and draw connections to similar practices in Franco-Cuban musical duo Ibeyi's song and video "Deathless" (2017).

This chapter's exploration of the ways Puerto Rican, Cuban, and other Caribbean activists, writers, and artists defend the dead offers a diachronic approach to disaster that shifts the focus of analysis from a specific disaster to what Bonilla (2020: 1) calls "the coloniality of disaster." Bonilla coins this phrase to underline the long-term processes, practices, and conditions of racio-colonial capitalism that have unevenly cultivated vulnerability to disaster and other systemic violence among particular populations—specifically among people of the circum-Caribbean and its diasporas. Although societies across the globe memorialize the dead, such practices take on special significance and added urgency as empowering forms of resistance for marginalized communities and colonized peoples in regions rendered especially vulnerable to the disastrous violence—slow, quick, and symbolic—of racio-colonial capitalism. Moreover, wake work in the circum-Caribbean is often rooted in syncretic cosmologies and spiritual practices such as Vodou and Santería that colonial powers have demonized and attempted to eradicate for centuries. In this particular context wake work then becomes not only a means to defend the dead and to resist the negative material and psychic effects of coloniality but also a strategy for maintaining, reclaiming, and renewing sacred forms of memorialization and relationality that connect Caribbean peoples to their ancestors. These connections to one's ancestors prove essential in the aftermath of disasters such as Hurricane Maria, in the midst of political crises such as the #RickyRenuncia protests of 2019, and in the long afterlives of colonization and slavery that make poetry such as Pietri's as relevant today as when he first performed it.

Post-Maria Wake Work

In her incisive meditation on Black culture in the long afterlife of slavery, *In the Wake: On Blackness and Being*, Christina Sharpe (2016: 10) asks, "What does it mean to defend the dead?" Sharpe stages this question among intimate accounts of the deaths of members of her family to illustrate how "racism, the engine that drives the ship of state's national and imperial projects . . . cuts through all our lives and deaths inside and outside the nation, in the wake of its purposeful flow" (3). Sharpe's turn to the autobiographical undisciplines her study, validates lived experiences, and illustrates the various ways that racism kills Black people—from the slow violence of hostile policies and bureaucratic negligence, to state-sanctioned murder by police, to the symbolic oblivion of erasure.

In response to these different modes of violence, wake work takes different forms as "a mode of inhabiting and rupturing this episteme with our known lived and un/imaginable lives," an analytic to "imagine otherwise from what we know now in the wake of slavery," and a method to "attend to physical, social, and figurative death and also to the largeness that is Black life, Black life insisted from death" (17–18). Despite the funereal contexts that make the defense of the dead necessary, Sharpe describes wake work in positive terms as resistance, imagination, and care narrated from the first-person plural of community and rooted in the insistent presence, creativity, and perseverance of Black life.

The question of defending the dead through collective forms of resistance, imagination, and care lay at the heart of the 2019 Puerto Rican protests. After Hurricane Maria hit the island on 20 September 2017, Puerto Ricans performed wake work on multiple fronts with social media playing a key role. When a May 2018 Harvard study in collaboration with Puerto Rican researchers revealed that Hurricane Maria caused 4,645 Puerto Rican deaths—a number that far surpassed the US government's original estimate of sixty-four (Hernandez and McGinley 2018)—Puerto Ricans took to social media using the hashtag #4645 to share the untold stories of their dead and to protest the lack of US governmental aid after the storm. When, on 13 July 2019, El Centro de Periodismo Investigativo (Center for Investigative Journalism) published the scandalous private chats between Roselló and his inner circle of bureaucrats and lobbyists, Puerto Ricans on the island and in diaspora used the hashtag #RickyRenuncia to organize and document the protests calling for the governor's resignation (Valentín Ortiz and Minet 2019).

The defense of the dead was particularly salient in the Puerto Rican public's reaction to Telegramgate. Among the many crass comments included in the leaked transcripts was a record of Christian Sobrino Vega joking about feeding the cadavers of victims of Hurricane Maria to the crows (Associated Press 2019). Sobrino Vega was chief executive officer and president of the Puerto Rico Fiscal Agency and Financial Advisory Authority (AAFAF, from its Spanish name) and the governor's ex officio representative to the Fiscal Oversight and Management Board (FOMB) established under PROMESA. In other words, Sobrino Vega served as the representative of the Puerto Rican people in bureaucratic structures imposed on the island by the US. Instead of using this platform to speak for Puerto Ricans, he ridiculed and disrespected their dead. Sobrino Vega resigned the day the transcripts leaked.

These events in the aftermath of PROMESA and Hurricane Maria provide powerful examples of the many possible manifestations of wake work. The research that revealed the actual number of Puerto Rican deaths caused by Hurricane Maria, the social media campaign to memorialize the dead, the investigative journalism that uncovered the leaked chats of Puerto Rican elites desecrating the memory of the dead, and the protests that eventually ousted Roselló all constitute strategies for defending the dead. These events also exemplify the capacious creativity of Puerto Rican and circum-Caribbean wake work. Despite the dire circumstances, the protests demonstrated the rich creative possibilities of wake work manifesting through joyful collective celebrations expressed creatively in unexpected forms of protests including horseback riding, acrobatics, scuba diving, boating, yoga, and more (Henríquez 2019).

One creative form of protest-cum-celebration that became common across multiple sites was the electric slide, a four-wall line dance with variants consisting of as many as twenty-four and as few as sixteen steps. The electric slide featured in videos from protests in Guaynabo, Puerto Rico; San Juan, Puerto Rico; Washington, DC; and New York City. Though some on social media dismissed it as frivolous or passé, the dance constituted a powerful manifestation of wake work that drew together multiple forms of protest, synced protesters through movement, made their presence and will known, and helped ease, if only temporarily, the traumatic effects of the disaster and its aftermath (Roy 2020).

As the protests unfolded, one particular video of protesters dancing the electric slide resonated on social media. On 22 July 2019, Puerto Rican poet Ricardo Alberto Maldonado posted to Twitter a thirty-three-second clip of protesters filling New York City's Grand Central Station.[1] Throughout the video, the Puerto Rican flag dominates, adorning the bodies of protesters and waving from poles. Alongside the original red, white, and sky blue *monoestrellada,* flies the black and white Puerto Rican flag that signaled the call to anticolonial resistance after PROMESA and to mourn the dead after Hurricane Maria (Newman 2018).[2] As the protesters dance the electric slide, individuals embellish turns and dips with personalized flourishes—a raised fist here, a shoulder shimmy there. The dancers also double as percussionists beating drums, scraping guiros, and banging pots. The crowd repeats the dance and chants in unison following the beat, the steps, and the lead of an amplified voice heard from off-screen shouting, "¡Yo soy boricua, pa' que tú lo sepas!" The refrain, popularized in the titular chorus to Puerto Rican rapper Taíno's 1995 song, declares, "I am Puerto Rican, let it be known!" After several rounds, the chorus shifts to "¡Ricky renuncia y llévate la junta!" demanding that Roselló resign and take the Fiscal Oversight and Management Board with him. The first chant exclaims in words the Puerto Rican presence on display in the mass of protesters and their ubiquitous flags, both colorful and somber. The second chant asserts that despite the festive atmosphere the crowd has gathered to demand concrete change in the governance of Puerto Rico.

This short clip of Puerto Rican protesters dancing the electric slide and chanting together in unison provides just one example of how the 2019 protests performed wake work by interweaving activism, cultural expression, and celebration to defend the dead. Through dancing, chanting, and the display of Puerto Rican flags, old and new, the protesters inhabited the public space of Grand Central Station to make their community visible and their voices heard. Their collective action defended the dead of Hurricane Maria, demanded a better future for Puerto Rico, and provided a glimmer of how solidarity and creativity could make that future possible. Finally, while the protest raised consciousness of the physical, social, and symbolic death that plagues Puerto Rico and its diaspora, the collective joy of the protest also insisted Puerto Rican life from death.

Wake Work in Puerto Rican Cultural Production of Protest

Though the 2019 protests represent an exceptional moment in the history of the island, these manifestations of wake work blending activism, creativity, and celebration form part of a longer tradition of Puerto Rican cultural production of protest. This tradition cultivates an active, symbiotic, cyclical relationship in which the dead empower the living to defend the dead; this interdependent and dynamic relationship of the living and the dead alloys cultural production and political protest, suffusing popular culture with historical import and communal purpose. Pietri's "Puerto Rican Obituary" exemplifies this tradition of Puerto Rican wake work, blending activism and performance. As scholar William Luis explains, "Nuyorican poetry developed in the decade of the sixties, concurrently with the civil rights movement, the Black Panthers, the Young Lords, and other organizations promoting black and Puerto Rican pride" (Luis 1997: 46). Pietri, a member of the Young Lords, performed "Puerto Rican Obituary" at party meetings—most famously at the People's Church, the name the Young Lords gave to the First Spanish United Methodist Church in East Harlem after they occupied it in 1969. The poem first appeared in print in the Young Lords' newpaper, *Palante*, and then in the 1971 book *Palante: The Young Lords Party*. Many scholars today consider "Puerto Rican Obituary" the quintessential example of the aesthetic of this historic moment; poet and scholar Urayoán Noel, for example, calls it "the Puerto Rican Movement's emblematic poem" (Noel 2014: 17).

"Puerto Rican Obituary" interweaves the narratives of five fictional Puerto Ricans who fail to achieve the American dream despite their backbreaking efforts. The poem's opening stanza sets the stage for their stories through the impersonal and monotonous repetition of labor and death.

> They worked
> They worked
> They worked
> and they died
> They died broke
> They died owing.[3]

Yet as the poem's chorus reveals the protagonists' names, it becomes clear that the implications of their deaths far exceed the linear, the literal, and the individual.

> Juan
> Miguel
> Milagros
> Olga
> Manuel
> All died yesterday today
> and will die again tomorrow.

The surreal temporality of these repeating deaths blurs the boundaries between past, present, and future, indicating that this is not a realist portrayal of the literal deaths of discrete individuals. Rather, "Puerto Rican Obituary" riffs on these figures as iterations on a common, collective experience of social death that all but forecloses the possibility of achieving the American dream. Like dancing protesters individually improvising over the same cycle of repeating steps, Juan, Miguel, Milagros, Olga, and Manuel each undertake their own particular Sisyphean march towards the same morbid fate.

Through these five figures, Pietri portrays as a foregone conclusion the social death of Puerto Ricans seeking to assimilate into the capitalist society that colonized their homeland—"They were born dead / and they died dead." This social death manifests as various forms of economic exploitation including unfair wages ("They worked / ten days a week / and were only paid for five"), inescapable debt ("passing their bill collectors / on to the next of kin"), endemic malnutrition ("hating the grocery stores / that sold them make-believe steak / and bullet-proof rice and beans"), and institutionalized discrimination ("*is* against the company policy / to promote SPICS SPICS SPICS").

Yet rather than portray these characters solely as innocent victims, "Puerto Rican Obituary" explores their self-destructive and ultimately unsuccessful attempts to assimilate in order to achieve the American dream. Perhaps the most concise example of the poem's critique of this drive to assimilate comes in its description of the impulse to purchase a home in a white neighborhood:

> Dreaming about queens
> Clean-cut lily-white neighborhood
> Puerto Ricanless scene
> Thirty-thousand-dollar home
> The first spics on the block
> Proud to belong to a community
> of gringos who want them lynched.

Pietri's portrayal of this fantasy of suburban home ownership stands in as a synecdoche for migration from the island to the mainland and emphasizes many of the negative aspects that the poem attributes to assimilation and the American dream: materialism; the abandonment of language, cultural identity, and community; and the acceptance of a subordinate, marginal role in a violently racist social order. Through these descriptions of the economic plight of Puerto Ricans, and through examples like the passage above and others pitting Juan, Miguel, Milagros, Olga, and Manuel against one another in petty, materialistic rivalries, Pietri attends to the material and psychological toll of social death on Puerto Ricans and paints these five figures as profoundly unhappy, jealous, unfulfilled, and disconnected.

"Puerto Rican Obituary" thus presents a bleak depiction of Puerto Ricans' life chances in the US and a sharp critique of assimilationist strategies for upward social mobility. Yet the poem nevertheless insists Puerto Rican life from death by lacing its critiques with humor and offering its protagonists and audience a hopeful path towards liberation through pride, love, and community. Though also evident on the page, Pietri's humor significantly shaped the reception of his live performances of the poem. The short film *El Pueblo Se Levanta* (The People Are Rising, 1971), for example, includes footage of Pietri performing "Puerto Rican Obituary" inside the People's Church. When he enunciates "make-believe steak / and bullet-proof rice and beans" the audience breaks into knowing laughter. Pietri's playful, oneiric language describing hunger transforms a common, difficult experience into a point of connection and solidarity among the audience. Through live performance featuring humorous depictions of painful lived experiences of his community, Pietri cultivated the self-reflection, camaraderie, and solidarity for which his poetry advocates and created a space where "you do not need a dictionary / to communicate with your people."

Pietri's poem clearly left its mark on Puerto Rican singer, songwriter, musician, and activist Alynda Segarra, who fronts the New Orleans–based Americana band Hurray for the Riff Raff. Their 2017 song "Pa'lante" announces itself as an homage to the Young Lords and Pietri through its iconic title and climactic sample of Pietri performing "Puerto Rican Obituary" in the People's Church. The song's lyrics reiterate the core themes and retrace the emotional arc of "Puerto Rican Obituary." For example, the opening verse of "Pa'lante" echoes the emphasis on labor in the first stanza of "Puerto Rican Obituary."

> Oh I just wanna go to work
> And get back home, and be something
> I just wanna fall in line
> And do my time, and be something
> Well I just wanna prove my worth
> On the planet Earth, and be something
> I just wanna fall in love
> Not fuck it up, and feel something.[4]

Despite clear similarities, "Pa'lante" makes significant alterations to translate the themes of Pietri's poem into a contemporary pop anthem. It shifts the narrative from third person plural to first person singular, providing an account of the narrator's emotions and motivations and thus facilitating the audience's identification with them. The song also exchanges Pietri's litany of unattainable signifiers of the American dream for the more nebulous epistrophe "be something."

The second verse of "Pa'lante" echoes Pietri's critique of aspiring to assimilation and of capitalist notions of success as a colonial subject of US empire.

> Colonized and hypnotized, be something
> Sterilized, dehumanized, be something
> Well take your pay
> And stay out the way, be something

> Ah do your best
> But fuck the rest, be something.

The first two lines contrast "be something" with an oblique but devastating gloss of Puerto Rico's colonial history, including eugenicist US policies encouraging sterilization. This bleak context shifts the meaning of "be something" from the narrator's internalized desire for a successful and meaningful life in the first verse to a sinister and externally imposed command in the second. In the final four lines of this verse, the imperative to "be something" becomes a dehumanizing bludgeon driving home a zero-sum-game mentality that accepts injustice and abandons community to seek personal gain.

In contrast to "Puerto Rican Obituary," references to death in "Pa'lante" are minimal but nevertheless key. As the song builds to its climax, the narrator hints at suicidal ideation—"Lately I'm not too afraid to die / I wanna leave it all behind / I think about it sometimes." This seemingly casual admission sets the stage for the revelatory sample of Pietri performing "Puerto Rican Obituary."

> Dead Puerto Ricans
> Who never knew they were Puerto Ricans
> Who never took a coffee break
> from the ten commandments
> to KILL KILL KILL
> the landlords of their cracked skulls
> and communicate with their latino souls[5]
>
> Juan
> Miguel
> Milagros
> Olga
> Manuel
> From the nervous breakdown streets
> where the mice live like millionaires
> and the people do not live at all.

The recording of Pietri reciting these words plays a key role in the sonic and thematic composition of the song. With the insertion of the sample, the voice of an ancestor returns to the song's soundscape to illuminate the narrator's encounter with social death as part of a larger collective Puerto Rican experience and to chart a path towards liberation. The opening lines of the first stanza—"Dead Puerto Ricans / Who never knew they were Puerto Ricans"—equate the ruptured transmission of cultural heritage with social death. As antidote to this social death, Pietri prescribes that Puerto Ricans "KILL KILL KILL / the landlords of their cracked skulls," a violent metaphor mobilizing fantastic imagery of internalized capitalist slumlords, mental anguish, and death to colorfully depict the difficult process of decolonizing one's mind.

This sample of Pietri performing "Puerto Rican Obituary" unlocks the song's incandescent conclusion, which charts an affective geography of diasporic belonging through a dedicatory list of locations, ancestors, and elders:

> From el barrio to Arecibo, ¡Pa'lante!
> From Marble Hill to the ghost of Emmett Till, ¡Pa'lante!
> To Juan, Miguel, Milagros, Manuel, ¡Pa'lante!
> To all who came before, we say, ¡Pa'lante!
> To my mother and my father, I say, ¡Pa'lante!

The coda replaces the three syllables of the epistrophe "be something" with those of "Pa'lante," sung over the same notes, in a new, higher key. The substitution effectively rejects the equation of human worth with labor and material wealth, replacing it with "Pa'lante," an expression of solidarity and perseverance used in the face of adversity to encourage oneself and others to push forward, onward, together. While this affective map highlights key Nuyorican signifiers such as "el barrio," and four of the five figures from "Puerto Rican Obituary," it also outlines an inclusive coalition of solidarity among all marginalized people, saying "¡Pa'lante" to "all who had to hide," "all who lost their pride," and "all who had to survive."[6] Notably this intersectional coalition of solidarity extends Puerto Rican wake work's defense of the dead to include Emmet Till, the lynching victim whose 1955 open-casket funeral produced shocking photographic images credited with galvanizing the civil rights movement. The affective map of Segarra's wake work follows the example of the Young Lords and Pietri, who recognized Puerto Ricans as part of the African diaspora and built strong coalitions with Black activists.

Circum-Caribbean Wake Work

In 2018, Puerto Rican filmmaker Kristian Mercado Figueroa wrote and directed the music video for "Pa'lante," dedicating it to his "grandfather Felipe Figueroa Rosa, who died in the aftermath of the hurricane but will not be forgotten. And to all the Puerto Ricans struggling after Maria. Pa'lante Siempre."[7] The video sets the song against the story of one fictional family's difficulties in the aftermath of the hurricane as the father returns to them in Puerto Rico from New York City. Mercado Figueroa depicts labor conditions and economic hardships similar to those found in "Puerto Rican Obituary" and the lyrics of "Pa'lante." Yet before the song begins and after it ends, the video frames the narrative with sights and sounds from the ruins of Hurricane Maria. The footage is not the sensationalized, apocalyptic imagery of cable news or Hollywood blockbusters. The ruins, as Mercado Figueroa captures them in a series of haunting images, are quiet, exist on a human scale, and are shot through with signs of survivors attempting to make do: a small pile of wood gathered from a collapsed home, a roofless house partially covered in blue tarps, a utility worker and his truck parked near a pole with downed lines, interiors and exteriors of roofless homes in which people seemingly still live, and a tattered Puerto Rican flag wrapped around a pole, flapping in the wind.

These real images of the hurricane's aftermath document what happens when colonization, social death, and catastrophe combine. The results, as Mercado Figueroa reminded a stunned audience when accepting the Best Music Video Award for "Pa'lante" at the 2019 SXSW Film Festival, are neither abstract nor theoretical: "We lost 5,000 people. On fucking American soil. 5,000 DEAD PUERTO RICANS. Where is the response? WHERE IS IT?" (Jackson 2019). "Puerto Rican Obituary" and "Pa'lante" describe long-term, systemic patterns of slow violence that set the stage for disaster by rendering specific communities vulnerable to catastrophic events. These patterns predominate across the circum-Caribbean, in diasporic Caribbean communities and among marginalized populations at large in what Puerto Rican anthropologist Yarimar Bonilla (2020: 2) calls an "archipelago of racialized neglect." This archipelago connects communities whose life chances are fundamentally diminished by the coloniality of disaster, or "how catastrophic events like hurricanes, earthquakes, but also other forms political and economic crisis deepen the fault lines of long-existing racial and colonial histories" (2020: 1). Wake work proliferates across this archipelago of racialized neglect because death disproportionately accumulates across this archipelago. This accumulation of death—symbolic, social, and clinical—makes wake work necessary.

In the summer of 2020, a year after Roselló's resignation, the electric slide also became a staple of Black Lives Matter protests in the US. The use of the electric slide as wake work by both Black and Puerto Rican activists is not, however, surprising given the rich collaborative history of Black and Puerto Rican activism, the fact that many Puerto Rican activists are also Black, and the origins of the dance. Dance critic Sanjoy Roy (2020) explains:

The dance has a long pedigree, with black roots and widespread branches. The step sequence was first devised by Broadway dancer Ric Silver in 1976 to an upbeat reggae song by Bunny Wailer, Electric Boogie, a hit in Jamaica that went on to become a more mainstream US success for his compatriot Marcia Griffiths, in 1982 and 1989. . . .

In the 1990s, the sequence was styled for American line-dancing and became a genre staple. It got another big boost through the 1999 black romcom The Best Man, here danced to Cameo's 1986 hit single Candy. It has become massively popular at parties and weddings, and is often called the Candy Dance.

The prominence of the electric slide in both the Ricky Renuncia protests of 2019 and the Black Lives Matter protests of 2020 suggests that in response to the violence of racialized neglect, the archipelago develops transnational, transcultural forms of wake work to attend to its dead, resist violence, and insist life from death.

Similarly to the broadly inclusive affective map of diasporic belonging that Segarra charts in the conclusion of "Pa'lante," Puerto Rican scholar Beatriz Llenín Figueroa (2019) theorizes a regional network of solidarity rooted in

> a Caribbean-wide history of maronage, resistance, and endurance that travels and unites us, as Brathwaite famously declared, submarinely. We honor the submarine corals made from the bodies of our enslaved, our migrants, our poor, our women, our queers, our dispossessed, our freedom-seekers. In and through them, we, Antilleans, islanders, Caribbean peoples, stand united. The maroons are deathless. We are deathless.

Llenín Figueroa identifies the marginalized dead—those who historically have defied hierarchies of race, class, and gender, those who often remain unrepresented in the historical archive, and those whom Roselló, Sobrino Vega, and company ridiculed in their leaked chats—as foundational figures of this circum-Caribbean tradition of wake work. Further still, Llenín Figueroa claims deathlessness for all Caribbean peoples, living and dead, and thus effectively defines the Caribbean community not only across time and space but beyond the boundaries of mortality.

Llenín Figueroa borrows this concept of deathlessness from the lyrics of Ibeyi's song "Deathless" (2017). French-Cuban musicians Lisa-Kaindé Díaz and Naomi Díaz of Ibeyi—twin sisters and daughters of celebrated Cuban percussionist Anga Díaz—composed "Deathless" in response to an incident of racial profiling Lisa-Kaindé experienced in the Paris Metro at age sixteen (Younes 2017). Yet despite the song's bleak topical origins, Lisa-Kaindé explains the song's title and chorus—"Whatever happens, whatever happened, we are deathless!" (Ibeyi 2016)—as a profound, joyful, and defiant optimism rooted in their Yoruban faith: "To be 'Deathless' means that there's no end. . . . It means there's no end to love, there's no end to joy, there's no end to music" (Edes 2017). Ibeyi's video for "Deathless" figuratively stages this deathlessness through the repeated, cyclical emergence of the twins from the red garments of one another's prostrate bodies. In the video, Lisa-Kaindé and Naomi Díaz provide an embodied performance and visual representation of the empowering, symbiotic, cyclical relationship between the living and the dead cultivated through wake work. While the protests Puerto Ricans undertook in the aftermath of PROMESA, Hurricanes Irma and Maria, and Telegramgate provide powerful examples of wake work in action, they also form part of a longer tradition of Puerto Rican cultural production of protest that invokes the dead to empower the living. In turn, this Puerto Rican tradition connects to broader circum-Caribbean networks of resistance in which the dead empower the living to defend the dead, insisting life from death through care, resistance, and joy.

John Ribó is assistant professor of English at Florida State University, where he specializes in contemporary Latinx literatures and cultures. His work has appeared in *Chiricú*, *The Journal of Haitian Studies*, *Cuban Studies*, and *ASAP*. He is currently completing his first manuscript, tentatively titled *Haitian Hauntings*.

Notes

Portions of this chapter first appeared online in 2019 in *ASAP/J* in an essay titled "'The Power of Memorializing People Not Memorialized': The Wake Work of the Shadowshaper Cypher Series and #RickyRenuncia." It was part of a cluster on Latinx speculative fictions edited by Renee Hudson with additional editorial assistance from Abram Foley. Thanks to Renee and Abram for their invaluable and insightful feedback and to *ASAP/J* for allowing me to reprint these portions here.

1. Ricardo Alberto Maldonado (@bookswimming), "Grand Central en NYC," Twitter post, 22 July 2019, https://twitter.com/bookswimming/status/1153448850872553473?s=20.
2. See also La Puerta, "Carta abierta: un llamado a la solidaridad," Facebook post, 7 July 2016, https://www.facebook.com/notes/la-puerta/carta-abierta-un-llamado-a-la-solidaridad/1756205121315928/.
3. All quotes of this poem are from Pedro Pietri, "Puerto Rican Obituary," in *Pedro Pietri: Selected Poetry* (2015). Copyright © 2015 by The Estate of Pedro Pietri. Reprinted with the permission of The Permissions Company, LLC, on behalf of City Lights Books.
4. Track 11 on Hurray for the Riff Raff's 2017 album *The Navigator*, ATO Records.
5. Though the published text reads "latino souls," Pietri says "latin souls" in the sampled audio recording.

6. Though "el barrio" literally means the neighborhood, in the Nuyorican context it has historically denoted East Harlem, also often referred to as Spanish Harlem.
7. Hurray for the Riff Raff, "Pa'lante," YouTube video, 8:34, 21 May 2018, https://www.youtube.com/watch?v=LilVDjLaZSE.

References

Associated Press. 2019. "Puerto Rico CFO and state secretary resign over profanity-laced chat." *CBS News*. 13 July, https://www.cbsnews.com/news/puerto-rico-cfo-and-state-secretary-resign-over-profanity-laced-chat-today-2019-07-13/.

Benyshek, Denita. 2020. "Our Time of Coronavirus and Black Lives Matter: Loss, Grief, Trauma, Resilience, and Healing Change." *Coreopsis: A Journal of Myth & Theater* 8(2): 109–31.

Bonilla, Yarimar. 2020. "The Coloniality of Disaster: Race, Empire, and the Temporal Logics of Emergency in Puerto Rico, USA." *Political Geography* 78.

Edes, Alyssa. 2017. "Ibeyi on Spirituality and Joy In 'Ash.'" NPR *Morning Edition*. 4 October, https://www.npr.org/2017/10/04/555046429/ibeyi-on-spirituality-and-joy-in-ash.

El Pueblo Se Levanta. 1971. Directed by Robert LaCavita. New York: Third World Newsreel.

Henríquez, Charo. 2019. "Puerto Rico Protesters Got Creative: Dancing, Singing, Diving . . ." *The New York Times*. 24 July, https://www.nytimes.com/2019/07/24/us/puerto-rico-governor-ricky-renuncia.html.

Hernández, Arelis R., and Laurie McGinley. 2018. "Harvard Study Estimates Thousands Died in Puerto Rico Because of Hurricane Maria." *Washington Post*. 29 May, https://www.washingtonpost.com/national/harvard-study-estimates-thousands-died-in-puerto-rico-due-to-hurricane-maria/2018/05/29/1a82503a-6070-11e8-a4a4-c070ef53f315_story.html.

Hurray for the Riff Raff. 2016. "Pa'lante." Track 11 on *The Navigator*. ATO Records.

Ibeyi. 2016. "Deathless." Featuring Kamasi Washington. Track 3 on *Ash*, XL.

Jackson, Jhoni. 2019. "'Pa'lante' Director Kristian Mercado Explains His Powerful Love Letter to Puerto Rican Resilience." *Remezcla*. 19 April, https://remezcla.com/features/film/palante-director-kristian-mercado-interview-sxsw/.

Llenín Figueroa, Beatriz. 2019. "From Puerto Rico: The Maroons Are Deathless, We Are Deathless." *The Abusable Past*. 20 July, https://www.radicalhistoryreview.org/abusablepast/from-puerto-rico-the-maroons-are-deathless-we-are-deathless/.

Luis, William. 1997. *Dance between Two Cultures: Latino Caribbean Literature Written in the United States*. Nashville, TN: Vanderbilt University Press.

Newman, Andy. 2018. "Hurricane Maria Casts Shadow Over Puerto Rican Parade." *The New York Times*. 10 June, https://www.nytimes.com/2018/06/10/nyregion/hurricane-maria-puerto-rican-parade.html.

Noel, Urayoán. 2014. *In Visible Movement: Nuyorican Poetry from the Sixties to Slam*. Iowa City, IA: University of Iowa Press.

Pietri, Pedro. 2015. *Pedro Pietri: Selected Poetry*, ed. Juan Flores and Pedro López-Adorno. San Francisco: City Lights Books.

Roy, Sanjoy. 2020. "How the Electric Slide Became the Black Lives Matter Protest Dance." *The Guardian*. 11 June, https://www.theguardian.com/stage/2020/jun/11/how-the-electric-slide-became-the-black-lives-matter-protest-dance.

Sharpe, Christina. 2016. *In the Wake: On Blackness and Being*. Durham, NC: Duke University Press.

Valentín Ortiz, Luis J., and Carla Minet. 2019. "Las 889 páginas de Telegram entre Rosselló Nevares y sus allegados." *Centro de Periodismo Investigativo*. 13 July, https://periodismoinvestigativo.com/2019/07/las-889-paginas-de-telegram-entre-rossello-nevares-y-sus-allegados/.

Younes, Nadia. 2017. "Rising from the Ashes: Ibeyi Interview." *The Skinny*. 24 October, https://www.theskinny.co.uk/music/interviews/rising-from-the-ashes-ibeyi-interview.

CHAPTER 7

Art and Politics Facing Disaster in the Caribbean
Defining a New Cultural Diplomacy

VANESSA SELK

Lwa Goudou is the name that terrified millions of people during the Haitian earthquake on 12 January 2010. Shaking the earth from beneath with its crab-like hands, unleashing the terse but terrifying guttural sound of soil and debris ("goudougoudougoudou . . . "), the folkloric character Lwa Goudou has been haunting the imagination of Haitians for centuries. It is represented as a giant subterranean creature, a cross between man and fish, in Edouard Duval-Carrié's painting, commissioned by the Winthrop-King Institute for French and Francophone Studies in 2020, commemorating the tragic event. Memory, folklore, and traditions nourish Duval-Carrié's artistic practice, which showcases the rich and varied history and culture of the Caribbean on the international contemporary art scene. Lwa Goudou is also that Black, resilient, sometimes unconscious force that has been carrying the colonial pressure for too long and episodically needs to explode to shake existing structures and reassert its autonomy.

The need to express political discontent to a colonizing power is exacerbated in situations of disaster, such as earthquakes or hurricanes. Disasters can be defined as natural or human hazards impacting the environment or habitat of people by disrupting their daily lives through the breakdown of essential functions of society (Campbell 2016). In situations without environmental or human implication, "there is no disaster regardless of the actual occurrence of a hazardous event (e.g., an extremely violent and large tornado occurs in a totally uninhabited area of the country)" (Selves n.d.). Therefore, considering the impact on human lives and property, "all disasters are political." Two examples illustrate disaster politics and the attempts to reaffirm political autonomy in the Caribbean. First, the "disaster diplomacy," initiated by the US when offering disaster relief to Cuba after the

Figure 7.1. *Lwa Goudou*, 2020, mixed media on paper in artist frame, 52x52 inches. © Edouard Duval-Carrié.

passage of Hurricane Michelle in November 2001, appeared like a reassessment of the US's "usual enemies," which seemed less harmful after the 9/11 terrorist attack (Kelman 2001). But Cuba, refusing to rely on American assistance, made a counteroffer calling for the normalization of trade relations—turned down by the US—and eventually asked for assistance from Venezuela and Russia. A second example is the need for self-organization and civil solidarity in Puerto Rico after Hurricane Maria in 2017. Artist-led initiatives such as Beta-Local coordinated relief efforts as a direct response to the difficult recovery of the island, already worsened by Puerto Rico's ongoing economic crisis and colonial status. To keep more Puerto Rican artists from fleeing to the mainland, Beta-Local developed specific programs to generate a critical dialogue with the international art scene, and to address Puerto Rico's efforts to achieve material self-sufficiency and challenge the disaster narrative in the US media (Dawn Lyle 2018).

However, cultural considerations are more often neglected in situations of emergency. Political authorities are expected to have one priority: security, so as to ensure the safety of the population. The activation of security protocols and safety measures does not only concern government forces within their own borders, it also implies diplomatic services in a foreign country that collaborate with local authorities, neighboring countries, or international allies to ensure their citizens are safe. A comic drawing in a study led by Michael D. Selves shows different roles and needs in terms of reconstruction after a hurricane: carpenters, bakers, plumbers, doctors... and finally, the politician, whose presence might be perceived here as counterproductive ("we don't need more wind"), but who is expected to intervene at some point (2003: 77). Though the list might not be exhaustive, the absence of one professional category is not surprising—indeed, it is revealing of conventional disaster management theories. These are the creatives or cultural practitioners. Culture can be divided in this context into two components (Kulatunga 2010): first, material culture consisting of physical or tangible creations that members of society produce, use, acquire, or share, and which includes arts, crafts, and historic buildings (UNESCO 2003); and second, nonmaterial culture, including abstract, intangible creations shaping a society, such as beliefs, values, language, norms, political systems, and family patterns. Visual and performing arts can be considered as a segment of the material culture, contributing however to a larger intangible culture.

On an international level, cultural and political systems can meet through cultural diplomacy, defined as crossborder "actions [that] are based on and utilize the exchange of ideas, values, traditions and other aspects of culture or identity, whether to strengthen relationships ... [or] promote national interests" (Institute for Cultural Diplomacy 2022). Cultural Diplomacy is therefore a constituting tool of *soft power*, conceptualized by Joseph Nye (1990) as a noncoercive capacity to influence other nations' decisions, in contrast with *hard power*, which means ordering actions or using force. The three pillars of this noncoercive power—political values, foreign policy, and culture (Nye 2004)—precisely meet in cultural diplomacy through a set of cultural assets used in a foreign country, such as language and education, protection of cultural heritage, exports of a film industry, and the organization of an artistic performance or show abroad. Implemented through bilateral (from country to country) or multilateral (among several countries within a regional or international organization) channels, cultural diplomacy can reflect three types of intentions: realistic, when the goal is to defend a national, private, or collective interest; idealistic, if the objective is merely to enhance cooperation to equally enrich both sides; or colonial/postcolonial, if the actions represent a form of continued cultural or political domination.

In either situation—realistic, idealistic or colonial/postcolonial—cultural diplomacy is being challenged. First, through the diversity of new actors: practiced by the public sector, the private sector, or civil society, cultural diplomacy is not the monopoly of the state anymore, contrary to hard power attributes such as police or military forces, which are supposed to remain in the hands of a functioning government. Second, it is questioned in its supposedly noncoercive nature. In fact, the use of certain cultural tools, language, or representations can be experienced as violence or domination by a population. Third, the long-term crisis of the cultural sector due to shrinking government subsidies is enhanced not only by a pandemic and global lockdown but also by "the global movement for social justice, forcing cultural institutions to assume greater accountability for the historical exclusion of underrepresented communities" (Flores 2020). This global movement is particularly affected by sanitary and environmental disasters, which accelerate the claims to decolonize cultural practices.

But these challenges also represent a windfall for cultural diplomacy, a chance to reinvent itself and develop new tools to better cope with a permanent crisis situation. As disasters keep coming back in a Sisyphean mode, as hurricanes become more regular and stronger because of global warming (Freeman 2013), or as they keep progressing in a silently threatening mode (e.g., sea level rise), long-term material and nonmaterial assets of the cultural sector can play an increasing role in lasting disaster prevention and management. This chapter therefore will examine how culture can become a political priority during a catastrophe, and how art can be a matter of emergency, by analyzing the potential role of cultural diplomacy in various disasters. After exploring the situations where cultural diplomacy interacts with disaster politics, this paper will focus on specific case studies of disasters in the Caribbean, first by presenting some examples of multilateral cultural action, then by showing how artists, through their visual, audiovisual, or poetic language, can adopt a posture that has similarities with a diplomatic approach. Artists convey a message related to a sociopolitical concern or country, and they try to foster change or influence the way we act and think.

When Culture Meets Emergency: How Cultural Diplomacy Evolves from Soft Power to Hard Power.

Culture as a Healing Tool in the Aftermath of a Disaster

Culture is an element for the survival of communities after catastrophes and has been widely acknowledged as playing a constructive role in the immediate aftermath of a disaster (Kulatunga 2010). In terms of healing and recovery, culture can help overcome psychopathologies, mental health issues, trauma, or posttraumatic stress disorders resulting from natural disasters such as earthquakes, volcanic eruptions, and hurricanes. It is a precondition for any recovery: "An understanding of cultural values and factors is the basic first step in understanding what the patient is going through" (Bhugra and Bhui 2018: 110). Recognizing the victim's "cultural baggage," such as ethnic background, cultural environment, dietary habits, family pattern, or religion, so as to identify the sources of distress, can illuminate the pathways toward healing or more efficient treatment. For health professionals, such recognition also implies becoming aware of one's own cultural background and social biases that may be perceived as hostile or as a barrier to the patient's opening up.

Trauma can be generated by the loss of cultural pillars that do include neighborhood and housing but also artistic goods or habits, such as seeing the same artwork in a street for years, as it has become part of one's visual imaginary and artistic culture, or going to a museum. Meeting with the Haitian artistic community after the 12 January earthquake, journalist Bill Brubaker (2010) commented on the impact on the artistic scene of the destruction of Haiti's cultural landscape, already vulnerable and rare. The earthquake reduced to rubble the biblical murals of the Holy Trinity Cathedral, painted by several Haitian artists in the early 1950s; destroyed or damaged thousands of paintings and sculptures belonging to museums, galleries, collectors' homes, or ministries; cracked the Haitian Art Museum at College St. Pierre; and crumbled the renowned Centre d'Art, which gave birth to Haiti's primitive art movement. The violent and sudden disappearance of such significant artistic landscape causes deep grief that needs to be acknowledged and healed like any other loss.

From a public policy point of view, recognition of loss can be communicated through commemorative practices—official speeches, dedicated monuments or statues, ceremonies, celebrations, and holidays—that can be implemented through national policies or cultural diplomacy. Ten years after the 2010 earthquake, the United Nations (UN) decided to commemorate the tragic event with a memorial sculpture titled *A Breath*, created by Italian artist Davide Dormino in 2011 with pieces of rubble from the Christopher Hotel in Port-au-Prince, and finally installed at the UN Headquarters in New York in January 2020. The breath evokes the instant before the earth started shaking, showing a stack of sheet metal fallen to the ground, and naming the 102 international UN employees who lost their lives. In this case, the memorial serves an internal memorial goal rather than expressing direct empathy with Haiti. Selecting an Italian artist rather than a Haitian raises further questions about the decision process within the UN.

From an individual point of view, the healing process can be triggered by expressing loss through artistic survival reflexes. "My future paintings will be inspired by this terrible tragedy," admitted Haitian artist Préfète Duffaut (Brubaker 2010). For local art professionals such as gallery owners Nader Jr. and Toni Monnin, the imagination of Haitian artists can be stimulated through disasters, as they are "continuing to create, sell and survive through crisis after crisis" (Brubaker 2010). Inspired by Franketienne's constructive thought on catastrophes—"Great changes and metamorphoses," Franketienne's observed, "often happen in dark, chaotic, and painful phases"—Martin Munro studied the personal testimonies and creative productions of several authors after the seismic disaster. He raised questions about the temporary and enduring effects of disaster on political, social, and cultural structures by analyzing the roles of artists and writers in particular (Munro 2014: 1). As a matter of fact, language is part of the cultural framework that has to be taken into account when supporting the survivors. The choice of language in the healing process is not neutral, specifically in a postcolonial context. Combined with medical or technical language, language brings to the surface other types of trauma (Bhugra and Bhui 2018). In a similar way, Haitian author Edwidge Danticat (2017) examines the power of language and words when facing the ambiguity of death. On the one hand, death is an exceptional event "that surpasses all existing words and deed"; on the other hand, it is trivial and happening "all the time." She wonders how to find the right tone when narrating death, whether authors should use humor, cold dissociation, or spill their hearts: "How do we write about them without sounding overindulgent, self-righteous, self-piteous, melodramatic, sentimental, or a combination of some or all of the above?" (50.) The response lies in the horror of disaster itself, which constitutes "a basis upon which to create a new language" (55.) And while building a new language through tragedy, people learn how to speak to the dead, to say goodbye and move on: "Hundreds of people ... kept vigil near a pile of rubble and spoke to their trapped loved ones as they slipped away" (48.) Danticat concludes that art and language are the only way out, writing that "poems, essays, memoirs, stories, and novels can help fill depth gaps in a way that numbers and statistics can't" (49.)

Culture as a Matter of Security

Cultural property and heritage have been identified early on as objects of necessary protection by security forces in specific contexts, such as armed conflict or war. In 1954, the Hague Convention for the Protection of Cultural Property in the Event of Armed Conflict, recognizing "that cultural property has suffered grave damage during recent armed conflicts" and that it represents "damage to the cultural heritage of all mankind," called on countries to anticipate possible armed conflict and to prepare "for the safeguarding of cultural property situated within their own territory." In the 1970s, the protection of cultural property and heritage was extended to the prohibition and prevention of illicit trafficking of cultural property (UNESCO 1970) and to the protection of the world's natural heritage (UNESCO 1972).

But the shift to incorporating culture as a security matter during disaster happened only forty years later. In 2015, the United Nations Educational, Scientific, and Cultural Organization (UNESCO) adopted a strategy for the reinforcement of the organization's actions for the protection of culture and the promotion of cultural pluralism in the event of armed conflict. In that year, UNESCO notably established the Heritage Emergency Fund to enable the organization to quickly respond to crises resulting not only from armed conflicts but also disasters. The fund aims to help states incorporate the protection of culture into humanitarian action, security strategies, and peace-building processes through targeted financed actions. What is particularly notable is that such support includes not only movable and immovable material culture but also intangible cultural heritage, cultural services, and underwater cultural heritage.

Two years later, two other diplomatic steps were taken to further incorporate culture into security matters. For the first time, the Security Council of the United Nations, which controls the hard power at the UN by taking decisions about military interventions or peacekeeping missions (versus the soft power of the General Assembly representing all 193 states and able to adopt nonbinding resolutions), clearly recognized, by the adoption of historic Resolution 2347, the protection of cultural heritage as an issue for peace and security. "Defending cultural heritage is more than a cultural issue, it is a security imperative, inseparable from that of defending human lives," declared former UNESCO director-general Irina Bokova in March 2017 following adoption of the resolution (Lofstead 2015). In November of the same year, the General Conference of UNESCO decided to strengthen its strategy on culture in emergencies through the adoption of an addendum concerning disasters caused by natural and human-induced hazards. UNESCO pursued two objectives: on the one hand, strengthening countries' ability to prevent, mitigate, and recover the loss of cultural heritage and diversity resulting from disasters; and, on the other hand, incorporating cultural considerations into disaster risk reduction and humanitarian actions by engaging with experts from the security sector. This addendum fills a critical policy gap as culture can finally be treated by disaster experts as a priority. But why did it take the international community so long to join culture and security in this way? It seems that the diplomatic community needed another disaster as trigger. In fact, over the course of 2017, a high number of disasters, in particular devastating hurricanes in the Caribbean, highlighted the vulnerability and exposure of culture and the insufficient preparedness of the international community to cope with catastrophes (UNESCO 2017). However, in 2018, less than 8 percent of available funds were actually allocated to Caribbean states (compared to 35 percent to Arab states), 57 percent of which was implemented in conflict situations and 43 percent in disaster situations. So, there is still a long way before culture in the Caribbean actually becomes a diplomatic priority. In the next section, however, specific case studies will stress when cultural diplomacy deployed concrete tools to cope with disasters in the Caribbean, before exploring how Caribbean artists have dealt with the same situation through artistic and political language.

Case Studies: Multilateral Cultural Diplomacy versus Individual Artistic Diplomacy

Earthquake

How to Revive Language When Nothing Is Left

Context: Haiti, 12 January 2010, earthquake of 7.0 magnitude lasting less than thirty seconds; 3 million people are affected, 250,000 lives lost, 300,000 people injured, and 1.5 million persons displaced internally.

On a multilateral level, about $1.5 million was dedicated by UNESCO for the restoration of more than one hundred historic buildings (including the Palace of Sans Souci), the creation of cultural jobs, and technical missions to protect cultural artifacts. UNESCO also decided to help with the organization of the famous Jacmel Carnival, recognizing that performing and live arts may be as important as cultural historical preservation by playing a vital role in the recovery of the Haitian people. On a civil society level, public organizations and cultural institutions such as the Smithsonian Institution launched their own effort to help restore damaged Haitian cultural property, establishing a "cultural recovery center" at the former headquarters of the UN Development Program near Port-au-Prince" (Brubaker 2010).

Guy Régis Junior (1974, Haiti), Playwright and Director

"Listen to the silence, the fear[,] . . . it's ready to extinguish us again," says a surviving woman in Guy Régis Junior's theater play *And the Whole*

Art and Politics Facing Disaster • 143

Figure 7.2. Guy Régis Junior, *And the Whole World Quakes: The Great Collapse.* Reading at the Martin Segal Theater, directed by Kaneza Schaal, Caribbean Theater Project ACT, December 2019. © V. Selk.

Figure 7.3. *Tout Saintes*, 2010, acrylic canvas, 36x24 inches. © Michael Elliott.

World Quakes: The Great Collapse. The playwright narrates the trauma provoked not only by the catastrophe itself but also by the foreign humanitarian actors intervening in the wake of the disaster. Two women, sitting on a hill overhanging a city in rubble, reflect on the permanent "coming and going of catastrophes and people" while observing the general agitation of the international community in their devastated homeland: "Missionaries deciding what works or not[,] . . . they are analyzing our situation[,] . . . the specialists," as Haiti has been labeled an international "priority zone." "Let them accomplish their mission on our back," replies the older woman, resigned and exhausted, "until they find another place to help" (Régis Junior 2019). But the younger woman refuses to accept the situation, trying to escape and hope for a better future while chasing shooting stars in the dark sky. The coming and going of missionaries, diplomats, NGO representative, and so forth is experienced as a second violence after the disaster, like the return to an infantile state of assistance after having proudly fought for independence. The grief added to the humiliation of sovereignty makes the situation unbearable: at the end of the play, the two women have to hurt themselves physically to forget the psychological pain and find a way out. *Omnia mors aequat*, death equalizes everything, is the inscription carried by an angel on the reading setting directed by Kaneza Schaal. Through this play, which was presented at the Avignon Theater Festival in France in 2011, and read for the first time in English at the Martin Segal Theater in New York eight years later,[1] Guy Régis Junior, speaking from his home country, acts like a cultural diplomat. He expresses a national feeling of sadness and anger by addressing the international community, not to ask for help or support but to explain. His play turns into a political declaration.

Michael Elliott (1979, Jamaica), Visual Artist

"Even the earth seems to be angry, perhaps angry at what we have done to it and each other," reflects Michael Elliott, commenting on the "catastrophic events involving flooding, hurricanes, earthquakes and volcanic eruptions." In his hyperrealist painting *Tout Saintes*, produced in the aftermath of the Haitian earthquake in a gesture of empathic grief, Michael Elliott adopts a public posture with the goal to convey a message, not only of solidarity but of political power. For Michael Elliott describes his productions as "socio-political paintings," depicting the harsh daily realities of Caribbean societies, distressed not only by environmental disasters and colonial structures but also social inequalities and gun violence. "I believe it is my calling to use my art as a tool to raise social awareness and I would like to see Jamaican art as a tool for change that makes our society think and do better," Elliott writes. His paintings and photography are the mirror of a permanent disaster society, a permanent state of emergency: dead insects, sick birds, soldiers in war, drowning migrants, fossilized hands, human robots or explosives—each work functions as a memento mori reminding us of our fragile existence and the need to fight for it every day. Life is a battlefield when it's not already too late. The skull that depicts Haiti appears like a double signature of helplessness and acceptance. But it is not the end stage yet; four years later, Elliott painted another human skull that is decomposed and disaggregated, acting as a metaphor for humankind, which after death still continues its self-destruction. But rather than a scream of despair, the universality of Elliott's work, encompassing a large variety of human-provoked disasters, is actually an example of empathy and solidarity across the globe. What is true for Jamaica may happen somewhere else in the world. We are all in the same sinking ship, whether we are migrating to a new home or in a comfort zone enjoying royal tea. Jamaica is not worse off than the United Kingdom: *Omnia mors aequat*, everyone is equal before death.

Hurricane

Starting from Scratch: How to Break Sisyphean Cycles.

Context: Category 5 Hurricanes Irma and Maria, September 2017. Respectively, 134 and 3,059 deaths. Costs estimated at $77.16 billion (Irma) and $91.61 billion (Maria).

In 2017, Dominica was the first country to benefit from the new cultural postdisaster needs assessment of the United Nations' emergency strategy associated with disasters. The Heritage Emergency Fund helped restore Morne Trois Pitons National Park and other historical sites and cultural industries. On a regional level, joint efforts were taken in Sint Maarten[2] and in Suriname[3] in the following years to establish and reinforce a regional network of experts in Caribbean cultural heritage protection. In May 2019, the Understanding Risk Caribbean conference took place in Barbados,[4] gathering five hundred disaster experts, government representatives, and international organizations to share best practices on disaster risk reduction in the region, including through art. The organizers partnered with cultural institutions such as the Barbados Museum and Historical Society to explain the risks related to natural hazards through video installations, as well as with cultural spaces such as Fresh Milk Barbados to conceive creative projects scattered across the University of the West Indies Cave Hill Campus. A large sculpture, titled *Risky Timelines*,[5] to which several Barbadian artists contributed—Alanis Forde, Anna Gibson, Kia Redman, Akilah Watts, Kraig Yearwood—presented the timeline of natural disasters happening in thirty-three Caribbean countries from 1900 to 2019, and included data on the human and economic impact of each catastrophe ("Fresh Milk" 2019). The active participation of cultural practitioners in a conference dedicated to risk management represents a symbolic step in fostering the role of art in disaster reduction, and it enabled creatives to play their part as cultural diplomats to communicate with policymakers through a visual language.

Deborah Jack (1970, Netherlands/Sint Maarten), Multimedia Artist

For multimedia artist Deborah Jack, hurricanes act as a repeating catalyst for the historical trauma on Caribbean bodies and identities. Her installation *Shore*, presented at the Big Orbit Gallery in Buffalo, New York, in 2005, includes visual references to Atlantic hurricanes, serving as a natural memorial for bodies lost at sea during the Middle Passage. The use of water and salt in her work echoes the bodies made of water and hints at the corrosion affecting Caribbean borders. In her 2018 video *Drawn by Water:*

146 • Vanessa Selk

Figure 7.4. *Imagined Spaces*, photography series, 2002. © Deborah Jack.

(Sea) Drawings in (3) Acts, Act One: Wait (Weight) on the Water, Deborah Jack further reflects on the aftermath of hurricanes through more implicit messages. She mixes the sounds of a Methodist church, representing a colonial structure, and a song about a lighthouse, suggesting both the emotion and fear of a drowning seaman and the hope and necessary vigilance in the dark when the storm is close. By representing the shorelines as shared, temporary, and abstract borders between Sint Maarten and the Netherlands, Jack highlights a shared vulnerability (the risk of disappearing) and questions the political domination of the Netherlands over its overseas territory. Her reflection on border porosity also concerns the shared frontier with the French territory Saint Martin in the north of the island. The freedom of movement, permitted for both sides of the island since the 1648 Treaty of Concordia between the Dutch and the French, was suddenly interrupted in 2017, so as to keep French citizens from fleeing to the Dutch side. Three years later, during the coronavirus pandemic, the situation was inverted by Dutch protest against the closure of the French border that aimed at blocking Americans from importing the virus through the Dutch territory (Steel 2020). The colonial

Figure 7.5. *La Perla After Maria*, 23 minutes, Puerto Rico/Venezuela/Germany, 2018, film still. © Clari del Pilar Lewis.

situation contributes to turning disasters into a political debate about class, culture, and race. It further becomes a diplomatic competition between two territories in the race for reconstruction, hence exacerbating existing tensions (Semple 2019). Through her installations and videos presented in various countries, Deborah Jack participates in this political debate about race and culture, between Sint Maarten, Saint Martin, the Netherlands, and France, and her visual language becomes a diplomatic tool of discrete but firm criticism.

Clari del Pilar Lewis (1971?, Venezuela/Puerto Rico), Filmmaker and Storyteller

In Puerto Rico, too, the colonial power relation with the United States seems to have exacerbated the impact of Hurricane Maria and the feeling of abandonment by the Puerto Rican population. "No Civil Defense forces came here, nor the National Guard . . . nobody." "No federal assistance. . . . If we don't take care of this, nobody else will." These are the words of the residents of the small coastal town La Perla in Puerto Rico, which was deeply affected by the hurricane in 2017, who narrate their loss in the short documentary *La Perla After Maria* (2018), directed by Clari del Pilar Lewis. But after observing that perceived lack of support, the director decides to insist on the social links built during reconstruction, leading to a certain rebirth of the community through solidarity. "We had forgotten many of our old customs, spending time with our neighbors. . . . It was a good experience," says a resident. "The community is more united now," observes another local. Narrating the construction of new social ties is key to asserting identity and self-confidence in a colonial relation. In fact, it is essential to show "Puerto Ricans speaking for themselves after months of receiving news about their condition from the outside," writes Marianne Ramirez Aponte, director of the Museum of Contemporary Art in Puerto, in her introduction to the exhibition *Entredichos* (2017). Whether through a film or an exhibition, the artists express the need in the wake of the disaster to "respond with (their) own voice to the greater level of international interest" in the socioeconomic situation of the island, and to the many visions of its complex political relationship with the United States (Acker 2018). By presenting the film in various festivals in the US, including in collaboration with French diplomatic services, del Pilar Lewis takes part in this sociopolitical construction as an audiovisual diplomat standing for the island, despite the recurring Sisyphean violence of disasters: "There is always a rebirth, and a start" (2018).

Flooding and Sea Level Rise

Going through Cycles: Gender Powers Strengthened by Waters

Context: Floods reaching a half meter above high-tide levels may become common throughout the Caribbean within the next several decades. More than six hundred thousand people occupy land less than a half meter above the tides. Guyana accounts for more than one-third of these totals; Haiti, Suriname, the Bahamas and the Dominican Republic are the other countries most likely to be affected. The Bahamas faces the greatest proportional threat: 32 percent of its land and 25 percent of its population are below a half meter above high tide.

Several regional conferences were organized to raise awareness about sea level rise in the Caribbean while giving art and culture progressively more attention. In 1992, CARICOM (Caribbean Community) adopted a regional development project with the United Nations Development Program and UNESCO for cultural conservation in the region. In 2015, the climate change conference "Voices and Imagination United for Climate Justice" established an informal group of Caribbean artists and journalists to raise awareness on climate change, with the participation of popular Caribbean musicians such as David Michael Rudder, Alison Hinds, and Gamal Doyle. In 2017, the Jamaican ministry responsible for culture and UNESCO organized a symposium on "Caribbean World Heritage and Climate Change," gathering participants from Caribbean countries owning world heritage properties, such as Antigua and Barbuda, Cuba, Curaçao,

Figure 7.6. Guy Gabon, *#AllClimateRefugees*, installation, mixed media, part of *Echos imprévus* at the Memorial ACTe, Guadeloupe, 2017. © Bernard Boucard.

Dominica, Haiti, Jamaica, and others. The operational outcomes and impacts of such conferences on the effective preservation of cultural heritage are, however, extremely hard to evaluate when they do not include immediate target numbers and actions.

Guy Gabon (1967, Guadeloupe/Guadeloupe),
Visual Artist, Ecodesigner, and Director

Guy Gabon defines herself as an "artivist" whose social and artistic practice is strongly driven by environmental concerns. Her installation *#AllClimateRefugees*, using mostly textiles such as jeans, initially created as part of the exhibition *Echos imprévus* at the Memorial ACTe in Guadeloupe,[6] reflects a wait-and-see attitude toward a water level that keeps rising before condemning communities to emigrate. In response to the annual climate conference, the artivist calls on cultural and educational actors to adopt a new approach towards ecological disasters. "Far from discourse and numbers," Guy Gabon's militant posture is intended to "reveal the importance of the threat that climate change represents for our island territories." The installation also includes a participatory creative process that involves the public, from the collection of (usually) used jeans, to sewing workshops to create the mannequins. A performance on the installation was added in 2018 through a collaboration with choreographers Myriam Soulanges and Anne Myer in a project titled *Yué#Sorority*. The project wove the links of solidarity through sisterhood, both between the three female artists and with local female communities who participated in the creation of the artwork and the final performance. The social link between all women appears as a resilient weapon, empowering them through their collectivity and presenting new paths to face the imminent threat of sea level rise. Traveling through the French Caribbean, the project gained an international and diplomatic dimension when it was presented at the waterfront of the Pérez Art Museum in Miami, Florida, with the support of the French Embassy. The message from this refugee installation is parlous: we are coming, we are already here. Similar to Deborah Jack, Gabon's installation exposes the shared ecological vulnerabilities between Guadeloupe and Miami.

Dominique Hunter (1987, Guyana), Visual Artist

During a residency at the Vermont Studio Center in January 2017, Dominique Hunter unexpectedly revived the memory of the 1927 flood of Vermont's Gihon River. Before embarking on her trip to the US, Dominique Hunter decided to pack only one material: sanitary napkin wrappers, which she had been collecting obsessively for years without knowing how and when to use them. After her arrival, upon learning about the 1927 Vermont flood, the idea for *And Then It Came* began to germinate. She started imagining the potential overwhelming force of the swelling Gihon River pouring through her window and flooding furniture and artwork in her studio. The installation *And Then It Came* suggests not only the duality of water but also speaks to the ideas of feminine strength and resilience as the artist incorporates specific resistant materials to hold the piece together (e.g., painter's tape, aluminum foil tape). As an extension to this piece, Dominique Hunter produced another installation with a suggestive title, *Downpour*, developed in collaboration with Trinidadian artist Shanice Smith. The use of recycled material in each version, augmenting the integrity of the wrappers by the use of tape, hints towards a gradual process of disintegration, both of the artwork and of the human body affected by time, disasters, and erosion. Finally, the threatening context of sea level rise in her own country, Guyana, where two hundred thousand people live on land less than a half meter above the tides (Strauss and Kulp 2018), may have played a conscious or unconscious role in the conceptualization of the work by the artist. The concept of "black Anthropocene," referred to by geographer Kathryn Youssef as the "absorbent qualities of black and brown bodies to take up the body burdens of exposures to toxicities and to buffer the violence of the earth" (Youssef cited in Loichot 2020: 4), may offer an interpretation of the embodiment by the artist of the Vermont

Figure 7.7. Dominique Hunter, *And Then It Came*, 2017, installation, mixed media. © Mark Reamy.

flood through her own menstrual cycle. Finally, the vision of water flooding the artist's studio raises the international question of urgent political action to adopt conservation measures to protect Caribbean artwork facing sea level rise in the region.

Oceanic Pollution

Awakening Apnea: Dive or Die

Context: About 80 percent of marine pollution comes from land-based activities. Nitrogen loads to oceans tripled from preindustrial times due to fertilizer and wastewater. More than 8 million tons of plastic enter the oceans each year, killing up to one million sea birds and a hundred thousand sea mammals, marine turtles and fish each year, causing a threat to the $57 billion of coastal tourism revenue (Sayed and Kemper 2019).

The United Nations proclaimed a Decade of Ocean Science for Sustainable Development, to be held from 2021 to 2030. The goal is to provide a framework in which ocean science can support and guide countries' actions to sustainably manage oceans. In its report on marine pollution in the Caribbean (Michele Diez et al. 2019), the World Bank makes twelve recommendations to take action on a national, regional, and international level. Beyond improved data collection and adopting new legislation, the strongest calls for action consist in reinforcing the control policies to reduce litter on coasts, the discharge of untreated sewage, and the use of industrial nutrients. It will take decades, however, for states to first adopt any necessary legislation and then enforce it through control mechanisms or sanctions. On a "glocal" level, the US Department of State launched the Greening Diplomacy Initiative in 2015, including an International Coastal Cleanup Day on 9 September, organized in partnership with Ocean Conservancy and with foreign diplomatic services (consulates and embassies) to help protect oceans and beaches and stem the tide of pollution. It is unusual and quite significant to see how various diplomats from all levels gather on American beaches on that day to actively collect litter.

Morel Doucet (1990, Haiti/USA), Multimedia Artist and Educator

Morel Doucet has been working over the last few years on the process of climate gentrification in South Florida. Highlighting how communities who don't have the means to escape natural disasters caused by climate change will be most affected by displacement, he notably stresses the precariousness of Black and immigrant lives. Studying the endangered ecosystems of coral reef colonies, green seas, and marine life, Doucet draws a parallel with the toxic exposure of Black bodies facing unstable environmental safety in Florida. Doucet makes a localized analysis about the ecologic volatility around Lake Okeechobee in Florida, where the unregulated use of sewage and other nutrients on farm fields leads to an increase of phosphorus in the lake's once fresh water, contaminating surrounding residents. Urban planning and dikes have further forced the lake to overflow into the Everglades and then into coastal saltwater, mixing with nitrogen and resulting in the proliferation of a new fluorescent blue-green alga (Staletovich 2016). Like intoxicated plant life and bleached coral reefs dying from an increase in water temperature, the survival of Black immigrant and low-income neighborhoods is compromised by the daily aggressions of the American way of life, reminding them of "the impossibility of attaining whiteness." Cast into delicate white porcelain by Doucet, the bodies, corals, and plants become one, calcified into decorative art objects, acting as a metaphor for the communities who have no seats at social banquets and whose future remains "a constant battle." He writes:

> WHEN A CORAL REEF DIES,
> Its body becomes a hollow memory
> Of its distanced past, the outer shell
> Is calcified, frozen in time. (Doucet 2018)

Art and Politics Facing Disaster • 153

Figure 7.8. *White Noise*, 2019, Ceramic sculpture. © Morel Doucet.

White Noise: When Moonlight Whisper & Raindrop Scream in Silence is the title of Doucet's ceramic series, which loudly proclaims the racial inequalities experienced by those communities and their cacophonous suffering. Each artwork serves as a megaphone speaking to Florida's politicians, lawmakers, and governmental agencies, who have failed to implement protective environmental measures.

Louisa Marajo (1987, Martinique/France), Visual Artist

It was during a yearly visit to Martinique in 2018 that Louisa Marajo started observing the proliferation of the sargassum algae on coasts. Due to polluting agricultural activities in the Americas and the rise of water temperature, these algae, naturally thriving between the coasts of West Africa and the Sargasso Sea not far from Florida, have drifted further toward the Caribbean and the Gulf of Mexico, where they started accumulating. The stagnation and decomposition in masses of the sargassum produces a toxic gas that causes severe health impacts, such as memory loss and respiratory diseases, and also kills marine life, leading to a social and economic disaster through the closing of schools and beaches. Marajo writes:

154 • Vanessa Selk

Figure 7.9. *Dismantling Sargasse Sea 3*, photography. © Louisa Marajo.

> Sargassum waves,
> Which carry away and restore
> The deepening of our pollution,
> Nauseating landscapes, Re-Mixed
> To Nature. (Doucet 2018)

However, in spite of the shared challenge posed to political authorities and scientists, Louisa Marajo does not blame the authorities or focus on the victims. Instead, she decides to confront the sargassum, embracing its proliferation and integrating its images into her work. In fact, the "nauseating landscapes" form a new state of coastal chaos, in which she sees an opportunity resulting from the unknown.

> From the ruins of the Sargassum shines beauty,
> From the unexpected,
> From the resilience.

Unlike the Sisyphean gesture of absurd repetition and endless despair, she reads meaning in each reconstruction effort. She cites German modernist artist Kurt Schwitters as her inspiration. "With a purpose," Schwitters believed, "we can destroy a world and, through the knowledge of possibilities, build a world with debris." This debris is part of her chaotic visual partition, in which paintings and photography are falling apart in conversation, forming a new orderly chaos, her sculptures. Her posture was more poetically personal until she decided to share her vision about the sargassum chaos with others, such as the Tout-Monde Art Foundation in 2019. Her initial idea was soon expanded beyond the Francophone territories, including West Africa, Latin America, and the USA, and beyond the art scene, by including scientists, researchers, anthropologists, and even business leaders who had been working on scientific solutions regarding the sargassum. The project tipped over into another dimension, becoming more international and political because it aims at raising awareness worldwide. The COVID-19 pandemic came to further shake the project, adding new surprises. The virus arrived as "a disaster after the disaster," increasing the vulnerabilities of the populations whose lungs had already been harmed by the hydrogen sulfide released by the sargassum. The sanitary emergency becomes even more obvious. The project quickly grew into a new hybrid form, ranging from art videos and film to an artist residency and exhibition, and announcing the advent of a new hybrid creature, *Homo sargassum*.

Conclusion

If these short case studies often seem to highlight how a disaster can be exacerbated in a colonial or postcolonial context, the relation to a continental power can also appear to be efficient as it can mobilize material, human effort, and financial means from an area that has not been affected by the disaster. Solidarity is easier and faster to execute when one of the parties is not in need.

But whether or not these power relations have a destructive or constructive impact on disasters, the fact that Caribbean artists raise their voices through different sociopolitical practices and artistic forms—film, poems, theater plays, installations, paintings, sculptures—to call for international attention to various disaster situations seems to announce a new generation of "cultural agents." They serve as inspiring examples to build a new cultural diplomacy, or rather a "cultural agency" (Summer 2006), in the region and beyond. Three lessons can be drawn from these cases for institutional cultural diplomatic players.

First, it is time to decolonize cultural diplomacy by accepting internal criticism of existing forms of domination and of the coercive force or hard power of certain cultural attributes. Such deconstruction goes through a stronger recruitment of underrepresented communities and a reorientation of existing programs toward more diversity. Second, the rarity of Caribbean art, considering sea level rise and recurring disasters, needs to be incorporated into art conservation programs, beyond existing cultural heritage preservation efforts. Expertise in water- or salt-damaged art and in evaluating the value of Caribbean art in a context of rarity and risk needs to be developed. Climate refugee artists who have lost their studio or material must be further supported through dedicated disaster residencies and long-term disaster-relief programs for artists, whereas galleries, museums, and collectors should be encouraged to acquire Caribbean art before it is too late. Last, cultural specificities of local communities or indigenous populations need to be more incorporated in diplomatic decision-making, taking into account specific languages, traditions, and memories.

Finally, after examining how cultural diplomacy can be implemented as a political priority in natural disaster situations in the Caribbean, one should now ask what the situation would look like in a disaster resulting from a human-made hazard, such as a military or biological attack. Is the Caribbean prepared to face such disaster? The question challenges the basis of the ruling security dogma in the countries possessing territories in the Caribbean—the United States, France, the United Kingdom, and the Netherlands, all founding members of the North Atlantic Treaty Organization. In fact, article 5 of the treaty ensures, in case of an armed attack against one of the members, that all parties will assist the attacked member, including through the use of force. However, article 6 explicitly excludes from this protection all the territories belonging to the countries situated south of the Tropic of Cancer, which means the Caribbean (NATO 1949). One can therefore wonder if Caribbean populations do represent a concern for NATO countries in terms of security for any potential human-provoked disasters affecting the region. Maybe it is time to rethink the Caribbean as a priority, at last.

Vanessa Selk is an independent political arts advisor, cultural programmer, entrepreneur, and former diplomat. She is the executive and artistic director of Snowblack, a company offering creative consulting, projects, and storytelling in the arts and media industry. In this role, she has been working as an art consultant for digital companies now expanding into the arts, such as chaching.nyc. She is also the founder and artistic director of the Tout-Monde Art Foundation, a nonprofit organization dedicated to supporting emerging Caribbean artists committed to sociopolitical work related to ecology, education, and equality. Prior to this role, she served as the cultural attaché/head of the Florida Office of the Cultural Services of the French Embassy in the US, where she was responsible for the French cultural programming in visual and performing arts and education in Florida and the Caribbean. In this role, she launched and directed the Tout-

Monde Festival dedicated to Caribbean contemporary arts, which has now become a regular year-round program. She would like to especially thank Dr. Tatiana Flores.

Notes

1. The reading of the play at the Martin Segal Theater, directed by Kaneza Schaal of the Caribbean Theater Project ACT (Cultural Services of the French Embassy in the US), took place in December 2019.
2. These efforts were organized in 2018 by the Caribbean branch of the International Council on Archives (CARBICA), with the support of the UNESCO's Heritage Emergency Fund.
3. CARBICA XI Conference Archives at Risk: Preserving Caribbean Heritage (2019)
4. The conference was organized by the World Bank and the Global Facility for Disaster Reduction and Recovery (GFDRR), in partnership with the Caribbean Disaster Emergency Management Agency (CDEMA) and financed by the European Union
5. Conceived by World Bank representative Janot Mendler de Suarez and by artist in residence Pablo Suarez.
6. *Echos imprévus/Turning tide* at the Memorial ACTe in Guadeloupe, held from November 2016 to April 2017, was curated by Johanna Auguiac and Tumelo Mosaka.

References

Acker, Jennifer. 2018. "After the Storm: On the Artist's Life in Puerto Rico, Post-Maria." *Literary Hub*, 13 September. Accessed 12/7/2022: https://lithub.com/after-the-storm-on-the-artists-life-in-puerto-rico-post-maria/

Bhugra, Dinesh and Bhui, Kamaldeep. 2018. *Textbook of Cultural Psychiatry*. Cambridge University Press.

Brubaker, Bill, 2010. "Haiti, the Art of Resilience." *The Smithsonian Magazine* (September). Accessed 12/7/2022: https://www.smithsonianmag.com/travel/in-haiti-the-art-of-resilience-53519464/

Campbell, Nnenia. 2016. "Looking through Different Filters: Culture and Bureaucracy in the Aftermath of Disaster." *Natural Hazards Center* website. 4 July, https://hazards.colorado.edu/article/looking-through-different-filters-culture-and-bureaucracy-in-the-aftermath-of-disaster.

Danticat, Edwidge. 2017. *The Art of Death: Writing the Final Story*. Minneapolis, MN: Graywolf Press.

Dawn Lyle, Erica. 2018. "After Hurricane Maria, Meet the Artists Challenging the US Media's Disaster Narrative." *Frieze City Report*. 11 April.

Del Pilar Lewis, Clari. 2018. *La Perla After Maria*. Film, 23 minutes. Puerto Rico/Venezuela/Germany.

Doucet, Morel. 2018. Poem, No title, Extract. Accessed 7 December 2022, https://www.instagram.com/p/CejNkYYFDrm/.

Flores, Tatiana. 2020. "Introduction to Newsletter n1." *Tout-Monde Art Foundation* (November).

Freeman, Andrew. 2013. "Hurricanes Likely to Get Stronger & More Frequent: Study." *Climate Central*. 8 July.
"Fresh Milk Contributes to the 2019 Understanding Risk Caribbean Conference." 2019. Fresh Milk Barbados website. 14 June, https://freshmilkbarbados.com/tag/understanding-risk/.
Hague Convention for the Protection of Cultural Property on the Event of Armed Conflict, Article 3: Safeguarding of Cultural Property. 1954. Accessed 7 December 2022, https://en.unesco.org/sites/default/files/1954_Convention_EN_2020.pdf.
Institute for Cultural Diplomacy. 2022. "What is Cultural Diplomacy?" Accessed 23 October, https://www.culturaldiplomacy.org/index.php?en_culturaldiplomacy.
Jack, Deborah. 2018. *Drawn by Water: (Sea)Drawings in (3) Acts, Act One: Wait(Weight) on the Water*. Digital Video, 6:01. Accessed 7 December 2022, https://vimeo.com/357098495.
Kelman, Ilan. 2001. "Hurricane Diplomacy for Cuba." *Disaster Diplomacy*. Accessed 7 December 2022, https://www.ilankelman.org/articles1/ddwxsoc1.pdf.
Kulatunga, Udayangani. 2010. "Impact of Culture towards Disaster Risk Reduction." *International Journal of Strategic Property Management, School of the Built Environment* 14: 304–13.
Loichot, Valérie. 2020. *Water Graves, The Art of the Unritual in the Greater Caribbean*. Charlottesville: University of Virginia Press.
Lofstead, Becky. 2015. "Defending our Right to the Past". West Virginia University Magazine. Accessed 7 December 2022, https://magazine.wvu.edu/stories/2017/08/06/defending-our-right-to-the-past#:~:text=UNESCO%20Director%20General%20Irina%20Bokova,enough%20to%20defend%20violent%20extremism.
Marajo, Louisa. 2019. *The Awakening of the Sargassum*. Poem extract.
Michele Diez, Sylvia, Pawan Patil, John Morton, Diego J. Rodriguez, Alessandra Vanzella, David Robin, Thomas Maes, and Christopher Corbin. 2019. *Marine Pollution in the Caribbean: Not a Minute to Waste*. World Bank Group. 1 March.
Munro, Martin. 2014. *Writing on the Fault Line—Haitian Literature and the Earthquake of 2010*. Liverpool, UK: Liverpool University Press.
NATO (North Atlantic Treaty Organization). 1949. "The North Atlantic Treaty." Last updated 10 April 2019, https://www.nato.int/cps/en/natolive/official_texts_17120.htm.
Nye, Joseph. 1990. *Bound to Lead: The Changing Nature of American Power*. Cambridge: Cambridge University Press.
———. 2004. *Soft Power: The Means to Success in World Politics*. Paris, France: Hachette UK.
Régis Junior, Guy. 2019 [2011]. *And the Whole World Quakes (The Great Collapse): Chronicle of a Slaughter Foretold*, trans. Judith Miller. Accessed 7 December 2022, https://www.youtube.com/watch?v=uE_RnnaVY0E.
Selves, Michael D. 2003. "The Politics of Disaster: Principles for Local Emergency Managers and Elected Officials." Journal of the American Society of Professional Emergency Planners 10:77-82.
Semple, Kirk. 2019. "After a Caribbean Hurricane, the Battle Is Where, or Even Whether, to Rebuild." *The New York Times*, 7 October.
Staletovich, Jenny. 2016. "Lake Okeechobee: A Time Warp for Polluted Water." *Miami Herald*. 13 August, https://www.miamiherald.com/article95442427.html#storylink=cpy.

Steel, Jenny. 2020. "Protest at Saint Martin Border: 'You Are Basically Blocking Us from Living.'" *Caribbean Network*. 9 August.

Strauss, Benjamin, and Scott Kulp. 2018. "Sea-Level Rise Threats in the Caribbean: Data, Tools, Analysis for a More Resilient Future." Inter American Development Bank. Accessed 7 December 2022, https://sealevel.climatecentral.org/uploads/ssrf/Sea-level-rise-threats-in-the-Caribbean.pdf.

Summer, Doris. 2006. *Cultural Agency in the Americas*, Durham, NC: Duke University Press.

Tout-Monde Foundation. 2019/2020. "Homo Sargassum." https://www.tout-monde-foundation.org/project-page.

UNESCO Convention on the Means of Prohibiting and Preventing the Illicit Import, Export and Transfer of Ownership of Cultural Property. 1970. Accessed 7 December 2022, https://en.unesco.org/about-us/legal-affairs/convention-means-prohibiting-and-preventing-illicit-import-export-and.

UNESCO Convention Concerning the Protection of the World Cultural and Natural Heritage. 1972. Accessed 7 December 2022, https://whc.unesco.org/en/conventiontext/.

UNESCO Convention for the Safeguarding of the Intangible Cultural Heritage. 2003. Accessed 7 December 2022, http://www.unesco.org/ culture/ich/index.php.

UNESCO Strategy Reinforcing Protection of Culture and Heritage from Natural Disasters, UNESCO Communiqué, Addendum. 2017. Accessed 7 December 2022, https://icorp.icomos.org/index.php/2017/11/23/addendum-to-unesco-strategy-reinforces-protection-of-culture-and-heritage-from-natural-disasters/.

CHAPTER 8

Marvin Victor's *Corps mêlés* and the Writing of Disaster in Haiti

MARTIN MUNRO

What are the effects of a catastrophic earthquake on a society, its culture, and its politics? Which of these effects are temporary, and which endure? Are the various effects immediately discernible, or do they manifest themselves over time? What is the relationship between natural disasters and social change? What roles do artists, and writers in particular, have in witnessing, bearing testimony to, and gauging the effects of natural disasters? These are some of the fundamental questions raised by the Haitian earthquake of 12 January 2010, a uniquely destructive event in the recent history of cataclysmic disasters, in Haiti and the broader world.[1] Haitian literature since 2010 has played a primary role in recording, bearing testimony to, and engaging with the social and psychological effects of the disaster. While Haitian writing has arguably always had a social and political function, the sheer scale of the destruction caused by the earthquake posed an unprecedented challenge to authors, as well as to other artists. Although many authors initially expressed their feelings of helplessness and of the futility of their art, virtually all established and many new and original voices published works soon after the earthquake, some of whom wrote directly of the event, while others made no reference to it at all. There was and has been no single, unifying literary reaction to the earthquake; rather, there is a proliferation of works that share certain thematic preoccupations but which insist on the freedom to express those themes in original ways, thus making new and daring explorations of form a crucial part of the meaning of the event as it is processed through the workings of the individual text. If, as many authors initially said, art is useless in the face of catastrophe, that uselessness has a paradoxical value in that it can be used to liberate an author from the potentially restrictive expectation to act as a faithful chronicler of a social event. In many cases, this freedom, and this fundamental inutility, have formed the basis for stylistic innovations that are meaningful in themselves in that they suggest potential new modes of thinking and being that are some of the unexpected creative effects of the disaster. Therefore, far from treating recent Haitian writing as a straightforward extension of social reality, or as a simple *littérature de circonstance*, I would argue that daring literary invention—what Edwidge Danticat calls "dangerous creation"[2]—constitutes one of the most striking and important means of communicating the effects of such a disaster, and that close engagement with the creative imagination is one of the most privileged ways for the outsider in particular to begin to comprehend the experience of living in and through a time of catastrophe. In this chapter, I engage with a singular piece of writing: Marvin Victor's *Corps mêlés*, a quite brilliant first—and to date, only—novel that was hailed as one of the first "postearthquake novels," but which is rarely discussed by scholars and risks being forgotten, itself a kind of tragically neglected ruin.[3]

The "writing of disaster" seems an apposite term to apply to postearthquake literature from Haiti. The phrase recalls the title of Maurice Blanchot's 1980 work *L'Ecriture du désastre*, which has been used by certain critics to refer to Haitian literature, both before and after the earthquake.[4] The fragmented narrative style of many contemporary Haitian novels is often a sign of the disrupted memory of the traumatized individual and a disjointed means of communicating between the traumatizing past and the traumatized present. The trope of silence that one finds in many works is a further example of "the writing of disaster," which, in Blanchot's terms, is a "discourse [*parole*] of waiting, silent perhaps, but which does not discard silence, but makes silence a statement in itself, which says in silence the statement that is silence. For mortal silence is never silent" (1980: 98). For Blanchot, therefore, the "writing of disaster" is characterized essentially by paradox: it is a silence that is nonetheless a statement, and one can in some senses say more by remaining mute. Fragmented narratives are born out of human catastrophes for, as Blanchot says, "the need for fragmentation is related to disaster" (99). The narrative fragmentation that often characterizes the writing of disaster amounts in Blanchot's terms to "the putting into pieces (tearing apart) of that which has never existed before as a whole" (99). Many Haitian novels are structured in such a way, as a "putting into pieces" of fragmented personal and collective history, a tearing apart of a plenitude that never truly existed at all.

There is moreover to some extent a critical expectation that the "writing of disaster" should bear in formal terms the physical and stylistic marks of catastrophe: prose will be "fractured," "fragmented," or otherwise show signs of rupture and violence. Short fiction may be a genre particularly suited to or representative of this fractured style. The sharp blasts of narrative from many different voices in, for instance, the short story collection *Haiti Noir* are suggestive of the difficulty of conceptualizing longer fiction at such a short remove from the earthquake. Also, with such a collaborative volume, one senses that no one person can own the event or its memory, and that it is something to be shared and constructed collectively. Indeed, it could be said that the short fiction mode has been the dominant genre in recent and contemporary Haitian fiction. Lyonel Trouillot writes short novels that could be categorized as long novellas, while Dany Laferrière's books are made up of episodic, fragmented narratives, and Yanick Lahens and Edwidge Danticat are accomplished short story writers whose respective novels *La Couleur de l'aube* and *The Dew Breaker* are also constructed around short, self-contained chapters that draw on the modes of short fiction.

Given the critical expectation for fragmented style and the apparent aptness of shorter fiction to the "writing of disaster," one might have expected that the great novels of the earthquake, those written on an epic, expansive scale, would take time to compose, and that they may not begin to appear for years or decades to come.

Marvin Victor's *Corps mêlés* (2011) confounds these expectations in spectacular fashion. A long, dense, fluid piece of prose fiction, it writes of disaster in a style that bears little relation to the dominant modes in contemporary Haitian writing. The book's style seems to owe more to non-Haitian writers such as Édouard Glissant, Maryse Condé, Patrick Chamoiseau, Gabriel García Márquez, James Joyce, Marcel Proust, William Faulkner, and even, in the attention paid to detailed descriptions of objects, Honoré de Balzac, than to the established Haitian authors.[5] As one of the characters says, "the novel owes everything and nothing" to Balzac, a phrase that perhaps refers at once to the general history of the literary genre and to Victor's novel, which, like Balzac's works, is rich in descriptions of characters' possessions, clothing, and living conditions (2011: 120). Moreover, Victor's first-person narrative of a country girl's experiences in a rural community recalls Condé's *Traversée de la mangrove*, while the intimate portrait of a female character's episodic madness echoes to some extent Glissant's Mycéa figure. The representation of life in the urban slums recalls Chamoiseau's *Texaco*, while the elaborate style and the *conteuse*-type storytelling mode is closer to Martinican *Créolité* than to the shorter, clipped style of many contemporary Haitian authors. The elements of the family saga are reminiscent of Márquez, while there are also traces of the influence of the European and North American masters listed above. These and other influences are hinted at in the book through various mentions of authors' names and choices of character names: there is, for instance, a Father Condé; the narrator's family name is Fanon; at one point she turns down rue Roumain; another character is "in search of lost time" (235). These influences say much about the book's ambitious scope and sophisticated style, which, although new in a sense to Haitian writing, owe much to established modes in other traditions and create a feeling that the new in this case is conceived with at least one eye on tradition and an ear finely attuned to the rhythms of classical prose writing.

Published in the Gallimard Blanche collection, the novel joins a very select group of Caribbean works thus recognized by Paris's most prestigious literary imprint; and for this reason Victor finds himself in the company of figures such as Glissant, Jacques-Stephen Alexis, Marie Vieux Chauvet, Saint-John Perse, and René Depestre. That this is Victor's first novel makes the work all the more impressive and unexpected. The earthquake invites the use of metaphors of rupture and seismic shifts, and it did seem that at the time of publication Haitian writing had in Victor a remarkable, new, and original author, one who was born one might say from the disaster, and whose work marked a new and distinctive mode, written as it were from the other side of the fault line.

It is perhaps fitting then that the book opens with a birth, that of the narrator, in the coastal village of Baie-de-Henne. The birth, however, is also a kind of death in that the narrator's godmother describes to her an infernal scene in which she came into being "like others enter into hell" (13). The moment of birth is also connected with notions of sterility, as the mother is called a "mule" by others in the community, given the number of lovers she had had before falling pregnant (13). The narrator, moreover, does not seem to want to be born and was a child who "said no to life" (13), refusing to leave the mother's womb (15). The time she is born into is the mid-1960s, a period that is now seen by the narrator almost as an ancient epoch, in which the people of the community "lived like beasts"; back then, the women wore very few clothes and bathed naked in the sea and rivers, and they had still "an almost Eden-like immodesty" (14). It is in the sea that the narrator is finally born: her grandfather is "taken by an excess of trance or drunkenness" and insists that the mother be taken to the shore, for "only the sea could deliver that which it had started" (16). The land is implicitly sterile and unable to give new life, while the people's origins are related to the sea, particularly in the case of the godmother, who traces their origins to the seas off the African coastline, which explains for her "our hatred of the sea, that secular hatred that leads us all to turn our backs on its turbulent immensity, another way perhaps of letting ourselves be all the more consumed by it" (18).

Despite being born in the sea, the narrator says she is "dust, forever attached to the land" (20), and will return finally to dust (18). This attachment to the land seems to be born of her own experience in the village, rather than from the stories of her origins that her godmother passed on to her. The narrator is decidedly skeptical about the worth of such oral accounts of history, and she wonders, "what is a child whose story of birth has been changed and then erased" (20). The godmother is particularly culpable in this regard, in that she is "more used to malicious gossip and fables than to the true evocation of the heart's passions" (24). More broadly, the narrator is similarly ambivalent about the value of orally related proverbs and metaphors, which seemed to the storytellers "to administer a balm for everything," but in which she seems to see little worth (27). The narrator's sense of her being is also defined to a large extent by the words of her daughter, who sees her as "finished," old and worthless, even at the age of forty-five (25). Just as she asks what a child is whose story of birth has been altered, so she asks through her own narrative what is a woman whose life has been shaped by migration, poverty, the words of others, and now by the earthquake of 2010. The earthquake has taken the life of her daughter, who lies beneath the rubble of their home, and whose death the narrator seeks to announce through her narrative, a task that is deferred throughout the novel as her story oscillates between the past and the present, the one time period radically separated from and yet intimately connected to the other. Fascinatingly, too, the time of the earthquake is already referred to as a past time, "that period," she says, as if the event seems at once recent and to have occurred a long time previously (60). Time in this sense contracts and expands in her memory, as it seeks to record, process, and express the intense trauma that the earthquake has added to her already difficult relationship to the past.

The earthquake brings the death not only of her daughter but of the entire country: "The country is dead," she says on the doorstep of her childhood friend Simon Madère (33). Or rather, she "thinks" she said to him, thus introducing an element of doubt and self-questioning that will characterize her account of her meeting with Simon and her recollections of the past (33). Her memory is imperfect: having been struck in the head by a falling piece of concrete, she forgets already the whereabouts of her daughter's body and everything else, including time, while realizing "that it is time that forgets us, and not the other way round, devouring our flesh and our memory with a demonic hunger" (33). Death brings certainty and truth, while life is somehow false, an invented story. The dead, she says, are now "in truth, and I in falsehood" (33), while she later says that the survivors of the earthquake must feel as if they are dead, more so than the thousands of bodies being burned or thrown into communal graves (127). The state of mind she writes in is one of shock and trauma: she has fled from the scene of her daughter's death, at which she remained unexpectedly calm, her eyes "strangely dry," and fixed on the blood of her daughter mixing with the dust of the ruined home (34). She also loses her speech for several minutes, only to recover it with the feeling that she remembered everything, or at least, she says, "everything that a human being would decide to retell, arming oneself with the magical, the benefit of doubt [and] this gift of lying about others and oneself that I take from my village" (34). She therefore aligns herself to some extent with the storytellers of her village, while remaining mindful of the certain betrayal of truth that her story will involve. Her narration is something of a journey, marking out a paradoxical inner topography according to which she feels that despite her leaving the village thirty years previously, in a sense she has "never budged" (34). The "real journeys," she says, are "interior," undertaken in dreams in the hope, she feels, that her "phantoms" will cease to chase her (35). The earthquake has not so much killed these phantoms as made it impossible to find answers to the questions she poses herself about her past, her daughter, and her own mother. These replies are, she says, "forever buried beneath the ruins, lost, returned to their silence, to the impossibility of their formulation" (36).

Her daughter deceased, she turns to her childhood friend Simon, who came to Port-au-Prince three years after she did, at the end of the 1970s. She had seen him on a few occasions and heard pieces of information about him during that time: he was earning a good salary as a photographer but was still as fragile as he had always been, drinking and smoking as a balm for the difficulty he had in "grappling with life" (36). Simon is the only remaining link to her past, to the childhood they spent together in Baie-de-Henne. Almost instinctively, she seeks him out to "find him again," realizing however that "one never rediscovers neither others nor oneself" (44). As such, what she perhaps seeks to rediscover, or at least feel once again, is something of the phantom of their shared past, to sense the people they were and indeed the ghosts of themselves that they have become.

The narrator's dialogue with Simon is characterized by silences; indeed, the narration is closer to an interior monologue, in which Ursula records what she wanted or intended to say or what she thought she said to Simon. "I have lost my daughter," she wanted to say to him first, but all she reveals is her identity (49). Her firm intention, she says, is to bring to Simon a "truth" that no longer belongs to her alone, so much so that she would have wanted to present herself naked at his doorstep, the truth being, she says, not only a sense of reality or that which is supposed to be true but the form of a naked woman (50). She brings in her large fake-leather Hermès handbag items that relate to their past together: a Billie Holiday record and a Canon camera that she stole for Simon from Father

Condé more than thirty years previously. As she crosses the threshold into Simon's apartment, which was built to resist earthquakes, she feels strangely liberated from her previous status as a woman alone suffering endless bad luck (52). "I was already," she says, "that woman who no longer asks for anything from life," or from the rich, whose charity, she now realizes, amounted to giving "junk" to the poor, "killing us more than doing us any good" (59). In a sense, she enters into another trajectory, one that began in the same place as hers, but which has brought a degree of professional success and material comfort to Simon. His photography has given him access to this lifestyle, but it is an ambiguous profession, and one senses that Simon's alcoholism may be related to his work, which involves tracking down "at once the ugly and beautiful poverty of people and things" in Haiti and collaborating with foreign newspapers, to which he sends images of the "eternal natural disasters, hunger riots, coups d'état" and other calamities (55). He therefore lives in a sense from the suffering of others, an activity that pays him well, but which he seems compelled to pay for too, with his own health and well-being. His certain recklessness with his health, and perhaps his ambivalence about continuing to exist in the way he does, is suggested in the way he does not leave his apartment on the evening of the earthquake to join his neighbors in the courtyard below. Apparently unconcerned about aftershocks, both Simon and Ursula remain in the building, "risking my life," she says, and "condemned" to spend the night together (57).

The night becomes a kind of wake, during which the two sit behind their "wall of silence," which to Ursula is "worth more than words" (57). They communicate through gestures and sharing cigarettes and rum—Ursula says she lights a cigarette as others light a candle "to invoke the gods, the saints, and the angels" (145), and that the rum is "the only connection" between Simon and her (184). The two are literally lost for words as their trajectories cross once again, and they can no longer ignore each other or deny the other's existence, as they had done for the thirty years when they had lived in the city, seeing each other intermittently but never acknowledging that they knew each other. This refusal to acknowledge each other amounts, for Ursula, to a "betrayal," as much of time (their shared childhood), and place (their native village), as of each other (62).

There is a real tension in the novel between the need for silence between Ursula and Simon and her equally pressing desire to bear testimony. Time and again her attempts to testify are frustrated or else murmured in a half voice that speaks to no one but herself. It seems more important to her to tell the story of her past than face the reality of the postearthquake present. She suggests as much when she writes of how her memory is "in shreds," with the "heavy shadows of the past triumphing over those of the present" (67). Indeed, it seems like she cannot engage fully with the present without telling her story and that of her family and the village of Baie-de-Hennes. Her own story, or at least her own torment, seems to relate to her mother, a troubled figure who had, the narrator recalls, a deep sadness, a "soft gravity" in her eyes, the result of a long psychological illness that led to her abandoning her daughter for long periods (70). The mother was later found dead, her body naked, covered with ants and maggots, her hair cut off by a broken bottle (87). A key scene recalled by the narrator relates a discussion between the mother and grandmother, where the former says she is leaving once again and that she has already "one foot in the grave" (71). As she does at other moments of crisis, Ursula immediately runs away from the scene, and crucially, this time she becomes aware for the first time of her breasts, which impede her running and which "hurt" her (71). This is significant as her awareness of her own changing body comes at the moment when her mother announces a further traumatizing departure. The narrator seems to relate motherhood and indeed womanhood to trauma and death, and to view her changing body as a foreshadowing of her own fated suffering as a mother. She sees in her body the sexual traumas of her mother, who quite publicly took her own virginity with a pestle at the age of thirty-three, the "age of Christ," the mother said to her father (73). As the narrator writes, the mother's departure and intimation of her death marked the beginning of Ursula's own "Way of the Cross" (71).

The intricate mixing of sex, love, bodies, and death is further suggested in Ursula's recollection of her first kiss with Simon, which took place at the graveside of one of their friends called Fanfan, and which led to them making love by the grave, before they had interred the body (75). Pushed by Ursula to duel with Fanfan, Simon had killed their friend with a punch that led Fanfan to fall and crack his head on a stone, which was, Ursula notes, to take the place of her heart for a long time (76). The lovemaking is recalled by Ursula as an "obscene and execrable" act that even as it was happening brought visions to her of their souls being consumed "by the fires of hell" (75). She says that she buried her love for Simon with the body of Fanfan, whose ghost visits her at night (75). The episode marked the end of her love for Simon, but it also created a bond between them, "a pact sealed forever in the silence and blood of that child" (76). The pact connects their destinies, however long they have been apart, and specifically links them bodily to the corpse of their friend: their own stories are entangled in a morbid relationship of sex, death, and silence, as their bodies were by the graveside.

This instance of connected, entangled bodies, or *corps mêlés*, seems to create in her an enduring revulsion about physical intimacy: "The idea of bodies entangled with each other has always horrified me," she says (183). It also functions in the novel and in their lives as a form of original sin, and this key aspect of the novel constitutes a further link to some of the classics of Caribbean and broader American fiction, namely those of Faulkner, Glissant, and Condé. Glissant, for example, sees in Faulkner's work a preoccupation with the origin of Southern society, which is damned or cursed by history, by the existence at its origin of a crime, or original sin. Glissant offers three possible sources of this original sin: miscegenation, the theft of the land, and slavery. These three crimes are related and intertwined in that miscegenation is the product of slavery—"the damnation and miscegenation born of the rape of slavery" (1999: 88)—while the appropriation of the land—a "perversion" according to Glissant—is "tied (secretly and nebulously) to injustice and oppression—namely, slavery" (122).

The theme of ancestral crime also appears in Glissant's own work, notably *Le Quatrième siècle*, an epic historical work that bears relation in terms of style and scope to Victor's *Corps mêlés*. In Glissant's novel, the Béluse family is descended from an African who betrayed his friend by selling him into slavery. This is the ancestral crime and original sin that haunts *Le Quatrième siècle*, and which complicates the question of lineage, all the more so because the crime is secret and known only to the storyteller, much like in *Corps mêlés*. Victor's novel can also be compared in this regard to Condé's *Traversée de la mangrove*, most directly in both works' presentation of closed, restrictive communities that are fixed to a large extent by their own histories, which limit individuals' capacity for self-determination and create a sense that each generation is condemned to live out the consequences of previous crimes and wrongdoings. In Condé's novel, the theme of ancestral crime is explored most extensively through the figure of Sancher, the enigmatic outsider and descendant of a male lineage that is characterized by premature deaths, which are ultimately related to a massacre of slaves committed by one of his ancestors. Sancher comes to Guadeloupe, where he has come to die, leaving no heirs, and thus to "terminer une race maudite" (put an end to a cursed race) (1990: 87). In Victor's novel, the murder of Fanfan and the morbid lovemaking of Ursula and Simon function in similar ways, as moments that in a sense fix the essence of the characters, condemning them to live forever the consequences of their crimes and their associated guilt. The sense of history and lineage as phenomena charged with inherited guilt is compounded in the case of Ursula, who refers regularly to the damnation of the Fanon family, "the cursed blood" that each generation shares (80). She feels she is born to suffer, "condemned to be naked," given her ample Fanon family chest: "A girl naked," as she says, "standing before her cross, on which she was ready to climb, to be ridiculed, crowned with thorns, and sprinkled with vinegar and spit" (157). In a more muted sense, one also feels that Simon is living not his own discrete existence, but a continuation of that of his father, who abandoned his family to live in the Dominican Republic, leaving Simon fatherless and apparently condemned to live a rootless, isolated life.

In Ursula's case, the family curse is more of a matrilineal affair, in that she seems to inherit from her mother a degree of emotional instability that she in turn appears to pass on to her daughter. Ursula foresees that her death will be like her mother's: she will die, she says, in "the most absolute deprivation, and in shame," as her mother did (110). The two women share the same great disappointment, expressed by the mother as being unable to "follow a trajectory, to move forward, instead of turning round on myself, like a top" (110). As an adolescent, Ursula "was not so different" from her own daughter (109). Ursula recalls wanting to bring her mother's life to an end (110), while she mutters to Simon, "My daughter killed me, devoured me" (103). She recounts to herself her daughter's decision to leave school early to become a prostitute on a night they had no food. Ursula recalls how her daughter burst into laughter then into tears just before she left to go to the streets, and how she took back to her a meal, which Ursula refused to eat, imagining that her first client had left in it "a few drops of his sperm" (104). The daughter's body is also a kind of family legacy in that she has inherited her mother's chest, "the well-known chest of the Fanon girls" (103). Bodies in this sense are not so much discrete objects or indices of one's individuality; rather, they are, as in the book's title, entangled, passed from one generation to the next as a curse, literally embodying the unfinished past.

The earthquake brings to the fore another of Ursula's family legacies: her madness. "I am going mad," she was going to say to Simon as an aftershock shakes her glass of rum and the apocalyptic scene of the devastated city unfolds outside the apartment window (107). The view stretches to the Champ de Mars, where thousands of survivors, among the corpses that litter the streets, wait desperately for water, food, and aid, and further to the destroyed National Palace, whose lawns are transformed into an "immense slum," the sight of which leads some to swear they would fight to the death to save the remains of the palace, and of the republic (107–8). The death that the earthquake brings now permeates life. As Ursula notes, "That death which, surged forth from the depths of the earth, had however already impregnated all of us." As she drinks the rum, she tries not to forget the event, but to "go along with it" (faire avec), which, she says, amount to the same thing (108). Both forgetting and accepting the event seem to lead to madness; folly appears in this sense to be the only possible psychological reaction to the earthquake.

Madness is also something she shares with Simon. "We were running," she says to him, "toward nothing, and madness caught up with us, no doubt the folly of running toward something" (111). One of their favorite activities as adolescents was to run endlessly until they were completely out of breath. When they did this, Ursula felt she was no longer in control of herself and had "fallen resolutely out of time" (114). They run in this sense to escape themselves and the lives they seem destined to live, carrying the curses of the past. They are drawn to traveling figures, notably Father Condé, the village priest who has traveled the world, and who introduces them to Billie Holiday, to reading, and less felicitously, to alcohol. Ursula finds in Condé's library worlds beyond those presented in the closed nationalist stories that she had been taught at school. After discovering the priest's library, she "no longer wanted to hear anything about our heroes murdered while in power or on the battlefield" (119). Likewise, reading the Bible only gave her migraines (148). National education, she says, did nothing but "return us to our ignorance, to our secular metaphors and proverbs—thus even closer to beasts" (129). Simon promised to go with her to Port-au-Prince, but he failed to appear at their meeting place. She was left alone, thus creating the rupture in their relationship, which she revisits on the night of the earthquake, time having only exacerbated her sense of betrayal (130).

Ursula associates her native village with ignorance, gossip, entrapment, and the various curses that limit her ability to define herself in terms other than those dictated by the closed traditions of Baie-de-Henne. On arrival in the city, she is surprised how quickly she forgets the village and finds the city streets to be "beautiful and numerous, irrigated by a dense, anarchic circulation" (134). When she hears of the death in the earthquake of a prominent feminist, Ursula recalls having heard a speech in which the woman spoke of leaving the city to live by the sea, and of the broader importance of a general "return to the sources, to the land" (146). As Ursula remarks, the feminist's speech contradicted her own movement and aspirations: "I wanted only to leave it, that land . . . for Miami, Florida, or anywhere else" (146). The city, however, reveals to her its own complex social relations when she arrives in the convent arranged and paid for by Father Condé, who was desperate for her to leave the village after a local scandal broke over Ursula staying overnight at his residence. The convent is a "golden prison," where the city's elite throws its "black sheep," girls involved in arson attacks, incestuous relationships, murder, and other episodes that brought shame to their "excellent families" (147). Tellingly, too, Ursula is unable to create any bond with her fellow boarder Adeline, who comes from a similar background, but with whom Ursula can only communicate in silence, and in "the complicity of glances and looks" (147). Their common social class offers no grounds for mutual support or empathy, for as Ursula states, "It is well known, the poor don't like the poor" (147).

Unable to form any friendships with either the middle-class or the poor girls, Ursula finds a kind of empathy and freedom in the city itself. "I was not made for the country," she says, "but for the capital, however crooked and stinking it is" (233). It is in the city that she finds a degree of liberty and the anonymity in which she can to some extent begin to define herself in relation to a space with which she has had no pre-existing relationship. Slipping out of the convent in the afternoons, she "surveys Port-au-Prince," discovering its dimensions, its tree-lined streets, especially rue Pavée, which she calls "my street," and where she feels "not in the least bit lost" (223). She walks the streets slowly, like a flaneur, visiting the seafront, the cathedral, and rubbing shoulders with the beggars, visitors, and pilgrims to the basilica, destroyed later by the earthquake (152). She finds beauty in the "frenetic fauna" (155) of the city, in the sun hanging over the bay down the Grand Rue, and says to herself, "How happy I am, how happy I am!" (153). The city by night takes on a different allure: on the street corners Dominican prostitutes vie for trade with the local women, while on the rue Ennery she mingles with the crowd surrounding a group of troubadours playing "soft and melancholic" music (159). However vivid these recollections of her earliest encounters are, her memory of many of these places is irreversibly changed by the earthquake, and she says she will from now see them only in dreams and "forever in ruins" (153).

The city is in another way unforgiving and consumes her identity. She is "tearing" herself, she says, from her own being and from others, so that she wants to invent "a different life," one that is worthwhile, in which she would wear a flower behind her ear, like in the picture of Billie Holiday on her album cover, her head thrown back, laughing freely and showing her white teeth (167). She becomes instead a "phantom" in the city, which "offers no gifts," and which she feels is ready to let her die as it did its own hungry children, "claiming without mercy its dues in flesh and blood" (168). The question of "phantom" identity is related obliquely in the novel to photography, through Simon's profession and the camera she stole from Father Condé and brings to Simon on the night of the earthquake. Her daughter is another phantom, in life and in death. Ursula recalls the student demonstrations of December 2003, a key moment in the eventual downfall of Jean-Bertrand Aristide, and how her daughter asked her to be taken to see the students. Ursula imagines that her daughter had a "secret plan": to be hit by a stray bullet, die as a martyr, and be photographed by Simon. Ursula pictures her daughter lying in blood, agonizing, but then "moved by a sudden desire for eternity, representation, *photogénie*"— the latter being the meeting of the photographic subject with the camera and the photographer, a process that defamiliarizes the subject, revealing in this case qualities and perhaps an identity that are imperceptible or unattainable in reality. In other words, the daughter, Ursula imagines, no doubt thinking of herself, seeks in death and photography an existence transformed and fixed to "make her beautiful, here and now[,] . . . claiming her own instant of fiction of herself, forever desiring that after her death the photos would speak of her, of her legend[,] . . . for time passes, dies" (173). The photograph would allow a transformation denied to her in life; it would be false in a sense (a "fiction," Ursula says), but would also express a truth in fixing in time an image of what she aspired to be—both memorable and remembered, an unforgotten phantom (173).

Ursula is herself a "revenant" (212), a ghost that returns through her narrative as much to her own previous self as to Simon, who remains in more or less complete silence, which seems to her like a "challenge," a way of forgetting oneself, and above all "a refusal of any and all act of memory" (192). Their encounter leads her to reflect that "to remember is perhaps a waste of time and the most horrible crime that one commits on oneself and on others" (200). Indeed, the past seems bound to play itself out again in commuted form in this new encounter, notably in a scene in which Simon takes a shower and she, for all her horror of entangled bodies, touches and masturbates him, "making him ashamed." (204). Following the act, she runs to the kitchen to light a cigarette, "ashamed in my own turn." From the window she watches a woman dying under a tree, says to herself that she cannot "fall any lower," and wishes for a new tremor to come to "swallow her up to the deepest parts of the earth" (204). The act, carried out with so many bodies lying unburied on the streets outside, seems to recall their lovemaking by the dead body of their friend Fanfan, and suggests something of the way that they are condemned to re-enact their past, particularly its most shameful and irredeemable moments. The past is not something to be saved or changed but a phenomenon that repeats itself almost inevitably, reminding them of the impossibility of redemption.

Their bodies carry the memory of their pasts and contain historical narratives that link them to the past and to each other. Ursula suggests this when she talks of her daughter and how her lips were like Ursula's own, her laughter was that of Ursula's aunt, her eyes were her grandfather's, and her hips were like Ursula's mother. Thus, she says, her daughter was nothing but "the sum of the multiple echoes of my dead, the result of a sort of puzzle of blood and flesh, and had nothing that belonged to her alone" (242). Identity is not in this sense a discrete, singular phenomenon but a complex amalgam of different parts, inherited from the past and communicated principally through the body. Any individual is a kind of revenant, a repetition of lives that have come before. In a sense, this is why Ursula finds it difficult to mourn her daughter, or even to announce her death. What is distinctive about and what is the value of a single death, she seems to wonder, when there are so many other people lying dead, their stories and bodies entangled and apparently undifferentiated?

In fact, Ursula begins to mourn only when she realizes the limits of this entangled, bodily identity. This happens during a fundraising event held in the courtyard below the apartment two days after the earthquake, when Ursula sees a woman that she at first thinks resembles her and her daughter. However, when she dances with the woman, she realizes that she was mistaken. "You don't look like her at all, in fact," she says to the woman (246). Following this realization, Ursula leaves the dance and begins to run away from the scene, tears of sorrow finally filling her eyes, as she reveals through the narrative that Simon was the father of her daughter. It is only when she becomes aware of her daughter's individuality that she can in a sense extricate her body from the hundreds of thousands of others and begin to mourn her as an individual. Her great fear—and no doubt that of many other grieving Haitians—was that her daughter's body be taken away in a truck to a communal grave, "mixing your body with the others," she says to her daughter (247). As Ursula runs away from the apartment, she imagines her daughter already returned to Baie-de-Henne, and herself running to join her there, to the house of the daughter's grandparents, who had only known the daughter through photographs. As Ursula imagines herself reunited with her daughter at the family home, she begins to tell her the story of her family through the photographs that hang there. The first photograph is of the grandparents posing formally in their garden; the second is of the aunt, Ursula's godmother, "majestic" in her Sunday clothing; the third is of Ursula's mother, barefoot on a beach, smiling, but in her eyes the "mark of sadness" that was always there; the fourth and final photograph is of Ursula herself, looking "very unassuming," against a background of green plants with, in her arms, her daughter, naked, she says, like a winged cherub in an Italian Renaissance painting (248–49). Ursula's final wish as she addresses and names her daughter, Marie-Carmen Fanon, for the first time in the novel, is that the wings grow not for her, who remains "in falsehood," but for the daughter, who is "in truth," and whom Ursula will now only see, she says, "in the fires of a January sunset," in the echo of that day of which the novel stands as a remarkable, lyrical, and finally beautiful testimony (249).

Martin Munro is Winthrop-King Professor of French and Francophone studies at Florida State University. His publications include *Writing on the Fault Line: Haitian Literature and the Earthquake of 2010* (Liverpool, 2014);

Tropical Apocalypse: Haiti and the Caribbean End Times (Virginia, 2015); and *Listening to the Caribbean: Sounds of Slavery, Revolt, and Race* (Liverpool, 2022).

Notes

1. Among the effects of the Haitian earthquake listed by the Disasters Emergency Committee are that 3.5 million people were affected by the quake, there were 220,000 estimated deaths, 300,000 were injured, and nearly 300,000 homes were destroyed or badly damaged. See "2010 Haiti Earthquake Facts and Figures," Disasters Emergency Committee website, accessed 9 November 2021, http://www.dec.org.uk/haiti-earthquake-facts-and-figures.
2. See *Create Dangerously: The Immigrant Artist at Work*. Princeton, NJ: Princeton University Press, 2010.
3. According to the website *Ile en île*, Marvin Victor "lives and works between England, Belgium, and France, whither he withdrew in a movement of voluntary exile in 2014." "Marvin Victor," accessed 8 November 2021, https://ile-en-ile.org/victor_marvin/. Gallimard offered him a contract for three or four novels, but Victor reported feeling unsupported by the publisher and has yet to produce a second novel. There is a short interview with him on the website *Small Axe*, published on 8 February 2012, http://smallaxe.net/sxsalon/interviews/marvin-victor. This article compares Victor to the Haitian poet Villard Denis-Davertige, both of whom were apparently hampered by early successes. See also Wébert N. Charles, "Le dernier Prix Goncourt n'est peut-être pas une bonne nouvelle pour Mohamed Mbougar Sarr," 8 November 2021, https://ayibopost.com/le-dernier-prix-goncourt-nest-peut-etre-pas-une-bonne-nouvelle-pour-mohamed-mbougar-sarr/.
4. See, for example, Martin Munro, *Exile and Post-1946 Haitian Literature: Alexis, Depestre, Ollivier, Laferrière, Danticat* (Liverpool, UK: Liverpool University Press, 2007), 244–48; and Deborah Jenson, "The Writing of Disaster in Haiti: Signifying Cataclysm from Slave Revolution to Earthquake," in Martin Munro (ed.), *Haiti Rising: Haitian History, Culture and the Earthquake of 2010* (Liverpool, UK: Liverpool University Press, 2010): 104–5. This chapter largely adapts analysis from my book, *Writing on the Fault Line: Haitian Literature and the Earthquake of 2010* (Liverpool, UK: Liverpool University Press, 2014).
5. There are also echoes in Victor's novel of Marie Vieux-Chauvet's *Fonds des nègres* in the issue of migration between the city and the hinterland, and in the tensions inherent to such movements.

References

Blanchot, Maurice. 1980. *L'Écriture du désastre*. Paris: Gallimard.
Glissant, Édouard. 1964. *Le Quatrième siècle*. Paris: Gallimard.
———. 1999. *Faulkner, Mississippi*, trans. Barbara B. Lewis and Thomas C. Spear. Chicago: University of Chicago Press.
Condé, Maryse. 1990. *Traversée de la mangrove*. Paris: Mercure de France.
Victor, Marvin. 2011. *Corps mêlés*. Paris: Gallimard.

CHAPTER 9

Beyond Malediction and Prophecy
Melovivi or the Trap

ALEX LENOBLE

Haitian playwright Franketienne's *Melovivi or the Trap* may be the only work considered to belong to the Haitian earthquake literary archive to have been written *before* the event. The anecdote, reported by Dany Laferrière (2011) in *Tout bouge autour de moi*, by Rodney Saint-Éloi, and by the author himself is well known: on the very day of the cataclysm, on 12 January 2010, minutes before the earth started to shake, Franketienne was rehearsing *Melovivi*. Stunned, disoriented, and struck by the enormity of the coincidence, his first reaction was to vow to never perform this play, almost as if he thought he was partly responsible for the catastrophe and that his words somehow materialized in the devastated Haitian landscape: "[The play] speaks of a Port-au-Prince that cracks, is torn apart. Franketienne makes the seism with his words. His prophetic solo. . . . Franketienne feels that he will never be able to perform this play that brings bad luck" (Laferrière 2011: 46-47).[1] After the cataclysm, he assumed and proclaimed the prophetic status of his writing, stating in an interview:

> I had a form of vision, a feeling of premonition that my land and the planet were threatened. And it turned out to be true when a voice spoke to me. . . . A voice spoke to me at dawn, at this time when the sun comes to earth full of energy, bearer of antennas that allow you to catch the passing messages, the inner music to which we do not pay attention, connected to the music of the world, of the cosmos. This voice told me: your country is threatened as well as the planet. Write a play about global ecology. (Guy 2010).

In this chapter, I question the characterization of the play as prophetic and examine how it led to the play's *misreception*. I contend that the earthquake of 2010 disrupted and threw off course the reception of the play, trapping Haiti and its people in a closed time and space. Instead, I want to propose a reading of the play that reinscribes *Melovivi* in Franketienne's overall disaster aesthetics and that actually accounts for the originality of the play: for the first time Franketienne addresses our environmental crisis and "global ecology." In fact, the problems with the reception of *Melovivi* reveal the "representational challenges" (Nixon 2011: 2) posed by the "relative invisibility" (2) of what Rob Nixon calls "slow violence" (2). In opposition to the violence of an event, such as a disaster, "immediate in time, explosive and spectacular in space," "erupting into instant sensational visibility," the slow violence of environmental degradation is "a violence that occurs gradually and out of sight, a violence of delayed destruction that is dispersed across space, an attritional violence that is typically not viewed as violence at all. . . . [It] is neither spectacular nor instantaneous, but rather incremental and accretive, its calamitous repercussions playing out across a range of temporal scales" (2). My claim is that Franketienne's intention was to design a performance that would expose the "slow violence" of our global ecological crisis, make it perceptible, especially for a public that is not in a vulnerable zone. What happened on 12 January 2010 disrupted this plan and obscured the play. In the aftermaths of the earthquake, it was impossible to see anything else or to think about anything else other than the actual disaster. *Melovivi* became a play about the 2010 Haitian earthquake.

A first version of this article was presented at the occasion of the conference organized by the Winthrop-King Institute at Florida State University to mark the ten-year anniversary of the Haitian earthquake. Ten years on, it is probably time to confront the play for what it is, without searching for the signs of a "future past" in the written traces of a prophetic text. It is probably time to consider the play in Franketienne's literary trajectory and to redirect our attention to aspects crucial to the reception of any work of art, yet widely ignored by the commentaries: its content, its literary strategies, and its intent. The play then appears in a different, more complex, spatiotemporal frame. It is not a representation of the aftermath of 12 January 2010, it is not even about Haiti—Haiti is never mentioned—and it does not foretell the earthquake or its consequences. Rather, it is a play about the planet—or even the cosmos—whose effects are meant to address at once the present and the deep time of our global ecological crisis. *Melovivi* is set out of time "in the wake of a disaster," in a "dilapidated, devastated space" (Franketienne 2010: 17). Two characters only designated by the letters A and B are trapped, with no way out, in this "place of confinement," which is also a space of nothingness. They talk and ramble (or "parlent et déparlent" (17) in Franketienne's parlance), seemingly without rhyme or reason, in Franketienne's unique language. In this postapocalyptic vision of a world in peril, the characters ponder the global ecological situation. They condemn the pseudoexperts of international institutions who do little more than utter verbiage and empty words. The world they inhabit, our world, goes round in circles and language reveals its vanity. In sum, *Melovivi* is a play about human-made disasters that are progressively ruining the planet, it is a play that questions the power of language in the face of disasters past and to come, and it is a play that proposes to turn our attention to the planet as our common embedded environment.

The twelfth of January 2010. The magnitude 7.2 earthquake that shattered the lives of hundreds of thousands of Haitians will mark this date in history. Incidentally, it also attracted the attention of critics and journalists to Franketienne's theater play. The analysis was unanimous: Franketienne had been a prophet and *Melovivi* had predicted the devastation of Port-au-Prince and its surroundings. A journalist, François Busnel, wrote in *L'Express* in June 2010, "Do you believe in the prophetic power of literature? Franketienne, one of the best living poets, felt it on January 12th when the earth shook in Haiti, his native island. . . . Today, we say that there are 400,000 or 500,000 dead or missing. A disaster. A disaster that the Haitian writer had envisioned a few weeks ago." In the preface to the 2010 edition of the play, Fabrice Hadjadj affirmed Franketienne's prescience: "The poet has been prophet. His text was the sole clairvoyant seismogram" (9). Rachel Douglas (2016), in her article about the necessity of reimagining the archive as a live process rather than a depository of inert ancient artifacts, introduced Franketienne's manuscript as his "premonitory play" (388). Prophecy, according to Martin Munro, is a recurrent motif in Haitian Literature. In a section titled "Prophets of the Past," he connects this predilection to a nonlinear apprehension of time in tune with Vodou and a Haitian history that seems to stutter and repeat itself rather than fulfilling the promises of its heroic origin as the first black independent nation. Quoting Paul Ricoeur, he affirms that "prophecy amounts to extrapolating from the configurations and concatenations of the past in the direction of what is still to come," and consists of speaking about the future "in terms appropriate to the past." For Munro, prophecy is a means of "'emplotting' time, and of clarifying poetically something of the nature of time, without offering a final theoretical resolution" (Munro 2014: 144).[2] It is indeed not surprising that one of the functions of Haitian literary narratives is indeed prophetic. Yet, is it reasonable to interpret Franketienne's play as literally prophetic? Is the play really (fore)telling the catastrophic event of 12 January 2010?

During the same period, reactions to the earthquake in newspapers and social media were turning to the idea of malediction: if this happened to Haiti, a country already plagued with poverty and political instability, rather than somewhere else, it must be because of a malediction. Televangelist Pat Robertson infamously accused Haiti of having made a pact with the devil. Referring to the Vodou ceremony of Bois Caiman, prelude to the slave revolt that led to the Haitian Revolution, he proclaimed on a radio show that "ever since, the Haitians have been cursed by one thing after the other" (James 2010). This anecdote would not be worth mentioning if this idea of a curse did not become mainstream in the way the media reported the event. In reputable newspapers, journalists considered trustworthy used the exact same rhetoric. On 14 January, the newspaper *Le Monde*—one example out of many—published an article entitled "Haiti, la malédiction" (Gautheret 2010). Though the content of such articles could be nuanced and critical in their analyses (for instance, evaluating the impact of colonization, US imperialism, and corruption as primary factors for the scope of the catastrophe), few resisted the sensationalist headlines. "Tragedy" was another common designator for the earthquake in the first few days following the catastrophe.

Interestingly enough, "tragedy," "malediction," and "prophecy" all have something in common: they reorder time in the same way, that is by conflating past, present, and future. The three terms evoke the same worldview of human lives directed by fate and deprived of agency. "Prophecy," from the Greek *prophemi*, to foretell, refers to something that is told before it happens. "Malediction" implies that a wish of misfortune uttered in the past will necessarily befall its target in the future. And one of the defining characteristics of tragedy as a genre is the impossibility for the hero to escape *fatum* (fate), literally what has already been spoken. If *Melovivi* at the time of its performance exposes what has already happened, then it has nothing to tell us. In other words, deeming *Melovivi* as a prophecy traps Haiti once again in a closed space and time while sealing the gap between text and meaning, where the possibility of interpretation resides. Moreover, if the earthquake is the result of a malediction, there is neither historical, political, nor human responsibility behind the disaster. If *Melovivi* recounts the events of 12 January, then its purpose vanishes with the fulfillment of the oracle.

In the context of the aftermath of the earthquake, viewing the play as premonitory was perhaps a natural response. Because of their scope—by definition beyond the human capacity to cope—and because of their unexpectedness, disasters challenge rational or logic explanations. Of course, we know the scientific explanation: earthquakes occur at fault lines, when the pressure caused by the friction of two tectonic plaques is suddenly released. This scientific explanation, however, does little to quench our thirst for meaning when the explosion and its violent tremors cause death and devastation. Because they disrupt life as we know it, because they dislocate the flux of time, disasters interrupt our capacity for making meaning. And yet, at the same time, they demand an immediate cause, an ultimate justification. One of the only ways to reorder time in this context is to accept that what happened happened because it ought to have happened. As the etymology of the word suggests, every disaster (from the Latin *astrum*) must have been already written in the stars.

Since it became impossible to even mention *Melovivi* without referring to the earthquake that confirmed its alleged premonitory quality, most critics would ponder the eerie coincidence and would stop there. Very few actually grappled with the content of the play, its language, or its staging. It is as if the 2010 earthquake on top of the damage it caused and the lives it took also interrupted the regular order of critical reception, resulting in an incapacity for critics to apprehend the originality of the work. Believing Frankétienne's claim to prophecy was probably, again, a psychologically protective response. The prediction and its fulfillment re-inscribe the event in a linear temporality where the future is not totally unknown and the present not totally unexpected. Confirming the prophetic power of Frankétienne, one of the most celebrated voices in Haiti, could also have been an unconscious attempt on the part of scholars to reinstate some degree of agency to the Haitian victims, beyond their (in)famous resiliency. As I have shown, however, it might lead to the opposite effect: the Haitian people become powerless victims of a fate against which nothing could have been done since the "natural" disaster appears to be inscribed in a linear teleology. It is true that lines such as "collapse of cities, palaces, slums and castles in cacophonic hecatomb" (Frankétienne 2010: 50) and "Don't you feel the tremors transporting us, lifting us?" (30) are troubling in light of the earthquake. However, disasters of all kinds are omnipresent throughout the works of Frankétienne: earthquakes, cyclones, tornadoes and fires, shattered cities and collapsed palaces, ruins and dilapidation are common place in Frankétienne's devastated landscapes.[3] *Melovivi* is the exception in the sense it does not refer, even implicitly, to Haiti or Port-au-Prince.[4]

To understand the originality of the play, it is necessary to read the text with Frankétienne's other works. In fact, all his work can be—and has been—characterized as an aesthetics of "disaster" (Chancé 2004), a "writing of chaos" (2009), an "aesthetics of degradation" (Lucas 2004), or a "poetics of shock and explosion" (Douaire 2001). There is nothing new in these characterizations and this should come as no surprise to Frankétienne's readers since his creative process is grounded, as Rachel Douglas has established, in the constant rewriting of his own texts: he keeps "returning to his own texts and transforming them by superimposing swathes of new additions" (Douglas 2009: 7). It is a way of privileging "the process of writing over what is written . . . production over the finished product . . . the dynamic over the static" (160). This strategy prevents any fixation of meaning and allows the whole project to be always in movement in the manner of the spiral, Franketienne's favorite figure. Each text not only repeats previous themes and motives but also fragments of sentences, or even at times full paragraphs. *Melovivi* has also a lot in common with Franketienne's previous theater plays in which the influence of Samuel Beckett[5] and Antonin Artaud has been noted (Ruprecht 2018). "Rewriting in this senses feeds on repetition" (Douglas 2009: 7), and repetition is a distinctive feature in Franketienne's aesthetics. But it is also through the process of repetition that difference comes to life and transformation takes place. If we want to appreciate the innovative character of this play, we have to situate it in Franketienne's literary production. The spatiotemporal indetermination is here absolute. Rachel Douglas (2016) observes: "Everything remains anonymous and unspecific. There are no specific references in this play to a particular natural disaster; it could easily refer to *any* of the natural disasters which regularly attack Haiti, including hurricanes, landslides and floods" (394). Haiti—or any other place on the planet since, again, Haiti is never mentioned. In the manner of Beckett's characters, those of Melovivi are literally caught in a no-man's-land.

> A and B—We are everywhere. And we are nowhere.
> B—Without any identity. Totally cut off from the rest of the world. Absolutely lost.
> A—Space is no more.
> B—Time is no more. (Franketienne: 17–20)

In this space of nothingness, as in Blanchot's (1995) essay, the disaster is literal, it separates the characters from the stars.[6] "No light! Absolutely no light! No brightness! No glimmer on the horizon!" Franketienne writes (2010: 43). Without stars signaling the existence of a cosmic order, the characters lose their bearings, they are totally disoriented: "We are adrift. We are completely adrift. We are lost. We are on the edge of the abyss, on the borders of nonsense" (31). There is no meaning and no direction, and *Melovivi* echoes Blanchot (1995) for whom "the disaster disorients the absolute" (4). Everything vanishes in nothingness, except for the characters' words, which spiral and swirl in the void. *Melovivi*'s disaster aesthetic runs into the same aporetic logic as Blanchot's *Writing of the Disaster*: there is no language apt to express the experience of the disaster. According to Deborah Jenson, "Blanchot describes disaster as the 'unexperienced,' as the limit of writing, and as something that not only eludes description, but actively de-scribes" (Jenson 2010: 104). The writing of the disaster avoids making concrete references to any historical disaster. Rather, it seeks a form of expression that would resist the closure of meaning; hence it is a fragmented writing that repeats, contradicts itself, and vanishes in its own abstraction. As Marie-Hélène Huet writes, "Thinking through disasters is best exemplified in our incapacity to reassemble fragments into a reassuring whole" (2012: 12). Eventually, the disaster is present in its absence; it can only be read in the silence that the text bears into existence.

Melovivi never was the representation of the Haitian earthquake. In fact, it was never a representation or a narrative. It does not provide meaning, intellectual knowledge or a political analysis. The text is only a support for a performance where living bodies express and transmit affects to other living bodies. At the beginning of the third sequence, the tension between A and B is rising. They raise their voices at each other. B rebels against A, vociferating: "There is no order! There is no more logic! And I am not the slave of your text. I will not repeat your text. I will not memorize your text! I will not memorize anybody's text! I, myself, will not memorize anybody's text!" B responds with growing anger: "But what text are you talking about? I have never talked to you about a text. I never demanded that you memorize a text. There is no text!" (Frankétienne 2010: 30). There are several ways to interpret this short exchange between the two characters. In French the verb *répéter* is ambiguous, it means both "repeating" and "rehearsing." B seems to imply that A, the playwright, demanded that he memorize the text of the play and rehearse the dialogue. However, he refused vehemently to play by the established rules. What does this refusal signal? Frankétienne, when performing, likes to accommodate spontaneity and improvisation. It has to be a live performance after all, and allowing some space for the unexpected is what will make the experience unique to the spectators as well as to the actors. In this sense, *Melovivi*, even if the creole word means "trap," is the opposite of tragedy: if there is no pre-existing written text, there is no *fatum*, no destiny. If there is no text, there is no beginning, no end, everything is up in the air. Everything can still happen.

At another level, this revolt against the text, followed by the denial of its existence, indicates a defiance toward language and its power. The linguistic inflation at work in environmental and global politics is exposed and ridiculed: after A mentions the "problematic of global modernity," B enjoins him to "shut up" (31). The term "problematic" is then repeated more than twenty-five times, picked up in turn by A and B, until this "shitty repetitive formula" (31) becomes pure noise. When words are worn out by excessive meaningless repetition, the very own tools of the author become useless. It becomes impossible to believe that language might resolve anything. This kind of defiance toward language and its capacity to construct meaning is manifest in the dialogue. A and B are not real characters; they are interchangeable and lack individualized personalities.

This split dialogue is another literary strategy familiar to Franketienne. It is as if his own consciousness were split into two voices that intertwine and clash with each other to finally sound together in what the author calls "schizophonie."[7] As soon as one character affirms something with the appearance of confidence, the second ridicules the first. The only moments of consensus evoke generalized destruction or nihilism, and as if these moments were still too meaningful, they quickly turn into singing and gesticulating bouts in the style of a farce. In all these instances, it is finally, as in Blanchot, the closure of meaning that is refused: ultimately, "there is nothing to understand" (21). Against the "carcass of words" (21) of the dictionaries and lexicons, Franketienne proposes a living language full of "particles of sensual energy."[8]

> A—Set up your own personal lexicon. Modulate your own dictionary in step with the tempo of your body.
> Tempo of your hips
> Tempo of your dreams
> Tempo of your sex
> Tempo of your guts
> Tempo of your blood!
> As for semantic, it is nothing but bluff; it assassinates the imaginary and kills all life. (26)

If there is no text, what remains? In Franketienne's theater, language is affect. Reading the sentence "Il n'y a pas de texte" (There is no text) is very different from hearing the actor's speech. When you listen to the actor's speech, you are surprised by the sudden rise in the tone of the voice, you can feel the impatience and the exasperation; your body reacts to the vibration of the sounds before your brain tries to decipher the signification of the message. In other words, you are experiencing an affective response.[9] The truths to be found in *Melovivi* are not meant to be grasped by our reason, they are not intellectual. They reach us directly through our senses and thus resembles the more profound truths that Marcel Proust, inspiring Deleuze's affect theory, seeks to recover in his writing:

> The truths which intelligence grasps directly in the open light of day have something less profound, less necessary about them than those which life has communicated to us in spite of ourselves in an impression, a material impression because it has reached us through our senses. (Proust cited in Deleuze 2000: 95–96)

The purpose of Franketienne's performance is not to convey meaning (especially a closed meaning), information, or knowledge. As Claire Colebrook suggests, "what makes it art is not content but its affect, the sensible force or style through which it produces content. Why, for example, would we spend two hours in the cinema watching a film if all we wanted were the story or the moral message?" (2002: 24–25). And indeed, Frankétienne seeks to breathe life into language but also into space and time. This is one of the questions that constantly worries him: "Through breath and momentum how to re-fecundate time as well as a space caribbeanized with evil gold and painful cries?" (Frankétienne 2002: 155). His answer is to focus on the materiality of the voice, its bodily aspects, "the voice, the tongue, the mouth . . . in the art of saying what happens. Especially the lungs! And the intensity of the breath! The fury of the cry!" (2010: 29). What matters in *Melovivi* is the linguistic energy produced by the collision of words, neologisms, repetitions, code-switching, singing, laughter. It is language in its materiality, its sensuality, when the words become body parts. Frankétienne's metaphors make everything bleed: body parts, holes, and stars become blended in the bloody matrix of an aborted cosmos.

> A—Stars bleed!
> B—All the stars bleed!
> A—Our legs and our arms bleed.
> B—Our chests bleed.
> A—Our eyes and our lips bleed.
> B—There are difficult holes who bleed.
> A—There are impossible holes who bleed.
> B—There are imaginary holes who bleed.
> A—The sun vomited blood.
> B—The earth bursts with blood. (2010: 52)

Against discourses of globalization, Frankétienne (2010) deploys an affective poetics of the planetary. *Melovivi* recounts the conflict between the forces of globalization, the "predators of the planet," the international institutions, their ridiculous summits, and their empty discourses against the vital forces of the cosmos. He writes: "Our marvelous little planet, earth-blue, sea-blue, moon-blue, as blue as the poet's metaphoric orange, our little fabulous planet sinks in shipwreck, in the malouque waters and in the turbulence of savagely voracious flames" (50).

Here, it is useful to remember Gayatri Spivak's (2005) distinction between globalization and planetarity. Spivak calls for an epistemic shift from the global conceived as "a financially, economically, and technologically homogenizing force" (Elias and Moraru 2015: xvii) in the abstract to the planet as "world-ecology" (xii) where interdependency and relationality prevail over competition, nationalisms, and individualisms.

> I propose the planet to overwrite the globe. Globalization is the imposition of the same system of exchange everywhere. In the gridwork of electronic capital, we achieve that abstract ball covered in latitudes and longitudes, cut by virtual lines,

once the equator and the tropics and so on, now drawn by the requirements of Geographical Information Systems. To talk planet-talk by way of an unexamined environmentalism, referring to an undivided "natural" space rather than a differentiated political space, can work in the interest of this globalization in the mode of the abstract as such. The globe is on our computers. No one lives there. It allows us to think that we can aim to control it. The planet is in the species of alterity, belonging to another system; and yet we inhabit it, on loan. (Spivak 2005: 72)

Epistemic shifts cannot occur without imaginary projections, especially on this scale. Thinking the world as the planet and the human as a species is a challenge. The world "escapes us as comprehension and as concept," affirms Edouard Glissant, "it is through the imaginary that one can attempt to grasp it" (Rosemberg 2016: 2). Changing our vision of the world is necessary to making the world change. Theater, because it is a living art and because it relies on the audience's and actors' direct interaction, is probably more than any others "the art of affects more than representation, a system of dynamized and impacting forces rather than a system of unique images that function under a regime of signs," to quote Elisabeth Grosz (2020: 3). If it seems already too late for the characters trapped in a nonplace in a world irremediably damaged, perhaps the effects of the performance can contribute to awakening our awareness of the present. The specific temporality of *Melovivi* is not the "future past" of the prophecy. In so far as the art of performance is the art of the present, *Melovivi* accomplishes the tour de force of bringing together the deep time of the planet and our very present, making the unseen "slow violence" of climate change tangible to the audience. The capacity to be affected is what separates immobility from action, passivity from resistance, and fate from agency.

Do we have to wait for more disasters to come to gain awareness of the present ecological situations? Do people outside of Haiti have to experience them firsthand before they understand that ecological catastrophes are not only taking place in "shithole countries"?[10] Frankétienne's clairvoyance comes from his continuing presence in Haiti; his play is a gift to its global audience. It links Haiti and the rest of the world, us and them, in a call for awareness, to overcome immobility and passivity in the face of the environmental apocalypse that threatens us all.

Alex Lenoble is assistant professor of French in the department of world languages at the University of South Florida, which he joined in 2019 after completing his PhD at Cornell University. His research interests include Francophone and Caribbean literatures from the twentieth to the twenty-first century, with a special focus on Haiti. He has published numerous articles on the work of Frankétienne in French and American academic journals. He is working on a book project entitled "Postcolonial Literatures beyond Representation." It addresses the ways in which postcolonial literary works respond to a historical exclusion of certain subjectivities from the symbolic. Experimenting with literary forms is one of the strategies authors use to powerfully express traumatic postcolonial experiences.

Notes

1. Unless otherwise noted, all translations from the French are my own.
2. While Munro mentions *Melovivi* in the book, his analysis does not include a detailed reading of the play.
3. See for instance in Frankétienne, *Voix Marassas*: "L'inconcevable échec/L'insupportable désastre/L'intolérable catastrophe" (Frankétienne 1998: 75).
4. See, for example, his *Brêche ardente*, which Frankétienne explicitly devoted to the description of a dilapidated Port-au-Prince.
5. See Jean Jonassaint, "Frankétienne," Île en île (website), updated 28 June 2021, http://ile-en-ile.org/franketienne/.
6. "If disaster means being separated from the star (if it means the decline that characterize disorientation when the link from fortune from on high is cut), then it indicates a fall beneath disastrous necessity." (Blanchot 1995: 2)
7. The term "schizophonie" comes from *L'Oiseau schizophone*, published in 1998 and has been used by the author since then.
8. This expression appears on many back covers of Frankétienne's works.
9. "Brian Massumi defines affect in terms of bodily responses, autonomic responses, which are in excess of conscious states of perception and point instead to a "visceral perception" preceding perception." (Clough 2008: 3) This is exactly what Frankétienne seeks in his work in general and in Melovivi in particular.
10. President Trump allegedly used this expression at a White House meeting. The anecdote was reported in *The New York Times* as follows: "President Trump on Thursday balked at an immigration deal that would include protections for people from Haiti and some nations in Africa, demanding to know at a White House meeting why he should accept immigrants from "shithole countries" rather than from places like Norway, according to people with direct knowledge of the conversation" (Davis: 2018).

References

Blanchot, Maurice. 1995. *The Writing of the Disaster*, trans. by Ann Smock. Lincoln: University of Nebraska Press.
Busnel, François. 2010. "François Busnel a lu *Melovivi ou le piège* par Frankétienne." *L'express*. 2 June, https://www.lexpress.fr/culture/livre/francois-busnel-a-lu-melovivi-ou-le-piege-par-franketienne_896319.html.
Chancé, Dominique. 2004. "Astres et désastres dans *L'Oiseau schizophone*, de Frankétienne." *Ponti/Ponts* 4: 303–21.
———. 2009. *Écriture du chaos. Lecture des œuvres de Frankétienne, Reinaldo Arenas, Joël Des Rosiers*. Saint-Denis, France: Presses Universitaires de Vincennes.

Clough, Patricia T. 2008. "The Affective Turn: Political Economy, Biomedia and Bodies." *Theory, Culture & Society*, 25(1): 1–22. https://doi.org/10.1177/0263276407085156

Colebrook, Claire. 2002. *Gilles Deleuze*. London: Routledge.

Davis, Julie Hirschfeld, Sheryl Gay Stolberg, and Thomas Kaplan. 2018. "Trump Alarms Lawmakers with Disparaging Words for Haiti and Africa." New York Times, January 11, 2018. https://www.nytimes.com/2018/01/11/us/politics/trump-shithole-countries.html.

Deleuze, Gilles. 2000. *Proust and Signs: The Complete Text*, trans. by Richard Howard. Minneapolis: University of Minnesota Press.

Douaire, Anne. 2001. "Ultravocal de Frankétienne." Pierre Campion personal website. 15 May, http://pierre.campion2.free.fr/douaire.htm.

Douglas, Rachel. 2009. *Frankétienne and Rewriting: A Work in Progress*. Lanham, MD: Lexington Books.

———. 2016. "Writing the Haitian Earthquake and Creating Archives." *Caribbean Quarterly* 62(3–4): 388–405.

Elias, Amy J., and Christian Moraru. 2015. "Introduction: The Planetary Condition." In *The Planetary Turn: Relationality and Geoaesthetics in the Twenty-First Century*, edited by Amy J. Elias and Christian Moraru, xi–2. Northwestern University Press, 2015.

Frankétienne. 1998. *L'Oiseau Schizophone*. Paris : Jean-Michel Place.

———.1998. *Voix Marrassas*. Port-au-Prince: Spirale.

———. 2002. *H'éros chimères: Spirale*. Port-au-Prince, Haiti: Deschamps.

———. 2010. *Melovivi ou Le piège suivi de Brèche ardente*. Paris: Riveneuve.

Gautheret, Jérôme. 2010. "Haïti, La Malédiction." *Le Monde*. 14 January, https://www.lemonde.fr/ameriques/article/2010/01/14/haiti-la-malediction_1291437_3222.html.

Grosz, Elizabeth. 2020. *Chaos, Territory, Art: Deleuze and the Framing of the Earth*. New York: Columbia University Press.

Guy, Chantal. 2010. "Frankétienne: Le pilier d'Haïti." *La Presse*. September 18, https://www.lapresse.ca/arts/spectacles-et-theatre/theatre/201009/18/01-4316982-franketienne-le-pilier-dhaiti.php.

Hadjadj, Fabrice. 2010. Preface to *Melovivi ou Le piège suivi de Brèche ardente* by Frankétienne, 9–13. Paris: Riveneuve.

Huet, Marie-Hélène. 2012. *The Culture of Disaster*. Chicago: University of Chicago Press.

James, Frank. 2010. "Pat Robertson Blames Haitian Devil Pact for Earthquake." *NPR*. 13 January, https://www.npr.org/sections/thetwo-way/2010/01/pat_robertson_blames_haitian_d.html.

Jenson, Deborah. 2010. "The Writing of Disaster in Haiti: Signifying Cataclysm from Slave Revolution to Earthquake." In *Haiti Rising*, edited by Martin Munro, 103-112: Liverpool University Press.

Laferrière, Dany. 2011. *Tout bouge autour de moi*. Paris: Grasset.

Lucas, Rafael. 2004. "The Aesthetics of Degradation in Haitian Literature." *Research in African Literatures*. 35(2): 54–74.

Munro, Martin. 2014. *Writing on the Fault Line: Haitian Literature and the Earthquake of 2010*. Liverpool, UK: Liverpool University Press.

Nixon, Rob. 2013. *Slow Violence and the Environmentalism of the Poor*. Cambridge, MA: Harvard University Press.

Rosemberg, Muriel. 2016. "Edouard Glissant's Geopoetics, a Contribution to the Idea of the World as the World." *L'Espace géographique* 45(4): 321–34.

Ruprecht, Alvina. 2018. "Totolomanwèl: Frankétienne and the One Man Show." *Journal of Haitian Studies* 14(1): 18–36.
Spivak, Gayatri Chakravorty. 2005. *Death of a Discipline*. New York: Columbia University Press.

EPILOGUE

Disrupting Permanent Catastrophe through Commemoration, Grief, and Action

VINCENT JOOS, MARTIN MUNRO, AND JOHN RIBÓ

When the earthquake struck Haiti on 12 January 2010, amid the chaos of fallen buildings, dead bodies, and general panic, citizens of Port-au-Prince were heard to cry that it was the "fin du monde," the end of the world. To many, it was an apocalyptic moment, a cataclysmic end, but without the promise contained in biblical versions of the apocalypse of a new and better beginning. In short, there was a sense, expressed by authors such as Dany Laferrière, that the earthquake marked an ending, and that whatever came next would have to be different. And yet, the disaster appears endless, as Haiti experiences an ongoing social and economic catastrophe that shows no signs of ending. As far back as 2012, this experience was termed one of "permanent catastrophe" by the Haitian sociologist Laënnec Hurbon. Recognizing the apparent contradiction in the term, Hurbon writes that if every disaster supposes a rupture in time and experience, one should also be aware of the "before and after of the catastrophe" (2012: 8).[1] Disasters strike so often in Haiti—from the floods in Gonaïves in 2004 to the 2010 earthquake to the cholera epidemic to Hurricanes Sandy and Isaac in 2012 and beyond—that the population "risks taking as natural every calamity" (9). One effect of living in permanent catastrophe is that the memory of the deadliest of these events, the 2010 earthquake, fades quickly and the event loses its distinctiveness. One has the impression, Hurbon wrote in 2012, that nothing happened on 12 January 2010, and that a "leap has been skillfully made beyond that date" (8). The constant denial and annulment of the disaster leads to the general "permanent installation in catastrophe" (9).

This condition of permanent disaster has important political dimensions, for as Hurbon argues, at the heart of the situation "the leaders of the State seem to worry only about how to stay in power" (9). Disasters are moreover "godsends" for those in power in that they give the politicians a source of legitimacy, which otherwise they would not have (9).[2] There is even a "desire for disasters" in government, as these events allow the leaders to present themselves as victims to the international community, and to discharge their responsibilities in the economic, social, cultural, and political life of Haiti (9). At a global level, disasters create opportunities for creating new financial markets that thrive when a catastrophe occurs. They are also opportunities for international NGOs that pile up donations whenever a major disaster strikes. As many contributors to this volume show, NGOs often replace governmental agencies, but they do so temporarily, leaving a void once they depart. Decades of disaster studies have shown that disasters are the result of identifiable political and/or neoliberal practices of violence, dispossession, and exploitation. As Hurbon (2012) points out, though, various types of disasters feed off one other and, in a sense, "natural" disasters accelerate the decline of democracy in places weakened by decades of austerity politics, such as Haiti, but also in Puerto Rico or Florida.

Declaring a state of emergency is one of the key processes that leads to the demise of democratic practices. Disasters further social and ecological vulnerabilities by suspending all kinds of governmental regulations and by reinforcing top-down forms of power. At once, the state dwindles and, paradoxically, takes on a greater importance. In the wake of Hurricane Katrina, the US federal government showed its inability to help its own citizens and contributed to the permanent displacement of thousands of people. At the same time, the George W. Bush administration forcefully implemented educational reforms that led to the closure of public schools, hence to the withering of the Black middle classes in the Crescent City. Disasters are not one-off events. They compound and lead to a state of permanent and global catastrophe—to a state of opportunities for neoliberal and self-serving nationalist leaders. Hence, thinking outside of the crisis mode enables us to capture new temporalities, to shed light on new relations between humans, nature, and the spiritual realm. It allows us to take a pause and ponder past disasters, to describe their specificity, to learn from them. The fine-tuned analyses of historical and structural processes contributors put forth in this volume show where economic and political changes must occur. They show that neoliberalism, nationalism, and racism only fuel disasters and lead us, to take Mark Schuller's words, to "humanity's last stand." Additionally, paying attention to cultural productions and practices that emerge in the wake of disasters, and paying attention to individual narratives and indigenous solidarity systems, enable us to see disasters not as disparate and ineluctable crises but as symptoms of global disenfranchisement. In other words, listening to and reflecting on the voices that describe, explain, and dissect disasters from below opens new political and epistemological alternatives. They open a path to commemoration, grief, and action.

To live in a state of permanent disaster means that individual events are not memorialized in a way that would consign them to the past and allow a sense of time other than that characterized by catastrophe. People live, Hurbon says, "without a perceptible future" and "in the condition of being superfluous (floating between life and death)" (2012: 10). Hurbon points out that the government has no interest in a memorial for the 2010 Port-au-Prince earthquake, and thus the disaster is not considered past but part of the catastrophic present (9). This in turn has serious consequences for notions of reconstruction, as to be in a permanent state of catastrophe is to forget any time in which disaster was not a daily reality, and to lose awareness of what was there before to be reconstructed. As Hurbon puts it, the causes of permanent disaster are as much political as environmental (10). Indeed, the various signs of environmental degradation—deforestation, pollution, and so forth—can be read as "the expression of the failure of the Haitian State" (10).[3]

In turn, the failure of the Haitian state can be read as a legacy of colonialism, imperialism, and foreign interventions leading to the fraudulent election and support of authoritarian leaders. After the 2010 earthquake, the US again undermined Haitian sovereignty by supporting the campaign of Michel Martelly, an incompetent probusiness candidate who won the presidential elections thanks to the support of US institutions. The Martelly government implemented reconstruction projects that were either unfinished or directly harmful to the Haitian population. In other words, undermining democratic processes disempowers entire societies and opens forms of "reconstruction" that foster disaster vulnerability. A majority of Haitians lived in autarkic and self-sufficient communities that sustained their natural environments in the nineteenth century. However, the values and ecological practices of small-scale peasantries were at best mocked, at worst severely repressed during antisuperstition campaigns.

We observe the same processes in so-called developed regions of the circum-Caribbean, where politicians and their corporate allies sabotage state institutions meant to prevent disasters or to help local populations, and where disaster relief is increasingly being privatized. For instance, rural communities of Florida have to rebuild their towns themselves as local officials steal reconstruction funds ("Former City Official" 2020), or as state and federal agencies are too slow to bring help. In the case of Puerto Rico, the Trump administration even withheld relief funds to retaliate against political adversaries (Acevedo 2021). Decades of austerity measures in Puerto Rico and Florida led to the closing of fire stations and to the withering of state education, health, and emergency management agencies. At the federal level, the government-induced decay of the Federal Emergency Management Agency (FEMA) is yet another example of the dwindling role of the state when it comes to the welfare of its citizens when disasters strike. Not surprisingly, areas of Florida affected by Hurricane Michael and areas of Puerto Rico hurt by Hurricane Maria do not recover. Simply put, the demise of the welfare state is not only a social question. The withering of democratic institutions fuels natural disasters, and in turn, these catastrophes only accelerate the nefarious privatization of public goods and services.

We conclude this volume by reinvoking Hurbon, as his ideas seem not to have lost any of their relevance, and as Haiti and the broader Caribbean are increasingly prone to disasters, social, economic, and environmental. As scholars of the Caribbean working across disciplines in the humanities and social sciences, the question of how our work contributes to efforts to counter the long-term effects of disaster in the region is pressing and difficult. One possible answer this volume provides is the production of scholarship that mobilizes commemoration, grief, and action to disrupt ways of living, thinking, and governing that normalize a state of permanent catastrophe. The work included in this collection commemorates disasters long after they have left the nightly news and the front page. It grieves the long-term losses that these disasters produce in their particularities and structural similarities. And it calls for action so that past disasters do not become the norm in a state of permanent catastrophe. The recent challenges of creating policies and practices to manage the catastrophic effects of a global pandemic and climate change demonstrate that disaster in the circum-Caribbean—often considered an eccentricity of the region linked to its unique geography, weather, and history—is in fact a vital topic for understanding the future of humanity broadly. Lessons learned about disaster in the Caribbean become increasingly applicable elsewhere in the world in regions where people have imagined themselves immune to its effects. We finally encourage more work on these pressing themes and offer the volume as a token of our solidarity and respect for the people of the region.

Vincent Joos is an assistant professor of anthropology and global French studies at Florida State University. His work has appeared in *Economic Anthropology*, *Transforming Anthropology*, *Vibrant*, and *World Politics Review*. His work focuses on postdisaster reconstruction in the Caribbean. He recently published his first book, *Urban Dwellings, Haitian Citizenships: Housing, Memory, and Daily Life in Haiti* (Rutgers University Press, 2021).

Martin Munro is Winthrop-King Professor of French and Francophone studies at Florida State University. His publications include *Writing on the Fault Line: Haitian Literature and the Earthquake of 2010* (Liverpool University Press, 2014); *Tropical Apocalypse: Haiti and the Caribbean End Times* (University of Virginia Press, 2015); and *Listening to the Caribbean: Sounds of Slavery, Revolt, and Race* (Liverpool University Press, 2022).

John Ribó is assistant professor of English at Florida State University, where he specializes in contemporary Latinx literatures and cultures. His work has appeared in *Chiricú*, *The Journal of Haitian Studies*, *Cuban Studies*, and *ASAP*. He is currently completing his first manuscript, tentatively titled *Haitian Hauntings*.

Notes

1. See also David Scott's interpretation of the collapse of the Grenada Revolution as "merely one significant *episode* in a larger story of generations of conflict in what is now imagined and represented as the cyclical pattern of a general history whose generative logic is catastrophic" (2014: 74–75).
2. Jonathan Katz suggests that disasters are also godsends for donors, who by late March 2012 had delivered less than half of the long-term funding pledged for 2010 and 2011. Donor countries, he argues, let President René Préval carry the blame for the lack of reconstruction (2013: 207). He also says that with the huge logistical costs of the relief operation, "much of the money was a stimulus program for the donor countries themselves" (206). He further critiques the overall achievements of the foreign relief programs: "Having sought above all to prevent riots, ensure stability, and prevent disease, the responders helped spark the first, undermine the second, and by all evidence caused the third" (278). See also Myriam J. A. Chancy's argument that "the Duvalier regime was in large part supported and financed (with arms and funds) by the U.S. for a thirty-year period" (2012: 34). Raoul Peck's 2013 film *Assistance mortelle* presents a cutting critique of humanitarian and development aid in Haiti. For a critique of "military humanitarianism" in postearthquake Haiti, see Jennifer Greenburg, "The 'Strong Arm' and the 'Friendly Hand'" (2013).
3. See also Hurbon's critique of the "privatization of the state" in "De la privatisation de l'État ou les embûches de la reconstruction," *L'Observatoire de la reconstruction* 5 (November 2012): 2–4.

References

Acevedo, Nicole. 2021. "New Probe Confirms Trump Officials Blocked Puerto Rico from Receiving Hurricane Aid." NBC News. 22 April, https://www.nbcnews.com/news/latino/new-probe-confirms-trump-officials-blocked-puerto-rico-receiving-hurri-rcna749.

Chancy, Myriam J. A. 2012. *From Sugar to Revolution: Women's Visions of Haiti, Cuba, and the Dominican Republic.* Waterloo, ON: Wilfrid Laurier University Press.
"Former City Official in Florida Pleads Guilty in $5 Million Hurricane Fraud Scheme." 2020. *Orlando Sentinel,* 15 July, https://www.orlandosentinel.com/weather/hurricane/os-ne-ex-official-pleads-guilty-in-hurricane-fraud-scheme-20200715-pl6guwc2sfejfndtinj5cr7vbm-story.html.
Greenberg, Jennifer. 2013. "The 'Strong Arm' and the 'Friendly Hand': Military Humanitarianism in Post-earthquake Haiti." *Journal of Haitian Studies* 19(1): 95–122.
Hurbon, Laënnec. 2012. "Catastrophe permanente et reconstruction." *L'Observatoire de la reconstruction* 6: 8–10.
Katz, Jonathan M. 2013. *The Big Truck That Went By: How the World Came to Save Haiti and Left Behind a Disaster.* New York: Palgrave Macmillan.
Schuller, Mark. 2021. *Humanity's Last Stand: Confronting Global Catastrophe.* New Brunswick, NJ: Rutgers University Press
Scott, David. 2014. *Omens of Adversity: Tragedy, Time, Memory, Justice.* Durham, NC: Duke University Press.

Index

AAFAF. *See* Fiscal Agency and Financial Advisory Authority
Aceh, Indonesia, 29
ACRA 2, 35
Action pour la Reforestation et la Défense de l'Environnement (AREDE), 70
African Americans. *See* New Orleans; Puerto Rico
Aftershocks of Disaster (Bonilla and LeBrón), 100
Agier, Michel, 30
Alexis, Jacques Stephen, 65, 163
Alguera, Martha, 86
Almeida, Joselyn, 6
Altucher, James, 109
amouni (harmony), 42, 43
Anderson, Mark, 8–9, 14
andeyò, 51–54
And Then It Came (Hunter), 150, 151
And the Whole World Quakes (Régis Junior), 142–44
Anglade, Georges, 66
Aponte, Marianne Ramirez, 148
Les Arbres Musiciens (Alexis), 65
AREDE. *See* Action pour la Reforestation et la Défense de l'Environnement
Armstrong, Louis, 79
Artaud, Antonin, 180
Assistance mortelle (film), 23n4, 192n2

Baby Dolls, 82, 84, 87
Ballard, Ryan, 86
Balzac, Honoré de, 162
Bangerz (Cyrus), 83, 84
Bataille, Georges, 106
The Battle for Paradise (Klein), 99, 100
Bauman, Zygmunt, 115n1
Beckett, Greg, 3

Beckett, Samuel, 180
Bellande, Alex, 8, 74–75
Bellegarde, Dantès, 73
Benítez-Rojo, Antonio, 44
Benson, LeGrace, 10
Best, Lloyd, 7
Beta-Local, 136
Biden, Joe, 29
Big Freedia, 84
black Anthropocene, 150–51
Black Code *(Code Noir)*, 9–10
Black Lives Matter, 89, 130, 131
Black Mardi Gras, 81, 87
Black Panthers, 124
Black Skin, White Masks (Fanon), 80
Blanchot, Maurice, 161, 180
blank-slate mentality, 18, 65–66, 68, 75
block parties, 37, 82, 84, 91, 92
Bokova, Irina, 141
Bonilla, Yarimar, 3, 98–99, 100, 121, 130
Boukman, Dutty, 75n2
Bowie, David, 87
Braden-Perry, Megan, 92–93
Braziel, Jana Evans, 19, 114
A Breath (Dormino), 139
Brubaker, Bill, 139
Building Back Better Plan, 29, 30–33, 67
Bush, Barbara, 35
Bush, George W., 189
Busnel, François, 177
Bwa Kayiman, 43

CAJIT. *See* Youth Action Committee of St. Thomas Court
camp committees, 35–37
Caracol, 62–75
Caracol Industrial Park (CIP), 68–74
Caribbean. *See also specific countries and topics*

art and politics in, 135–56
cultural diplomacy in, 138
epistemology of disaster in, 44–45
Caribbean Catastrophe Risk Insurance Facility (CCRIF), 101, 115n2
Caribbean Community (CARICOM), 35, 148
Caribbean World Heritage and Climate Change, 148–49
CARICOM. See Caribbean Community
Casas, Bartolomé de las, 5
Castin, Milostène, 63, 65, 70–73
Castor, Suzy, 72
Castronovo, Russ, 108
Catastrophes in Context, 16
cat bonds, 19, 98–114, 115n3, 116n10
CCRIF. See Caribbean Catastrophe Risk Insurance Facility
Chalmers, Camille, 33
Chamoiseau, Patrick, 162
Chancy, Myriam J. A., 192n2
Cho, Daniel, 68
CIP. See Caracol Industrial Park
circum-Caribbean, 15–22, 190–91
financialization of, 19
wake work in, 121, 123, 129–32
Citizens United, 107
Clarke, Edith, 41
climate change, 5, 17, 45, 116n10, 148–51, 191
Clinton, Bill, 28–29, 67
Clinton, Hillary, 28–29, 35
Code Noir (Black Code), 9–10
Colebrook, Claire, 182–83
Collier, Paul, 67
colonialism, 3, 5–8, 17, 18, 63, 178
Columbus, Christopher, 5–6, 58, 63–64, 72
Condé, Maryse, 162, 168, 170
conjunctural or intersecting crisis (kriz konjonktirèl), 28
Consultation and Investigation Mechanism (MICI), 71
CoreGroup, 39
Corps mêlés (Victor, M.), 21, 160–73
Cortés, Jason, 108–9
Corvington, Georges, 10
La Couleur de l'aube (Lahens), 162
COVID-19 pandemic, 27, 29, 155, 191

Cramer, Jim, 109–10
Cuba, 135–36, 148–49
cultural appropriation, in New Orleans, 83–85
cultural diplomacy, 20, 137, 138–42
climate change and, 148–51
in earthquake of 2010, 139, 142–44
in floods and sea level rise, 148–51
multilateral, 142–55
for oceanic pollution, 151–55
security in, 140–42
curse (malediksyon), 18, 63, 64–65
Cyrus, Miley, 83–85

Danticat, Edwidge, 34, 140, 161, 162
Dash, J. Michael, 14, 23n8
Dauphin Plantation, 72–73
Davis, Angela, 41
"Deathless," 121, 131–32
Decade of Ocean Science for Sustainable Development, 151–52
De Coppet, Andre, 72
DeCoste, Kyle, 89
defending the dead, 19–20, 121–23
deforestation, 7–8, 12, 18, 70
dehumanization, 17, 43–45, 106
Denis-Davertige, Villard, 174n3
Desir, Charlene, 40
Depestre, René, 163
The Dew Breaker (Danticat), 162
Díaz, Lisa-Kaindé, 131–32
Díaz, Naomi, 131–32
Diermeier, Daniel, 109–10
disaster capitalism, 17, 29–30, 98, 99, 100, 113
Disaster Capitalism (Lowenstein), 99
disaster diplomacy, of US, 135–36
The Disaster Profiteers (Mutter), 99
Disasters, Vulnerability, and Narratives (Mika), 99
disposable economies, 19, 98
Disposable Futures (Evans and Giroux), 115n1
Dominica, 6, 145, 149
Dominican Republic, 148
donor countries, 23n4, 40, 192n2
Dormino, Davide, 139
Doucet, Morel, 152–53
Douglas, Rachel, 177, 179, 180

Downpour (Hunter), 150
Doyle, Gamal, 148
Drawn by Water (Jack), 145–47
Duffaut, Préfète, 140
Duval-Carrié, Edouard, 135, 136
Duvalier, Jean-Claude, 66–67, 72–73, 192n2

earthquake of 2010, 18, 27–45, 62, 67, 99, 188, 190
 blank-slate mentality after, 66
 Corps mêlés and, 21, 160–73
 cultural diplomacy in, 139, 142–44
 deaths from, 31–32, 67, 174n1, 177
 lakou after, 39–40
 Melovivi and, 21, 175–85
 NGOs after, 30, 31, 32, 33, 34–41, 44, 143
 violence against women after, 40–41
earthquakes, 3, 29
 executive silence to, 13
 in Haiti, 1–2, 9–11, 12, 13, 20–21, 23n9, 24n11
 political response to, 20
Easterly, William, 68, 86
Echos imprévus (Gabon), 149
Economic Emergency Recovery Program (EERP), 109
L'Ecriture du désastre (Blanchot), 161
Edwards, John Bel, 85
EERP. See Economic Emergency Recovery Program
electric slide, 120–21, 123–24, 130–31
Elliott, Michael, 144
Empire (Negri), 115n1
Enriquillo fault, 9, 11
Entredichos, 148
Etienne, Sauveur Pierre, 30
Evans, Brad, 115n1
executive silence, 13–14
Exeus, Anel, 35

Fallon, Jimmy, 89
family compounds. See *lakou*
Fanon, Frantz, 80
Fatal Assistance (Peck), 32
Fatiman, Cecile, 75n2
Fatton, Robert, Jr., 12, 13, 107
Faulkner, William, 162

Federal Emergency Management Agency (FEMA), 191
Ferdinand, Malcolm, 8
Ferguson, James, 36
Figueroa, Kristian Mercado, 129–30
Figueroa Rosa, Felipe, 129
Fils, Jean, 33
Fiscal Agency and Financial Advisory Authority (AAFAF), 123
Fiscal Oversight and Management Board (FOMB), 123, 125
Fisher, Carrie, 86–87
floods, 2, 12, 148–51, 180, 188
Florida, in Hurricane Michael, 17, 191
FOMB. See Fiscal Oversight and Management Board
Fonds des nègres (Vieux-Chauvet), 163, 174n5
Forde, Alanis, 145
Foxman, Simone, 110
France, 9–10, 39, 75n3, 109, 144, 146–47, 156
Frankétienne, 21, 140, 175–85
free-trade zones, 62, 67, 71
Fresh Milk Barbados, 145
From Communism to Capitalism (Henry), 116n6

Gabon, Guy, 149–50
gang violence, 2, 38–39
García Márquez, Gabriel, 162
General Assembly, of UN, 141
genetically modified organisms, 46n7
genocide, 5, 63
gentrification. See New Orleans
Gibson, Anna, 145
The Gift (Mauss), 38
Giroux, Henry A., 100, 107–8, 115n1
Girvan, Norman, 7
Glissant, Édouard, 162, 168, 184
global capitalism, 6, 17, 30, 44
Gonzalez, Johnhenry, 64
Goudougoudou, 19, 31, 99, 135
Governors Accord, 109
Gramsci, Sèk, 43
Grand'Anse, 18, 54, 55–56, 60–61
Grant, Eugene, 89–91
Greening Diplomacy Initiative, 152
Grenada Revolution, 192n1

Griffiths, Marcia, 131
Gros, Jean-Germain, 13
Grosz, Elisabeth, 184
Guacanagarix, 5–6
Guadeloupe, 8, 149–50
Guyana, 2, 148, 150–51

Hadjadj, Fabrice, 177
Hague Convention for the Protection of Cultural Property in the Event of Armed Conflict, 140–41
Haiti, 27–45. *See also* earthquake of 2010; *specific locations and topics*
    blank-slate mentality for, 18, 65–66, 75
    Caribbean World Heritage and Climate Change and, 149
    cat bonds in, 19, 98–114
    (neo)colonial development in, 62–75
    colonialism in, 178
    Corps mêlés and, 21, 160–73
    countercapitalism in, 62–75
    cultural diplomacy in, 139
    deforestation in, 7–8, 12
    earthquakes in, 1–2, 9–11, 13, 20–21, 23n9, 24n11
    executive silence in, 13–14
    floods in, 12, 148, 188
    genetically modified organisms in, 46n7
    history of, 14–15
    necrocapitalism in, 19, 98–114
    politics of catastrophe in, 12–13
    revolution of, 43, 64, 75n2, 178
    Trump on, 185n
    tsunami in, 10, 11
    US in, 7–8, 178
Haitian Platform to Advocate for Alternative Development (PAPDA), 33
"Haiti Memory Project," 23n5
Haiti Noir, 162
hard power, 137, 138–42
harmony *(amouni)*, 42, 43
Hartman, Saidiyah, 41
Henry, Michael, 116n6
Heritage Emergency Fund, 141, 145
Hinds, Alison, 148
Hispaniola, 3, 5–6, 9, 65

Hold Tight, Don't Let Go (Wagner), 61
Holiday, Billie, 170
Huet, Marie-Hélène, 181
Hunter, Dominique, 150–51
Hurbon, Laënnec, 11–12, 13, 188–89, 190, 191
Hurray for Riff Raff, 120, 121, 127–30
Hurricane Andrew, 101
Hurricane Harvey, 102, 111–12
Hurricane Irma, 98, 102, 111–12, 120, 132, 145–48
Hurricane Katrina. *See* New Orleans
Hurricane Maria, 19, 98, 99, 102, 111–12, 136, 191
    cultural diplomacy in, 145–48
    wake work after, 120–32
Hurricane Matthew, 18, 50–61
Hurricane Michael, 17, 191
Hurricane Michelle, 135–36
hurricanes, 3, 9, 12
    cultural diplomacy in, 138
    political response to, 20
    reconstruction after, 137

Ibeyi, 131–32
IDB. *See* Interamerican Development Bank
IDPs. *See* internally displaced people
IFIs. *See* international financial institutions
ILS. *See* insurance-linked securities
IMF. *See* International Monetary Fund
Indigenous peoples. *See also* Native Americans
    in Caracol, 62–75
    Columbus and, 5–6, 64
Indonesia, 29, 98
insurance-linked securities (ILS), 101–2, 103, 104, 113
Interamerican Development Bank (IDB), 43, 67–68, 69, 70, 71
internally displaced people (IDPs), 2, 34, 35, 36
international financial institutions (IFIs), 67, 69, 107
International Monetary Fund (IMF), 42, 43, 67
international multi-peril cat bonds, 104
In the Wake (Sharpe), 19–20, 122

Jack, Deborah, 145–47
Jamaica, 9, 144, 149
James, C. L. R., 7
Janvye, Douz, 45
Jazz Festival, of New Orleans, 81, 89
jazz funerals, in New Orleans, 87
Jenson, Deborah, 180
Jeudy, Wilson, 35
Joos, Vincent, 18, 22, 59, 75, 191
Joseph, Mario, 42
Joyce, James, 162
Joyner, April, 112

Kanaran, 32–33, 43–44
Katrina babies, 83, 87
Katz, Jonathan, 23n4, 29, 192n2
Kay Joe (Unscripted), 91–92
Killing with Kindness (Schuller), 100
Klein, Naomi, 99, 100, 111
KOD-15, 43–44
Kohl's, 68
Kolbe, Athena, 1
Komite Tè Chabè (Kolektif Peyizan Viktim Tè Chabè—the Peasant Collective of the Chabè Land Eviction Victims), 70
Konbit, 43
Krewe of Chewbachus, 86
kriz estriktirèl (structural crisis), 28
kriz konjonktirèl (conjunctural or intersecting crisis), 28

Laferrière, Dany, 162, 175
Laguerre, Michel, 44
Lahens, Yanick, 23n9, 34, 162
lakou (family compounds), 39–40, 52, 55
Lamour, Sabine, 44
La Navidad, 5, 63
landslides, 180
Lasalin massacre, 39
Lazzarato, Maurizio, 109
LeBrón, Marisol, 100
left hand of empire, 30
Lenoble, Alex, 21, 184–85
Lespinasse, Collette, 44
Llenín-Figueroa, Beatriz, 121, 131
London, Dianca, 80
Louisiana Fair Housing Action Center, 78
Louis XIV, 9

Lowenstein, Anthony, 99
Lucien, Georges Eddy, 72
Luis, William, 124–25
Lundahl, Mats, 75n4, 99
Lwa Goudou (fictional character), 135, 136
Lwijis, Janil, 43

Madère, Simon, 163
Magnolia Shorty, 84
Makandal, François, 10
The Making of the Indebted Man (Lazzarato), 109
Maldonado, Ricardo Alberto, 123
malediction, 63, 177–78
malediksyon (curse), 18, 63, 64–65
Marajo, Louisa, 153–55
Mardi Gras, 81–82, 89
Mardi Gras Indians, 82
Marshall Plan, 106
Martelly, Michel, 35, 190
Martinique, 8, 153–55
Massumi, Brian, 185n9
Mauss, Marcel, 38
Mbembe, Achille, 28
Melovivi (the Trap) (Frankétienne), 21, 175–85
MICI. *See* Consultation and Investigation Mechanism
Mika, Kasia, 99
military humanitarianism, 23n4
Mills, Charles, 109
Mills, Cheryl, 35
Mintz, Sidney, 7
Mòd Leta (Schuller), 17, 27–45
Moïse, Jovenel, 39, 43, 71
MOLEGHAF. *See* Mouvement de Liberté d'Egalité des Haïtiens pour la Fraternité
Molinari, Sarah, 100, 103
Monnin, Toni, 140
monocrops, 7–8
Monsanto, 46n7
Mont, Joe, 109–10
Montas, Michèle, 34
Moore, Clark, 5
Morales, Pablo, 100
Moreau de Saint-Méry, Médéric Louis Élie, 10–11

Morel, Daniel, 45
Morison, Samuel, 63
Mouvement de Liberté d'Egalité des Haïtiens pour la Fraternité (Movement of Liberty and Equality of Haitians for Brotherhood, 38–39, 43
Muggah, Robert, 1
Munro, Martin, 20–21, 22, 140, 173–74, 177, 192
Music & Culture Coalition, 88–89, 91
Mutter, John C., 99
Myer, Anne, 149–50

Nader Jr., 140
Nan Bannann Camp, 36
Native Americans, 63, 82
necrocapitalism, 19, 98–114
Necro Citizenship (Castronovo), 108
necromedia, 108–9
Negri, Antonio, 115n1
Nelzy, Sandy, 41
neoliberalism, 3, 19, 43, 98, 100, 107
Nesbitt, Nick, 13
the Netherlands, 145–47, 156
New Orleans (Hurricane Katrina, gentrification), 18–19, 35, 78–94, 99
  cultural appropriation in, 83–85
  physical and spiritual displacement in, 86–87
  police in, 85–86, 89–92
  population replacement in, 17, 189
  resistance to intrusions on cultural practices in, 87–92
  social media in, 92–94
  transplants in, 79, 80–83, 86, 94
New Orleans Police Department (NOPD), 85–86, 91–92
NGOs. *See* nongovernmental organizations
Nguyen, Cyndi, 91
Nixon, Rob, 176
Noel, Urayoán, 125
nongovernmental organizations (NGOs), 1–2, 5, 28, 45, 58, 189. *See also specific organizations*
  after earthquake of 2010, 30, 31, 32, 33, 34–41, 44, 143

NOPD. *See* New Orleans Police Department
Numa, Guy, 43
Nuyorican poetry, 124–25, 129
Nye, Joseph, 137

OAS. *See* Organization of American States
Ocean Conservancy, 152
oceanic pollution, 151–55
Odum, Brandom "B-mike," 93
O'Gorman, Marcel, 108
Olivier, Djems, 39
OPL. *See* Organization of People in the Struggle
OPs. *See* people's organizations
Organization of American States (OAS), 39
Organization of People in the Struggle (OPL), 30
Orphe Shadda, 35
Oxfam, 32
Oxygène, David, 38–39, 43

Padilla, Alejandro, 108
"Pa'lante" (Hurray for Riff Raff), 120, 121, 127–30
PAPDA. *See* Haitian Platform to Advocate for Alternative Development
Parr, Adrian, 114
party buses, in New Orleans, 82, 91, 92
the Peasant Collective of the Chabè Land Eviction Victims (Komite Tè Chabè), 70
peasant farmers, 6, 8, 65, 66, 69–71, 74–75
Petion-Ville Club, 32
Peck, Raoul, 23n4, 32, 192n2
people's organizations (Ops), 37–38
Péralte, Charlemagne, 73
La Perla After Maria (del Pilar Lewis), 147–48
permanent catastrophe, 11–12, 188–91
Perse, Saint-John, 163
Persinos, John, 111
Petit-Frère, Alain, 70, 75
PetroCarib, 36, 42
Pettigrew, Robert, 72
Philogène, Jerry, 73
Pierre, Ralph Penel, 52

Pierre-Louis, Odonel, 44
Pietri, Pedro, 120, 121, 124–30
Pilar Lewis, Clari del, 147–48
planetarity, 183–84
Plantain Garden fault, 9
plantations, 6, 7, 17, 44, 63, 65, 71, 72–73
Plas Lapè camp, 36, 37
Pleasure Club, 87
police, in New Orleans, 85–86, 89–92
The Political Economy of Disaster (Lundahl), 99
pollution, 12, 151–55
Polyné, Millery, 12–13
population replacement, 17. *See also* internally displaced people
Port-au-Prince, 18, 39, 51–53, 59, 62, 66–67, 139, 142. *See also* earthquake of 2010
Poto Fanm+Fi, 41
Prepetit, Claude, 11
Préval, René, 13, 23n4, 192n2
privatization, 19, 190
Production of Disaster and Recovery in Post-Earthquake Haiti (Svistova and Pyles), 99–100
PROMESA. *See* Puerto Rico Oversight, Management, and Economic Stability Act
prophecy, 177, 178
Prosper, Mamyrah Dougé, 43
Proust, Marcel, 162
El Pueblo Se Levanta (The People Are Rising) (film), 126–27
"Puerto Rican Obituary" (Pietri), 120, 121, 124–30
Puerto Rico, 3, 190–91. *See also* Hurricane Irma; Hurricane Maria
cat bonds in, 19, 98–114
defending the dead in, 19–20, 121–23
necrocapitalism in, 19, 98–114
wake work in, 20, 120–32
Puerto Rico Oversight, Management, and Economic Stability Act (PROMESA), 108, 120, 123, 132
Pyles, Loretta, 99–100

Le Quatrième siècle (Glissant), 168
QuestLove (Ahmir Khalib Thompson), 89, 90

The Racial Contract (Mills, Charles), 109
"The Ransom," 27
Redis Junior, Guy, 142–44
Redman, Kia, 145
reinsurance. *See* cat bonds
religion, 16, 64. *See also* Vodou
Renuncia, Ricky, 131
resilience, 29, 45, 52
Retkwa, Rosalyn, 115n2115n3
return on investment (ROI), 108
Ribó, John, 19–20, 22, 132, 192
RickyLeaks, 120
Ricoeur, Paul, 177
Risky Timelines, 145
Rivien, Melise, 18
Roberts, Shearon, 18–19, 94
Robertson, Pat, 74, 178
Robinson, Cedric J., 7
Rodney, Water, 7
Rogers, Joshua, 110–11
ROI. *See* return on investment
The Roots, 89
Roselló, Ricardo, 120, 123, 124, 130
Rosenez, Guy Lauore, 43
Roy, Sanjoy, 130–31
Rudder, David Michael, 148
Ruffins, Kermit, 88, 93

Sae-A Co. Ltd., 68–69
Saint Domingue, 65, 78
Sakakeeny, Matt, 87
Santa Maria (ship), 5, 63
Sarkozy, Nicolas, 38
Schaal, Kaneza, 144
Schuller, Mark, 3, 17–18, 45, 67, 100, 189
Schwartz, Timothy, 35
Schwitters, Kurt, 154
Scott, David, 192n1
sea level rise, 148–51
Security Council, of UN, 141
Segarra, Alynda, 121, 127
segregated portfolio company (SPC), 115n2
Selk, Vanessa, 20, 156–57
Selves, Michael D., 137
Sharpe, Christina, 19–20, 41, 120–21, 122
Sheller, Mimi, 2, 65
Shigematsu, Kiyoshi, 1
The Shock Doctrine (Klein), 99

Shore (Jack), 145–47
Short Account of the Destruction of the Indies (Casas), 5
Shum, Michael, 113, 116n10
Silencing the Past (Trouillot, M.-R.), 14–15
Silver, Ric, 131
Sint Maarten, 145–47
Skulls and Bones, 87
slavery, 3, 5, 9–10, 17, 45, 64, 122. *See also* plantations
Small Axe, 15
Smith, Shanice, 150
social media, 92–94, 122, 177
SOFA. *See* Solidarity of Haitian Women
soft power, 137, 138–42
Solidarity of Haitian Women (SOFA), 44
Soulanges, Myriam, 149–50
So Undercover (film), 83–84
SPC. *See* segregated portfolio company
Spillers, Hortense, 41
Spivak, Gayatri, 183–84
State Failure, Underdevelopment, and Foreign Intervention in Haiti (Gros), 13
Steinke, Andrea, 31
Stormy Weather (Giroux), 115n1
structural crisis *(kriz estriktirèl)*, 28
Summers, Lawrence, 114
Suriname, 145, 148
Svistova, Juliana, 99–100
Sylvain, Patrick, 13

Taíno (Indigenous people), 5–6, 63
Taíno (musician), 124
Take 'Em Down Nola, 93
tankou (curse), 63
Tè Chabè, 72–74
Tectonic Shifts (Schuller and Morales), 100
Telegramgate, 120, 122–23
Texaco (Chamoiseau), 162
Thalman, Matt, 111–12
This Changes Everything (Klein), 99
Thompson, Ahmir Khalib (QuestLove), 89, 90
To Be Continued Brass Band, 91
Toovey, Michelle, 110
Tout Saintes (Elliott), 144
tragedy, 109–10, 111, 140, 178
transplants, in New Orleans, 79, 80–83, 86, 94
the Trap (Melovivi) (Frankétienne), 21, 175–85
Traversée de la mangrove (Condé), 162, 168
Tremé, 78, 81, 88
Trouillot, Lyonel, 162
Trouillot, Michel-Rolph, 14–15, 23n8, 27
Trump, Donald, 85, 185n, 190
tsunamis, 10, 11, 20, 98
twerking, 84–85

Ulysse, Gina Athena, 27, 29
UN. *See* United Nations
Understanding Risk Caribbean conference, 145
UNESCO. *See* United Nations Educational, Scientific, and Cultural Organization
United Kingdom, 109, 156
United Nations (UN), 139, 141, 145, 151–52
United Nations Educational, Scientific, and Cultural Organization (UNESCO), 141–42, 148
United States (US), 7–8, 39, 178. *See also* Florida; New Orleans; Puerto Rico
  cultural diplomacy of, 156
  Dauphin Plantation and, 72–73
  disaster diplomacy of, 135–36
  Greening Diplomacy Initiative of, 152
United States Agency for International Development (USAID), 1, 40, 55, 57, 67–68
Unscripted (Kay Joe), 91–92
US. *See* United States
USAID. *See* United States Agency for International Development

Valcin, Pierre, 74
Valcin, Tony, 74
Vansteenkiste, Jennifer, 71, 74
Vaughn, Sarah, 2–3
Vega, Christian Sobrino, 122–23
Versace, Christopher, 111
Victor, Gary, 34
Victor, Marvin, 21, 160–73, 174n3
Vieux-Chauvet, Marie, 163, 174n5

"The Visual Life of Catastrophic History," 15
Vodou, 18, 43, 64, 65, 74, 75n2, 75n4, 121, 178
Voices and Imagination United for Climate Justice, 148

Wagner, Laura, 18, 33, 61
wake work, 20, 120–32
Walcott, Derek, 28
Walmart, 68
Wasted Lives (Bauman), 115n1
Watts, Akilah, 145
White, Millisia, 84
White Noise (Doucet), 153
WID. *See* Women in Development
Wilentz, Amy, 14
Williams, Eric, 7
Williams, Sean, 110
Winter, Sylvia, 7
women
  in NGOs, 37
  violence against, after earthquake of 2010, 40–41
Women in Development (WID), 40
World Bank, 43, 101, 102, 107, 151–52
The Wrath of Capital (Parr), 114

Yearwood, Kraig, 145
yellow T-shirt phenomenon, 38
Young Lords, 124–25, 129
Youssef, Kathryn, 150–51
Youth Action Committee of St. Thomas Court (CAJIT), 35–36, 37, 40
Yué#Sorority (Gabon, Soulanges, and Myer), 149–50

www.ingramcontent.com/pod-product-compliance
Lightning Source LLC
Chambersburg PA
CBHW051544020426
42333CB00016B/2093